Canyon Bravado *© Serena Supplee 2018*

THE WORLD

40TH EDITION OF WE'MOON

published by

Mother Tongue Ink

We'Moon 2021: Gaia Rhythms for Womyn

Spiral, Sturdy Paperback Binding, Unbound & Spanish Editions

Mother Tongue Ink

Estacada, OR 97023

All Correspondence:

P.O. Box 187, Wolf Creek, OR 97497

www.wemoon.ws

We'Moon Founder/Crone Editor: Musawa, *Special Editor:* Bethroot Gwynn *We'Moonagers:* Sue Burns, Barb Dickinson *Graphic Design:* Sequoia Watterson *We'Moon Creatrix/Editorial Team:* Bethroot Gwynn, Sequoia Watterson, Sue Burns, Leah Markman, Barb Dickinson *Production Coordinator:* Barb Dickinson *Production Assistant & Retail Sales:* Leah Markman *Proofing*: EagleHawk, Sandra Pastorius, Kathryn Henderson, Becky Bee, Amber Torrey *Promotion:* Leah Markman, Sue Burns, Susie Schmidt, Barb Dickinson *Accounts Manager:* Sue Burns *Order Fulfillment:* Susie Schmidt *Shipping Assistant:* Dana Page

<u>Astrological Data</u> graciously provided by Rique Pottenger.

This eco-audit applies to all* We'Moon 2021 *products:

Hansol Paper Environmental Benefits Statement:

We'Moon 2021 is printed on Hansol Paper using 60% recycled content: 50% pre-consumer waste, 50% post-consumer waste, with solvent-free soy and vegetable based inks with VOC levels below 1%.

By using recycled fibers instead of virgin fibers, we saved:

114 fully grown trees
45,717 gallons of water
31 million BTUs of energy
2,695 pounds of solid waste
8,066 pounds of greenhouse gasses

As a moon calendar, this book is reusable: every 19 years the moon completes a metonic cycle, returning to the same phase, sign and degree of the zodiac.

We'Moon is printed in South Korea by Sung In Printing America on recycled paper using low VOC soy-based inks.

<u>Order directly from Mother Tongue Ink</u>

To Order see p. 230. Email: weorder@wemoon.ws

Retail: 877-693-6666 or 541-956-6052 Wholesale: 503-288-3588

We'Moon 2021 Datebooks: • $21.95
Spiral ISBN: 978-1-942775-25-6
Sturdy Paperback ISBN: 978-1-942775-26-3
Unbound ISBN: 978-1-942775-27-0
Spanish Edition ISBN: 978-1-942775-28-7
In the Spirit of We'Moon • $26.95
Paperback ISBN: 978-1-890931-75-9
Preacher Woman for the Goddess • $16
Paperback ISBN: 978-1-942775-12-6
The Last Wild Witch • $9.95
Paperback ISBN: 978-1-890931-94-0
Other *We'Moon 2021* Products:
We'Moon on the Wall • $16.95
ISBN: 978-1-942775-29-4
Greeting Cards (6-Pack) • $11.95
ISBN: 978-1-942775-30-0
Organic Cotton Tote • $13
We'Moon Cover Poster • $10

2021

JANUARY

S	M	T	W	T	F	S
					1	2
3	4	5	6	7	8	9
10	11	12	13	14	15	16
17	18	19	20	21	22	23
24	25	26	27	28	29	30
31						

FEBRUARY

S	M	T	W	T	F	S
	1	2	3	4	5	6
7	8	9	10	11	12	13
14	15	16	17	18	19	20
21	22	23	24	25	26	27
28						

MARCH

S	M	T	W	T	F	S
	1	2	3	4	5	6
7	8	9	10	11	12	13
14	15	16	17	18	19	20
21	22	23	24	25	26	27
28	29	30	31			

APRIL

S	M	T	W	T	F	S
				1	2	3
4	5	6	7	8	9	10
11	12	13	14	15	16	17
18	19	20	21	22	23	24
25	26	27	28	29	30	

MAY

S	M	T	W	T	F	S
						1
2	3	4	5	6	7	8
9	10	11	12	13	14	15
16	17	18	19	20	21	22
23	24	25	26	27	28	29
30	31					

JUNE

S	M	T	W	T	F	S
		1	2	3	4	5
6	7	8	9	10	11	12
13	14	15	16	17	18	19
20	21	22	23	24	25	26
27	28	29	30			

JULY

S	M	T	W	T	F	S
				1	2	3
4	5	6	7	8	9	10
11	12	13	14	15	16	17
18	19	20	21	22	23	24
25	26	27	28	29	30	31

AUGUST

S	M	T	W	T	F	S
1	2	3	4	5	6	7
8	9	10	11	12	13	14
15	16	17	18	19	20	21
22	23	24	25	26	27	28
29	30	31				

SEPTEMBER

S	M	T	W	T	F	S
			1	2	3	4
5	6	7	8	9	10	11
12	13	14	15	16	17	18
19	20	21	22	23	24	25
26	27	28	29	30		

OCTOBER

S	M	T	W	T	F	S
					1	2
3	4	5	6	7	8	9
10	11	12	13	14	15	16
17	18	19	20	21	22	23
24	25	26	27	28	29	30
31						

NOVEMBER

S	M	T	W	T	F	S
	1	2	3	4	5	6
7	8	9	10	11	12	13
14	15	16	17	18	19	20
21	22	23	24	25	26	27
28	29	30				

DECEMBER

S	M	T	W	T	F	S
			1	2	3	4
5	6	7	8	9	10	11
12	13	14	15	16	17	18
19	20	21	22	23	24	25
26	27	28	29	30	31	

● = NEW MOON, PST/PDT

○ = FULL MOON, PST/PDT

Shakti Rising

Cover Notes

Fatima* © *Shauna Crandall 2019

Symbolically giving birth to the planet, Fatima is robed in textiles representing various cultures as a nod to the women of these regions for the hope and wisdom brought to humanity. A planetary upheaval of long held paradigms that don't promote peace is shifting with a stronger yin energy. Fatima cradles the earth with the intention to raise its vibrations to the endless energy of love.

Female Strength* © *Helena Arturaleza 2016

The woman is standing in complete balance on the moon, connected to the lunar phases. The spiral of creation is spiraling to her fertile womb, the origin of growth and life. The outer masculine forces (from outside the spiral) permeate her with balance and inspiration. Female strength is the representation of the female energy in every human being that is responsible for nurturing our planet. May the feminine and masculine find inner balance within all of us and restore balance to humanity with pure and loving care. The universe lives inside of us.

Dedication

Every year, we donate a portion of our proceeds to an organization doing good work that resonates with our theme. This year, with *The World* as our guide, we dedicate *We'Moon 2021* to TreeSisters.

TreeSisters is a UK based non-profit whose mission is to fund tropical reforestation and protection. They focus on mobilizing and empowering women, "through the gateway of their femininity and their desire to restore Nature." TreeSisters donates 80% of funds raised to existing reforestation organizations, and the remaining 20% funds education, behavior change and consciousness shift work "in support of humanity's identity shift from a consumer species to a restorer species."

TreeSisters' goal is to plant 1 billion trees annually. As of February 2020, TreeSisters has funded over 8 million trees across their projects in Kenya, Madagascar, Brazil, Cameroon, Nepal and India.

Join TreeSisters in re-covering our world under a green canopy, to increase life diversity, mediate climate change, and empower women in global conservation leadership roles. treesisters.org

Barbara Dickinson
© Mother Tongue Ink 2020

Baptism © *Zena Carlota 2012*

Table of Contents

Introduction

Moon Calendar: The World

Appendix

We'Moon 2021 Feature Writers:

We'Moon Wisdom: Musawa **Astrologers**: Rhea Wolf, Heather Roan Robbins, Sandra Pastorius, Gretchen Lawlor, Susan Levitt, Mooncat!, Beate Metz **Introduction to We'Moon 2020**: Bethroot Gwynn **Holy Days**: Maeanna Welti **Lunar Phase Card**: Susan Baylies **Herbs**: Sue Burns **Tarot:** Leah Markman

What Is *We'Moon*? A Handbook in Natural Cycles

We'Moon: Gaia Rhythms for Womyn is more than an appointment book: it's a way of life! We'Moon is a lunar calendar, a handbook in natural rhythms, and a collaboration of international womyn's cultures. Art and writing by wemoon from many lands give a glimpse of the great diversity and uniqueness of a world we create in our own images. We'Moon is about womyn's spirituality (spirit-reality). We share how we live our truths, what inspires us, and our connection with the whole Earth and all our relations.

Wemoon means "we of the moon." The Moon, whose cycles run in our blood, is the original womyn's calendar. We use the word "wemoon" to define ourselves by our primary relation to the cosmic flow, instead of defining ourselves in relation to men (as in woman or female). We'Moon is sacred space in which to explore and celebrate the diversity of she-ness on Earth. We come from many different ways of life. As wemoon, we share a common mother root. We'Moon is created by, for and about womyn: in our image.

We'Moon celebrates the practice of honoring the Earth/Moon/Sun as our inner circle of kin in the Universe. The Moon's phases reflect her dance with Sun and Earth, her closest relatives in the sky. Together these three heavenly bodies weave the web of light and dark into our lives. Astrology measures the cycle by relating the Sun, Moon and all other planets in our universe through the backdrop of star signs (the zodiac), helping us to tell time in the larger cycles of the universe. The holy days draw us into the larger solar cycle as the moon phases wash over our daily lives.

We'Moon is dedicated to amplifying the images and voices of wemoon from many perspectives and cultures. We invite all women to share their work with respect for both cultural integrity and creative inspiration. We are fully aware that we live in a racist patriarchal society. Its influences have permeated every aspect of society, including the very liberation movements committed to ending oppression. Feminism is no exception—historically and presently dominated by white women's priorities and experiences. We seek to counter these influences in our work. We'Moon does not support or condone cultural appropriation (taking what belongs to others) or cultural fascism (controlling artistic expression). We do not knowingly publish oppressive content of any kind. Most of us in our staff group are lesbian or queer—we live outside the norm. At the same time, we are mostly womyn who benefit from white privilege. We seek to make We'Moon a safe and welcoming place for all wimmin, especially for women of color (WOC) and others marginalized by the mainstream. We are eager to publish more words and images depicting people of color created by WOC. We encourage more WOC to submit their creative work to We'Moon for greater inclusion and visibility (see p. 236).

Musawa © Mother Tongue Ink 2019

How to Use This Book

Useful Information about We'Moon

Refer to the **Table of Contents** to find more detailed resources, including: World Time Zones, Planetary and Asteroid Ephemeris, Signs and Symbols, Year at a Glance, and Month at a Glance Calendars.

Time Zones are in Pacific Standard/Daylight Time with the adjustment for GMT and EDT given at the bottom of each datebook page.

The **names and day of the week and months** are in English with four additional language translations: Bengali, Spanish, Irish and Mandarin.

Moon Theme Pages mark the beginning of each moon cycle with a two-page spread near the new moon. Each page includes the dates of that Moon's new and full moon and solar ingress.

Susan Baylies' **Lunar Phase Card** features the moon phases for the entire year on pp. 228–229

There is a two-page **Holy Day** spread for all equinoxes, solstices and cross quarter days, from a Northern Hemisphere perspective. These include writings by a different feature writer each year.

Astro Overview gives a synopsis of astral occurrences throughout the year from one of our featured astrologers, Heather Roan Robins, on pp. 8–10.

Read the **Astrological Prediction** for your particular sign on the pages shown on the right —>

Born of the Elements
© Colleen Koziara 2017

Astrological Overview: 2021

How do we define community, our people, our circle? What philosophy and vision guide us? At the end of 2020 and through early 2021, Jupiter and Saturn, the two arbiters of social consciousness, conjunct in the communal fixed air-sign Aquarius. Like the Sun and Moon on the New Moon, when two planets conjunct they begin a new chapter; this one instigates a 30-year revolution in our Aquarian concept of community and social responsibility.

Aquarius calls us to expand our horizon, to think globally, idealistically, philosophically. The trap can be to see everything through the filter of our philosophy and lose the ability to see what's really going on, or to try and control others to fit our concept. Aquarius can bring stubbornness. Under this influence, fanatical people can run full steam ahead and start conflicts around political mind sets, their own world-views, or religious theory.

To bring out Aquarius's gift we need to keep it authentic and responsive, to observe what's really happening, incorporate multiple points of view, and develop a healthy, flexible philosophy that pulls us out of the pettiness of the single story. Let's think about our personal and collective vision for the future.

Jupiter and Saturn, and soon Pluto in Aquarius, call us to truly think globally and act locally. But this is just a taste—preparation for the big social and political work we'll need to do when Pluto enters Aquarius in a few years, from 2023–2044. The last such relationship occured was from 1777–1798, when the USA labored to form a country that embodied its Constitutional vision statement.

Saturn, and soon Pluto in Aquarius, need us to investigate how we can save our ecosystem and create a mutually beneficial world without oppressing the freedom of the individual. Form communes and circles that support the good of the whole, while fostering unique creative process as well. We need to dust off our assumptions and ask fresh questions, particularly where we think we know the answer.

The New Year kick-starts metamorphosis as motivating Mars forms an exciting, uncooperative conjunction with change-maker Uranus—squaring Jupiter, January 20–23, just as America inaugurates a president. We'll either be working with a new government or building up resistance to old ways. Mercury retrogrades 1/30– 2/20 and lets us catch up, reorganize and repair. Our community and our beloveds will need pragmatic loving compassionate action as Venus conjuncts Pluto, Saturn, and Jupiter through mid-February.

February ends as Mercury enters Aquarius and gives voice to the Jupiter-Saturn debate. We can sketch out the grand landscape but may become too far-sighted. We have to carefully look for the needs of our beloveds.

Because we've been so busy with politics and community, it's important that we put relationships and creativity back on the front burner in March as Venus conjuncts Neptune and calls us back to our heart and our muse.

In April we can feel the enthusiasm build towards new possibilities. Spring fever can call us into new relationships and revolutionary adventures as Venus conjuncts Uranus. Discontent can be productive as fire simmers under the kettle. Towards the end of April, watch for a political crackdown or relationship issues around control wherever people feel insecure, as Venus squares Saturn and Pluto retrogrades. Build real security instead.

Jupiter enters Pisces on May 13, retrogrades June 20 and reenters Aquarius July 28–December 28. Jupiter and Saturn both intermittently square change-maker Uranus throughout the year, keeping politics and tectonic plates restless; we may be unable to settle, but that helps us continue an evolution. Transformation is inevitable, but which way that change goes will be up to us.

A lunar eclipse in Sagittarius on May 26, and a solar eclipse in Gemini on June 10, emphasize the need to celebrate true diversity—the real gift of myriad different voices and perspectives. Let's celebrate by finding someone way outside of our comfort zone and respectfully share stories.

Retrograde season: Every summer brings retrogrades; this one brings quite a lineup: Pluto turns retrograde April 27, Saturn on May 23, Jupiter June 20, Neptune June 25, and Uranus on August 19. Mercury retrogrades January 30–February 20, May 29–June 22, and September 26–October 18. These retrogrades ask us not to push forward but to hold our ground, renew, garden, and review the events of the year. Take time to investigate, fix mistakes, clarify problems, and fine-tune future plans.

From June 26–July 22 Venus and Mars are both in extroverted Leo; they stay active throughout the summer and inspire personal and political drama/melodrama. Life is performance art. Summer romances have a certain unrealistic flare; arts festivals can flourish, and the arts change our cultural understanding. Politics will be either heart-centered or ego-grandstanding.

We get a fresh sense from September 6 on that we have work to do, and it's time to get back to it as Mars trines Pluto and Saturn. Don't get discouraged if old problems need our attention—ones we thought we'd already conquered—as October dawns with six planets and a few asteroids retrograde.

Between October 6–18 Mercury, Jupiter, Saturn, and Pluto create tumult as they all station to turn direct. Then the channels clear and give us a green light forward. Mars in social-justice-loving Libra then trines Jupiter, squares Pluto, and nudges us to clear up misunderstandings and heal a rift. If conflicts are not resolved now, they may come to a boil after Mars enters Scorpio and opposes energizing Uranus through November. If we're not in a fight, this aspect powers our efforts. Mars enters Sagittarius on December 13 as Venus conjuncts Pluto; together they encourage us to finish the year with a flare of competence, forgiveness, and travel in mind, body, or spirit. Come back to that deep Aquarian understanding that we are unique selves intricately connected to all our relations.

Heather Roan Robbins © Mother Tongue Ink 2020

2021 Sacred Work Through the Signs

We have work to do this year. We may have to rethink our whole philosophy and approach in some quadrant of our life to bring it into line with our present understanding. Then take action. Read your Sun sign, Moon sign, and ascendant. Your ascendant points to the practical components where work needs to be done, the Sun to the evolution of your core personality, and the Moon to where you're challenged to stretch your heart.

Aries: Your relationship balance between your deeply-loved independence and your interrelatedness to community begins a new cycle. Instead of ambivalence towards connection, with fear that you'll be trapped, engage community with healthy boundaries. You need them, and they need you to help this world improve. This begins to heal some lingering self-doubts and, towards the end of the year, helps create an opening in your dream world or spiritual path.

Taurus: You've been evolving a new philosophy, a new need to walk your talk and have your work matter in the grander scheme. Stabilize teams. Ask yourself and others to review, question, and then apply beliefs, test great ideas, and investigate best practices to help them consolidate the next step. Manifest. As you step into more internal integrity, doors can open to new connections which can leave you both supporting and feeling supported.

Gemini: Take an opportunity to open up your relationship to the world at large, to start a new cycle of learning and understanding, and to public relations. Feel your global citizenship, reach out and connect through the web, politics, and human connections. You see where people have so much work to do to support integrated empowerment: call it out with openness and integrity. New connections can bring new work opportunities later in the year.

13th Moon *© Leah Marie Dorion 2018*

Cancer: Bring a light to dark corners of your life this year; start a new cycle in relationship to your body and your relationship to other people's bodies—to sex, healing, and material dependency. Poke at the monsters in the corner of your psyche and help them see it could be a new day. Freeing energy in these far corners can develop a fresh sense of safety in the world, which encourages exploration later in the year.

Leo: You're called to stretch in your relationships of all types, to really feel you are equal to anyone you deal with, and they are equal to you. Whether a romantic partner, business partner, or stranger, drop your preconceptions and explore with curiosity. Question your interpersonal habits which might arise out of insecurity, or that create distance—they no longer serve you. Explore the comfort of mutually empowering relationships, and watch this create generous safety.

Virgo: Investigate the relationship of your feelings and daily habits with the subtle gauge of your health; make sure your habits honestly support you. Find direct and conscious ways to listen to your emotional wisdom before it signals to you through your body. As you drop habits of anxiety, walk your talk on health, and create a more spacious, integrated attitude; a new and freeing sense of partnership can arise.

Libra: Explore a new creative relationship with all the children of your body, mind, and spirit. Notice if you were held back by family training, a philosophy that has served others but not you, or has just come to its completion. Examine and release preconceptions and explore life as an art form. From this authenticity a new philosophy arises. You can create safe ways to be sensitive, and your health can feel more robust.

Scorpio: Take a long deep look at your societal gestalt and the belief systems of your family of origin: how they formed you, where you've rebelled against them but still let them define the paradigm. Now reach farther back to your long-ago lineages, and bring old strength up the roots in a way that liberates you and grounds you. Dissolve those old restraints from these new healthy roots, and feed your capacity to love and create.

Sagittarius: You may have a philosophy of honesty, be direct and straightforward, and this can truly help your community. But this year asks you to investigate the levels of that honesty—do you leave out nuances? Are the gray areas actually more honest representations? Notice where you simplify in the name of a clear point. Develop a more subtle relationship to the truth, and then notice that people feel more at home with you and your ideas.

Capricorn: Your strong philosophy around material resources will be pushed and expanded. Examine how your resources really support your vision of your life, how they can be freeing for you rather than entrapping. Put quality of life for you and all sentient beings first, and notice how that could change your goals and ambitions. This exploration can take you into a deeper relationship with community and free up a layer of worries.

Aquarius: Tests and gifts, the best and worst of luck could stretch your sense of self this year. Face the challenges and take advantage of new opportunities; this gives you the chance to transform how you see yourself, and that changes how others see you. In your transformation, you help them ask the liberating questions. From this stronger and more expanded self-identity, your healthy generosity becomes a resource for others.

Pisces: Look at how your self-concepts and world-view have affected your health, your spiritual practice, your role within large organizations and groups. Question assumptions that affected your health and soul. Let this investigation liberate the corners of your psyche, integrate into your body, and create room to dream. This work is so deep it takes a while for it to integrate, come to the surface and evolve your worldly identity.

Heather Roan Robbins

Peace © Rosella 2007

Sky Map 2021

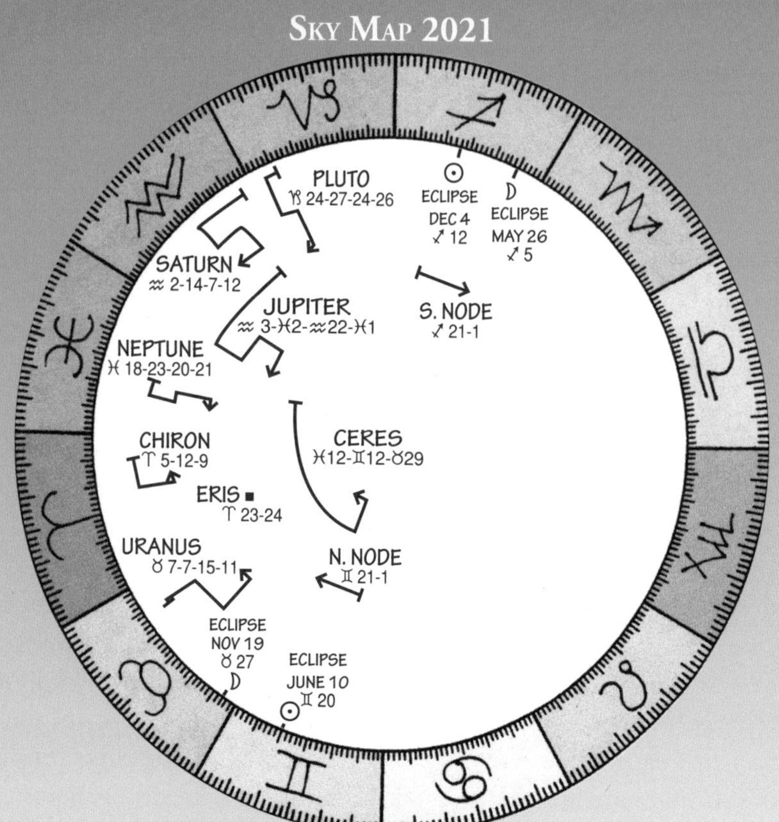

The sacred circle of the Zodiac is like a mandala, illustrating the major planetary movements of 2021. It's a way to explore the year's potential, especially for visual learners, for artists, and when words seem inadequate.

For those who wish to use this mandala as a contemplative tool, you might sit quietly and with soft eyes, gaze upon these celestial patterns. Allow the symbols, patterns, and colors to activate your own deep understanding. Let the mandala remind you of truths: That the planets move eternally through great circles and cycles, each with their own speed and style. That they cluster and scatter in different patterns each year. That change is constant and inevitable, and that every ending is followed by a beginning.

The synchronicity—or meaningful occurrence—between what we can see in the skies above and what is going on within, has been studied for thousands of years, through many countries and cultures. Many believe that just looking at a mandala is profoundly calming and centering. Try it yourself in a quiet moment, or when you need to invoke your own deep wisdom.

Astrological Year at a Glance Introduction

Goddess of Unity
© Elspeth McLean 2016

This year begins with a surge of energy to kick-start change in your life. The theme of the year is INSPIRATION, as we step back from the daily grind to see the bigger picture. The root of the word inspiration means "to breathe," reminding us that to find hope for the future, we need to get some fresh air—a revitalizing perspective to create a more just and beautiful life on Earth.

The World card is about endings and beginnings. We churn the compost of what has passed and imagine what might come. Tumultuous 2020 might have left us exhausted, but this is the perfect time to seize opportunities for renewal. Transits for the United States instigate radical shifts in which we wrestle with the negative roots of its founding: racism, sexism, colonialism. Personal as well as collective growth is a major theme for 2021.

The passage of Jupiter and Saturn through Aquarius brings us aspiration for something better, coupled with the practical follow-through to make those dreams reality. These planets have begun a new cycle to help humanity hit the reset button on its ethics, ideals, and morals. To align with this transit, consider your own values and connect with others who share them. Practice simple acts that bring your ideals to life.

If the past few years of dire circumstances have left you cynical, remember that just when you think everything is dead, something new starts to sprout. We are now in the emergent part of the process, breaking free from limiting beliefs. What's weird is in. A new generation of great thinkers is bringing us innovative theoretical understandings of social conditions. We must listen and be ready to reform the broken world we've inherited. Are you one of those voices? Don't stifle your budding vision for the future. This is the year to let the freak-flags fly and shed constricting worldviews that tell us we should just give up. Together, we can re-enchant the world.

Rhea Wolf © Mother Tongue Ink 2020

To learn more about astrological influences for your sign, find your Sun and Rising signs in the pages noted to the right.

Streaming the Archetypes in 2021

The mythopoetic World: an inter-connective totality
of all known and unknown realms.
In a constant dance of creativity,
a unified Whole offering Sacred space for all.

2021 arrives on the heels of the 2020 conjunctions of planets Saturn and Pluto in Capricorn, cycling until they meet again in 2045, and the twenty year cycle of Jupiter and Saturn in Aquarius. As these planets initiate their new cycles, our collective spirit gets activated. We may tune in by opening ourselves up for personal and collective epiphanies, for gathering the best of our contributions and advocating for the ripened revelations that we place at the feet of the future.

As the Saturn / Pluto cycle in Capricorn unfolds, we witness an intensifying clash of world views. Pluto rules the shadow archetypes created from limiting judgments, and unexpressed and denied heart expression. The collective shadow runs on fear, offering falsehoods for facts. May we be led to acknowledge and heal from the collective traumas that have followed us throughout human history.

While the cycle of Jupiter and Saturn gets underway in Aquarius, we find our relational fields beginning to expand and shift, evolving our capacity for collective action. This twenty year cycle offers us a fresh template to draw up plans for the Aquarian Age cresting our horizon. Look for opportunities for attuning group coherence, for the healing of social divides, and the revival of spirit. Horizontal power starts to take hold when we open the love field beyond previous boundaries, allowing the era of polarity and separation to wane.

Saturn and Pluto evoke a major archetype; the World Soul or the *anima mundi*: a reflection of Love awakened, and the vital force that permeates all. This eternal, yet evolving archetype streams through the generations, becoming re-expressed, re-mapped, and re-constituted in the collective unconscious.

Archetypes offer us reflections of consciousness that enlighten our Sacred play in all the realms. They are essentially neutral and manifest in both light and shadow attributes. We each carry patterns of archetypal energy, and may draw on this connection to take the higher roads necessary to transcend our othering and to advance the evolutionary path, both personal and collective.

Raven's Key *© Elizabeth Diamond Gabriel 2019*

Archetypes are recurring primal patterns of behavior in the human psyche that exist in the collective unconscious. While seemingly worlds apart, our personal inner world is connected to the archetypal realms. We may activate this connection through engaging myths and metaphorical understandings with symbol systems like tarot and astrology. When we grapple with how to respond to the pressing personal and global issues of the times, we fill the world with our life stories. We grow our individual character and the legacy of our humanity as the World Soul.

Bring the following archetypes forward in your life energetically to express and affect the changes most meaningful to you, and become a force of nature for the World.

Stream The Mother archetype to extend Her arms and heart into the world. Offer your devotion to grow the circle of kin, and let Love spread throughout the realms. Our ancestors guard over us in these challenging times with the medicine of inclusion for future generations. The Thirteen Indigenous Grandmothers celebrate all our relations—join them.

Stream the Revolutionary/ Liberator archetype to encourage an inspired group agency that advocates for a just and caring society. Risk rising up with courageous aspirations and actions that offer reforms for justice. Let civic grace transform the commons. Harriet Tubman lives through us—unleash the dream.

Stream the Healer/ Alchemist archetype to acknowledge the spell of duality. Use an alchemy of the heart to transmute the patterns that fueled our multi-generational traumas, and let our life-giving values become the precious gold of healing. Make ethical upgrades that bring empathy and kindness worldwide. Committing ourselves to be carriers for the common good allows us to grow our intent and unify with what we love. Life is magic in action.

Sandra Pastorius © Mother Tongue Ink 2020

Eclipses: 2021

Solar and Lunar Eclipses occur when the Earth, Sun and Moon align at the Moon's nodal axis, usually four times a year, during New and Full Moons, respectively. The South (past) and North (future) Nodes symbolize our evolutionary path. Eclipses catalyze destiny's calling. Use eclipse degrees in your birth chart to identify potential release points.

May 26: Total Lunar Eclipse at 5° Sagittarius underscores our need for reality checks. Let the shadow reveal what wisdoms you are holding within. When the light returns, bring what inspires to the fore. Help create fields of coherence and clarity.

June 10: Annular Solar Eclipse occurs at 19° Gemini while Mercury retrogrades. The air waves get lively with shadow dancing. Decode from the heart, and decide on what shared realities work in your world. Keep your gaze on the what rings true for you.

November 19: Partial Lunar Eclipse at 27° Taurus. Let the Shadow reveal the material attachments you hold dear and what you may give up for them. Bring forward where true satisfactions lie, and what sustains your desires. Be your own precious cargo.

December 3: Total Solar Eclipse at 12° Sagittarius. During the shadow period entertain what underlying unconscious biases you may hold. In the returning light allow your real values to uplift and guide social interactions.

Mercury Retrograde: 2021

Mercury, planetary muse and mentor of our mental and communicative lives, appears to reverse its course three or four times a year. We may experience less stress during these periods by taking the time to pause and go back over familiar territory and give second thoughts to dropped projects or miscommunications. Breakdowns can help us attend to the safety of mechanics and mobility. It's time to "recall the now" of the past and deal with underlying issues. Leave matters that lock in future commitments until Mercury goes direct.

Mercury has three retrograde periods this year in air signs:

Jan 30–Feb 20: During this Aquarius period attend to any meaningful communications left unsaid or needs unmet. Offer sharing from the heart for getting current. Let the healing begin with authentic attention.

May 29–June 22: Let's slow down the pace. Remember Gemini mimics the mind's many paths into the unknown. When you retrace your steps, practice being steady, read the Signs and go with what you know. Keep sight of the near and dear.

Sept 27–Oct 18: Libra reflects the Other and we see mirrors everywhere. During this period notice who offers their honesty and compassion. Chose reflections that value your true worth, including your own.

The Year of the Ox: 2021

Sacred Catalyuhule Cow *© Jakki Moore 2018*

The Year of the Ox begins on February 11th, the second New Moon after Winter Solstice. In agricultural societies, Oxen are reliable and strong work animals. They were responsible for the survival of humanity. That same sense of power and dedication are goals to strive for in Ox year, a time of focused work to complete what was started in Rat year 2020. Success is achieved through diligent and conscientious effort.

A good place to start is by putting your financial affairs in order if you didn't structure your resources in Rat year. Then tend to your home, and the personal needs of yourself and others. The element Metal represents a clean, pristine, even shiny environment in feng shui. 2021 is a Metal year to clear out, pare down, and simplify. Save new designs and risky ventures for Tiger year 2022.

We'moon born in Ox years (1925, 1937, 1949, 1961, 1973, 1985, 1997, 2009, 2021) are steady, loyal, and true. Ox values honesty, integrity of character, and reward from hard work. Like an Ox plowing the fields, she can firmly persevere, and is not swayed by opinions. Rarely does Ox make an effort to seek social connections to achieve success. Ox believes that if she applies herself and performs, she will be recognized and rewarded. But in today's work environment, where advancement often depends on how you sell yourself, the Ox we'moon can feel under-appreciated. So keep firm boundaries this year, and do not take on the workloads of others.

In relationships, Ox is a good provider. The surprises and thrills of romance may not be Ox's forte because she may not be overtly romantic. Nor is an Ox we'moon the first to try new things, set trends, or take the initiative. Ox is home oriented, and appreciates both a secure home and work environment. Ox enjoys feasts, and is often happiest when in her kitchen, cooking for friends and family.

Ox's most fortunate season is winter. Ox is most compatible with another Ox, Rat, Snake, or Phoenix (Rooster). Ox correlates to the Western sign Capricorn.

Susan Levitt © Mother Tongue Ink 2020

Mountain Mysteries *© Bernice Davidson 2018*

Decolonizing Herbalism

To my white herbalist sisters! This is for you. I am writing to you as a white woman myself. We have work to do.

Herbalism has a history rife with cultural appropriation, colonization, racism, and oppression. Particularly during the resurgence of western herbalism in this country in the 1960s and 70s, white herbalist culture left out the contributions of black and indigenous people of color—or worse, co-opted the contributions of many indigenous and communities of color without giving credit. This disrespect continues today. To move forward in integrity, we must interrupt further oppression of indigenous and marginalized peoples who are most greatly impacted by the degradation of our planet. Let us amplify the resiliency of the many individuals and communities who have carried their healing traditions into current day practice, despite the impacts of violent oppression. Donate to the organizations restoring herbal heritage. Volunteer with the tribe whose land you live on. Ask permission to harvest plants where you live. Respect the answer.

Let's recover the herbal heritage of our own blood ancestors. All peoples the world over used plants for medicine, food, and ritual. Do you know where your people lived, and what they practiced? What plants did they use for healing? How did your ancestors live in relationship to the earth? Can we honor our ancestors through ritual, offerings, prayers, or food? Put a cannoli on your altar—spirit food for your Italian ancestors. Use meadowsweet to ease your headache, if your people hail from Europe. The Celtic tradition of burning herbs to cleanse with smoke is called *saining*, and a bit of smoke from a bundle of dried mugwort will ready your bedroom for sweet dreams. If your ancestors were involved in the colonization of indigenous peoples and lands, hold yourself accountable to not repeat their behavior. Pray for their continued evolution beyond the grave; develop a connection to older, wiser ancestors, and model better behavior for the children.

Grow your own herbs; find and practice traditions that are rooted deeply in your heritage. When healers share their own culture's herbal wisdom and practices, it supports their well-being, their community, the earth, the world as a whole.

Sue Burns © Mother Tongue Ink 2020

Tarot Card #21: The World

The World card signifies clarity about where we have come from. We look behind us as we walk forward into the future. What's ahead is unknown, clouded in mystery and risk. We enter into this space prepared, carrying with us the baggage of our past mistakes, lessons learned through trial and error, and treasures from our triumphs. Our magic has manifested; we hold our tools in both our hands, ready to cast our spells for change.

A new cycle begins. Nothing is ever static. We dance through this passage with the joy of the Fool, the tricks of the Magician, secrets from the High Priestess and new perspectives from the Hanged One. What have we learned so far? We know not to repeat the mistakes of our ancestors, but to honor their memory and dig deep in their knowing. Our work still calls.

The World card is ruled by Saturn, a queen of structure, responsibility, discipline and ambition. This energy asks us to bring greater meaning and purpose into our lives—the embodiment of our successes. We have been tested, and have proven ourselves to the stars. Our limitations have been revealed to help us learn how to properly break through them. We must know our limits in order to know ourselves. The bounds of reality have called us back to Earth in order to rebuild her. The Earth is reaching her brink; how can we work to repair her using our own limitless imagination?

When this card reveals herself to you, be grateful. Be proud! This card is the one that speaks to your tune, a manifestation of your conjuring. What do you bring to the world? How does the earth speak through you? What makes you unique? Hold tight these tools—you have earned them. You are now armed with these teachings! How does this energy swirl into and blend with the greater rivers of humanity? What traits, skills and tools have you picked up to help nurture the earth? We can now use this mastery as we carry onward to dance in the spirals of fate.

Leah Markman © Mother Tongue Ink 2020

"I am a Secret agent of the Moon... "
© Sudie Rakusin 2003

Can A Move Change Your Destiny?

Astrologers have identified powerful zones in the astrological chart where your potential and destiny are amplified. These four power zones are the "angles" of your chart: ascendant, descendent, midheaven and *imum coeli* (or i.c. "the bottom of the sky"). Love, success, creativity, abundance all manifest with more certainty when the planet representing that theme is in one of your power zones (i.e. Venus here for love, Mars for passion and drive, Sun for vitality and recognition).

Your birth horoscope may have planets in these zones, showing dominant lifelong themes. But if you were born on the same date and same time, but in another city or country, other planets move into these zones, amplifying their influence in your life. That place holds this potential for you and is activated when you are there.

Will a holiday in a new location be enough to change your life? Your birth chart shows underlying potential, but your best stars may shine more brightly under a different sky. A technique called relocation astrology, or Astrocartography, shows which planets will move into power zones, or lines, as you travel or relocate. Online sites such as astro.com map out your power lines, or contact me.

On a **Sun Line** you shine. Here you are noticed, maybe famous. Leadership, self-confidence and audacity are accentuated. Health and well-being improve. If you feel lost or confused, spend time here. Potential challenges here: narcissism, arrogance, insensitivity.

On a **Moon Line** you feel like you've found your soul home. Here you could settle, create family. Customs and culture feel familiar and comforting, as though you've been here before. You're more sensitive, sentimental, childlike. Watch for moodiness, taking everything too personally.

On a **Mercury Line** you find your voice. Your ideas are appreciated, conversations flow, connections come easily. Great for teaching, writing, studying, learning a foreign language. Potential challenges here: nervous exhaustion, distractibility, fickle changeability.

A trip or a move to a **Venus Line** brings out your goddess self. Attractiveness and bonding urges draw friends and lovers to you. Life is languid here; artistic talents and material abundance flourish. Challenges here: laziness, extravagant indulgences, indecisiveness.

On a **Mars Line** you find your passion and courage. You make things happen with your "let's just do it" infectious boldness. You take up sports, win marathons, feel alive. Watch for impatience, ruthlessness, aggression.

Visit a **Jupiter Line** to discover new worlds and opportunities. Here hope, faith and optimism are restored. Anything feels possible; luck and prosperity abound. Potential challenges: overextending, promising or expecting too much, weight gain.

On a **Saturn Line** you accomplish great things, achieve life-long aspirations. Resourcefulness and self-reliance are strengthened, patience and dignity gained. Watch for overworking, melancholia, frugal self- denial.

It may be hard to stay long on a **Uranus Line**, full of lightning bolts to banish slumbering predictability and awaken your rebel genius. You won't come back the same. Be careful with hasty decisions, erratic behavior, contrariness just for the sake of it.

On a **Neptune Line** come illuminating dreams and visions. Spirits, ancestors and guardians feel close. Your inner artist/poet/musician is inspired here; intuition and psychic gifts flourish. It's easy here to feel vulnerable, hypersensitive, indulging in numbing escapes.

Go to a **Pluto Line** to transform your life. Here you strip away the past, let go of anything/anyone and start over. Your resilience is awesome, you thrive on the intensity. The relentless crises of a prolonged residence here can be draining and isolating.

On **Chiron Lines** your deepest wounds are soothed. Suffering diminishes in importance as healing skills take over. Heed calls to share these magical gifts. Don't wallow in your suffering here nor forget to care for yourself.

If you feel stuck or frustrated with some aspect of your life, go try life under a different sky. Visit or relocate to one of your specifically targeted power zones. And if you can't get there, their influence may come to you, especially through people from that place.

Gretchen Lawlor

Guardian □ *Jana Parkes 2012*

Light Work © *Autumn Skye 2016*

Coming Full Circle: The World (XXI)

We have drawn the World card for 2021 in We'Moon Tarot: a picture of harmony, cooperation, balance. The Earth is held in the center of a circle of hands weaving together a vibrant rainbow web of individual life threads. As of this writing (Leap Day in the Quantum Leap Year of 2020), that picture is rapidly disintegrating in the mind's eye, with the increasing systemic breakdown the World is now embroiled in on all fronts.

Tarot provides a framework for understanding the larger picture of human consciousness—as a creative resource for guidance on our life paths. And the We'Moon Tarot re-frames that picture in the universal language of the Mother Tongue. When you draw a card that does not fit the picture you are seeking guidance about, look again, from different angles: What is the reverse meaning? Are there hidden nuances? Look deeper: Do new insights emerge from the shadows of your unconscious?

As the last card in the cycle of spiritual growth represented by the Major Arcana in Tarot, the World completes one full swing of the pendulum: from Spirit beginning to emerge in the world of Form (O. The Fool / Open) . . . to the Form it takes upon completion of that cycle (XXI. The World), setting in motion the beginning of the next. The apparent duality between Spirit and Form is the portal we must pass through, coming into and going out of the World—and it serves as the training wheels for cycling throughout life.

Somehow, we seem to be reverting to an infantile stage of human development (the Terrible Two's?!)—that perceives differences as a threat to one's own power (the ones in power / the individual ego?) and seeks to maintain control by dominating and controlling all Others. Patriarchy is an unsustainable system of human relations which feeds on this divisive paradigm—becoming all the more entrenched as things fall apart. The prolonged stress of patriarchal dysfunction has resulted in massive PTSD—a fractured response to chronic distress that has now spiraled virally out of control in a pandemic that endangers the Earth's life-support systems, as well as our own. The great potential of human nature—as manifested in the World card, left—seems to be matched equally by the destructive nature of human divisiveness (its reverse meaning): a perfect storm of contradictory forces at work.

Meanwhile, the Moon and the Sun continue to shine on us from above, regenerating life energy by day, and illuminating the dark by night. As the left and right eyes of heaven, they are equally empowered and mutually empowering resources for renewing a healthy sustainable way of life on Earth. Like the right and left hemispheres of the brain within each one of us, the Sun and Moon are a universal source of creative life force. The Star is our third eye, continually streaming ancient wisdom, recycling as stardust in the blueprint of our genetic memory. The living Mother Earth embodies all the elements that channel the domains of the Sun, Moon and Stars in our day-to-day life on Earth.

May we take heart in the one power that is greater than all the discord mankind can stir up: the living Mother Earth's natural power of regeneration. Can we step up to reclaim these astounding gifts of Nature, the Original Blessings of creation, as part of our own human nature? It is now up to us—we who are the first generation of the 21st century, just coming of age at 21 this year. What life threads do you hold in the weave of the World? Look again at the World card: We are giving Her life support now, as She has given us all along: Coming Full Circle!

© Musawa 2020

Luna *by Cathy McClelland*
© Mother Tongue Ink 2020

Receiving
© Francene Hart 2003

Manifestation Chamber
© Mosa Baczewska 2016

A Prayer *© Lupen Grainne 2009*

Introduction to the Holy Days

We turn the wheel of the world. We are time unfolding—seasons following seasons flowing through us, bodies, hearts, minds. As I walk through the graces of the year, my wholeness is revealed. As I move through the paces of the year, I am made.

We turn the wheel of the world. We are made by the seasons, and as we love them, so they unfold. As we love them, so they unfold.

Have you any real idea of the power of your love? We cannot care for what we do not love. Love is the miracle of your breath hanging before you in the cold air. It is steam curling up as the winter sun melts the frost. It is the piercing radiance of the stars in the endless night. It is the gift of decay, the relief of death, the exquisite difficulty of the between times when surrender breathes over our skins, calling us to submit.

If you would care for the health of the Earth, you must love it in all its moods. If you would see to the continuance of its gifts, you must learn to let Earth move you through the graces and paces of your seasons. The needs of the Earth are calling us, urgent and demanding like the promise of a cat's claws, ready to unsheath. The needs of the Earth are the siren songs of our very own hearts, bringing us to realms, loves and depths unknown until the moment we melt into the beauty that surrounds us. The needs of the Earth are the gentle promise of home, the challenge of belonging, the gift of a love that will break us and remake us. We walk through the graces of the year, and our wholeness is revealed.

We are wise and withered, we are naked and new, we are rich and sumptuous, we are the wild harvest. We are steady commitment and the queerfire laughter of change. Turning the wheel.

Maeanna Welti © Mother Tongue Ink 2020

The Wheel of the Year: Holy Days

The seasonal cycle of the year is created by the Earth's annual orbit around the Sun. Solstices are the extreme points as Earth's axis tilts toward or away from the sun—when days and nights are longest or shortest. On equinoxes, days and nights are equal in all parts of the world. Four cross-quarter days roughly mark the midpoints in between solstices and equinoxes. We commemorate these natural turning points in the Earth's cycle. Seasonal celebrations of most cultures cluster around these same natural turning points:

February 2 Imbolc/Mid-Winter: celebration, prophecy, purification, initiation—Candlemas (Christian), New Year (Tibetan, Chinese, Iroquois), Tu Bi-Shevat (Jewish). Goddess Festivals: Brigit, Brighid, Brigid (Celtic).

March 20 Equinox/Spring: rebirth, fertility, eggs—Passover (Jewish), Easter (Christian). Goddess Festivals: Eostare, Ostara, Oestre (German), Astarte (Semite), Persephone (Greek), Flora (Roman).

May 1 Beltane/Mid-Spring: planting, fertility, sexuality—May Day (Euro-American), Walpurgisnacht/Valborg (German and Scandinavian), Root Festival (Yakima), Ching Ming (Chinese), Whitsuntide (Dutch). Goddess Festivals: Aphrodite (Greek), Venus (Roman), Lada (Slavic).

June 20 Solstice/Summer: sun, fire festivals—Niman Kachina (Hopi). Goddess Festivals: Isis (Egyptian), Litha (N. African), Yellow Corn Mother (Taino), Ishtar (Babylonian), Hestia (Greek), Sunna (Norse).

August 2 Lammas/Mid-Summer: first harvest, breaking bread, abundance—Green Corn Ceremony (Creek), Sundance (Lakota). Goddess Festivals: Corn Mother (Hopi), Amaterasu (Japanese), Hatshepsut's Day (Egyptian), Ziva (Ukraine), Habondia (Celtic).

September 22 Equinox/Fall: gather and store, ripeness—Mabon (Euro-American), Goddess Festivals: Tari Pennu (Bengali), Old Woman Who Never Dies (Mandan), Chicomecoatl (Aztec), Black Bean Mother (Taino), Epona (Roman), Demeter (Greek).

October 31 Samhain/Mid-Fall: underworld journey, ancestor spirits—Hallowmas/Halloween (Euro-American), All Souls Day (Christian), Sukkoth (Jewish harvest). Goddess Festivals: Baba Yaga (Russia), Inanna (Sumer), Hecate (Greek).

December 21 Solstice/Winter: returning of the light—Kwanzaa (African-American), Soyal (Hopi), Jul (Scandinavian), Cassave/Dreaming (Taino), Chanukah (Jewish), Christmas (Christian), Festival of Hummingbirds (Quecha). Goddess Festivals: Freya (Norse), Lucia (Italy, Sweden), Sarasvati (India).

*** Note: Traditional pagan Celtic / Northern European holy days start earlier than the customary Native / North American ones—they are seen to begin in the embryonic dark phase: e.g., at sunset, the night before the holy day—and the seasons are seen to start on the Cross Quarter days before the Solstices and Equinoxes. In North America, these cardinal points on the wheel of the year are seen to initiate the beginning of each season.**

 Sources: The Grandmother of Time *by Z. Budapest, 1989;* Celestially Auspicious Occasions *by Donna Henes, 1996 &* Songs of Bleeding *by Spider, 1992*

Introduction to We'Moon 2021

Let yourself be wrapped in the warm embrace of *We'Moon 2021*; let the Mother hold you in Her arms, and give yourself over to trust in Her. This does not mean that you do not hear the shrill alarms that call out Doom upon land and sea and all creature life. Oh no: Soft with heartful care for the World, you are nonetheless fierce and loud and sharp to insist on Reparative Justice and Radical Intervention wherever humans oppress one another and endanger the viability of life on earth.

We'Moon 2021 is inspired by the final card in Tarot's Major Arcana series: Card 21, The World. Completion. Resolution. Restoration. The World theme celebrates the majesty of the natural world, and cries out attention to its fragility. This edition of the datebook especially highlights the diversity of the world's many peoples—its disparate tribes and clans, held in the web of one common humanity. "Love is the force that greens and grows us all," (Ellen S. Jaffe, page 158). And the drumbeat for women's empowerment sounds page after page, with vibrant art and soulful writing that embody women's leadership, unwrapped and raw in its revolutionary work to incite justice, embody compassionate nurture, weave global sisterhood. "Ride uncertainty and tumult/Dance bedlam—into balance," (Susa Silvermarie, page 52).

Yes, Dance and Song and Poem, Story and Gardens and Protests and Children: women insist on performing righteous action; they tender young life, and offer devoted attention to an imperiled Earth. This work is framed by Prayer and Ceremony, grounded in quiet openings to Spirit, deep-sourced by ancestral reverence, eager to be led by wisdom from the next generation's wild imagination.

Is this creative revolt in the name of Love preposterous? Are there not monumental forces of greed and corruption, misogyny and racism, weaponry and violence arrayed against these waves of everyday passion? Passion erupted into irresistible, determined brilliance of women who never give up. Listen:

"We are asked ... To give voice to the voiceless/And translate light to language,/To cast the widest net,/To include everything inside of it,/To crack the heart wide open/And never close it again," (Emily Kedar, page 30).

You heard that right: Never! Ever!   Blessed Be.

Bethroot Gwynn © Mother Tongue Ink 2020

Recurring Dream © Dorrie Joy 2016

MA! O MA! We call you with the oldest word of all.
O Mother of Everything—at the very center of Being
Where we full-circle over and over again
The End devours The Beginning. The New digests The Old
And every morsel of life is nourished by Your devotion
Every iota of existence is destroyed by Your rigorous benediction
then spirals—Surprise!—into renewal.
We are So full! We are So grateful!
This world is radiant with gifts of Earth Fire Water Air
We gasp at golden sunfall through magenta sky,
We bow before towering trees, vast sparkles of star-fire.
BUT MA! Dare we say BUT? These multitudes of hungry children!
These parched riverbeds, vanishing beasts, brutalities people to people!
We crowd the streets with rage.
We crowd the streets with hope.
We gather our disparate clans around the hearth of peace,
the altar of forgiveness
Yes! We dance, Yes! Shadow and all, into Your wide embrace.
Even Now, You ignite unimagined possibility
And we rise up to fulfill The World's blessed promise.

Earthside

We are asked to arrive here, earthside,
To occupy every inch of the body we're given,
To learn its language, its needs and gifts.
We are asked to use it as a compass
To harbour us in safety
And lead us through the wild.

We are asked to care for this place,
With the grit and grace of dirt on our hands.
We are asked to speak,
To give voice to the voiceless
And translate light to language,
To cast the widest net,

To include everything inside of it,
To crack the heart wide open
And never close it again.
When we are pulled apart by longing,
We are asked to keep showing up,
To follow this soft, insistent tether:

To become what we love,
To pour ourselves into the hands of the ancestors,
To be held by them like water,
To quench the mouths of our children,
To nourish them with who we become.
We are asked to belong, finally

To ourselves, to each other, to the land,
To our own shapeshifting shadows,
To our own threadbare, indelible light.
We are asked to belong to the old tales that brought us here
And to the new ones that will keep us alive,

We are asked to belong to the Great Turning Wave
Of this time and this place.
We are asked to punctuate our breath
with both sorrow & praise
We are asked to answer by becoming
Again and again the way.

¤ *Emily Kedar 2019*

I. OH, MAMA GAIA!

Moon I: December 14, 2020–January 12, 2021

New Moon in ♐ Sagittarius Dec. 14; Sun in ♑ Capricorn Dec. 21; Full Moon in ♋ Cancer Dec. 29

Unbridled *© Lindsay Carron 2015*

December 2020

Ogrohaeon

☽☽☽ sombar

♓
♈

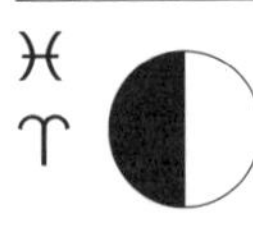

Monday 21

☉→♑ 2:02 am
☽✶♇ 2:24 am v/c
♃☌♄ 10:20 am
☽→♈ 2:32 pm
☽✶♄ 3:33 pm
☽✶♃ 3:36 pm
☉□☽ 3:41 pm
☽□☿ 6:04 pm

Winter Solstice

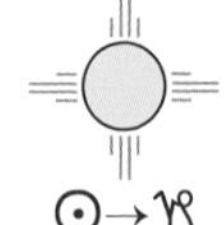

Sun in ♑ Capricorn 2:02 am PST
Waxing Half Moon in ♈ Aries 3:41 pm PST

♂♂♂ mongolbar

♈

Tuesday 22

☽△♀ 7:56 am

☿☿☿ budhbar

♈

Wednesday 23

♂□♇ 6:53 am
☽□♇ 2:36 pm
☽☌♂ 2:51 pm v/c
☿□⚷ 6:11 pm

♃♃♃ brihospotibar

♈
♉

Thursday 24

☽→♉ 2:55 am
☽□♄ 4:31 am
☽□♃ 5:10 am
☽ApG 8:35 am
☉△☽ 9:48 am
☽△☿ 3:57 pm
☽☌♅ 4:56 pm
☿△♅ 11:05 pm

♀♀♀ sukrobar

♉

Friday 25

☽✶♆ 4:10 pm
☉□⚷ 11:37 pm

Mama Gaia

She walks dark
earthen places,
Her light shines
in all faces
She's fierce
and fires burning
hurrah
She's tree fern
and fishes,
the source
of earthly blisses
She's kindness
in a rainbow
hurrah
Oh Mama Gaia

excerpt © Akefa Azu 2015

Unity *© Melissa Winter 2018*

♄♄♄ sonibar

♉
♊

Saturday
26

☽△♇ 3:32 am v/c
☽→♊ 3:32 pm
☽△♄ 5:41 pm
☽△♃ 6:54 pm

☉☉☉ robibar

♊

Sunday
27

☉△♅ 7:25 pm
☽☍♀ 10:47 pm

Dec. '20–Jan. '21

Mí na Nollag / Mí Eanair

Rebirth © Tamara Phillips 2016

☽☽☽ Dé Luain

♊

Monday 28

☽□♆ 3:59 am
☽⚹♂ 7:01 pm v/c

♂♂♂ Dé Máirt

♊ ♋

Tuesday 29

☽→♋ 2:28 am
☽⚹♅ 3:32 pm
☉☍☽ 7:28 pm

☿☿☿ Dé Céadaoin

Full Moon in ♋ Cancer 7:28 pm PST

♋

Wednesday 30

♀□♆ 2:19 am
☽☍☿ 8:04 am
☽△♆ 1:31 pm

♃♃♃ Dé Ardaoin

♋ ♌

Thursday 31

☽☍♇ 12:10 am
☽□♂ 5:45 am v/c
☽→♌ 10:58 am
☽☍♄ 1:56 pm
☽☍♃ 4:05 pm
☽□♅ 11:26 pm

♀♀♀ Dé Haoine

♌

Friday 1

January

☿⚹♆ 3:18 am

Infinite Expansion

"Infinite expansion," my midwife spoke as she gazed deeply into my eyes. I was beginning to doubt myself. I was there, right in that place during birth when you want to run away, where it feels like if you don't go to the place you are so much avoiding, you'll be lost forever . . . "Infinite expansion" she spoke the words again, but this time with her soul. Then I felt it. I thought that birth surge would split me in two, but I breathed her words into me and let them vibrate into the universe. And I expanded. And I birthed. And I healed . . .

As we walk into the space that we are so afraid of—afraid to be trapped, afraid of losing ourselves altogether—we must remember those two words, "infinite expansion." Despite our fears, we can go there—can still breathe and allow our souls to expand there. That is our gift as women. We can plant the seeds to heal ourselves and our Mama Earth. That is the birth energy we have deep inside—hidden, where only the strongest contractions can beckon it out of us.

The world has been working hard on us lately, hasn't it? The contractions are getting stronger. The easiness of breath that we once had now requires work and attention. We could get lost in this darkness, this political climate, this environment that no longer suits us, this busy world that squeezes our spirits so tightly that we want to give them up altogether. We could stay here, but we won't . . . It's time to expand. We will remember the words of the midwife, of all the midwives who taught us that in this place, in this darkness, we can find our strength. This is our birthright. This is where we heal. This is the place of infinite expansion.

¤ *Alexandra Kisitu 2019*

♄♄♄ Dé Sathairn

♌ ♍ Saturday 2

☽△♀ 3:24 am
☽△♂ 2:00 pm v/c
☽→♍ 5:13 pm

☉☉☉ Dé Domhnaigh

♍ Sunday 3

☽△♅ 5:12 am
☉△☽ 5:44 pm

January
enero

This earth was given.
Not to us.
It was not given to us,
It was just given,
Life arising out of itself,
For its own sake.
excerpt ¤ Maya Spector 2019

☽☽☽ lunes

♍
♎
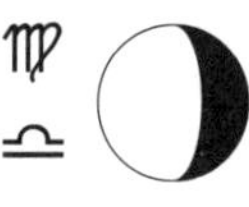

Monday
4

☽☍♆ 1:49 am
☽△☿ 11:11 am
☽△♇ 11:52 am
☽□♀ 1:34 pm v/c
☿☌♇ 4:58 pm
☽→♎ 9:42 pm

♂♂♂ martes

♎
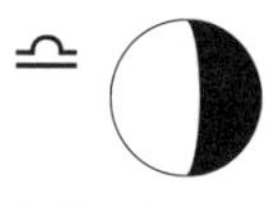

Tuesday
5

☽△♄ 1:22 am
☽△♃ 4:17 am

☿☿☿ miércoles

♎

Wednesday
6

☉□☽ 1:37 am
♂→♉ 2:27 pm
☽□♇ 3:23 pm
☽□☿ 9:21 pm
☽✶♀ 9:54 pm v/c

Waning Half Moon in ♎ Libra 1:37 am PST

♃♃♃ jueves

♎
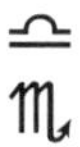
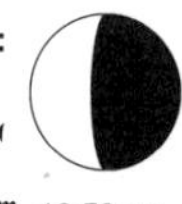

Thursday
7

☽→♏ 12:53 am
☽☍♂ 1:14 am
☽□♄ 4:54 am
☽□♃ 8:11 am
☽☍♅ 12:15 pm

♀♀♀ viernes

♏

Friday
8

☿→♒ 4:00 am
♀→♑ 7:41 am
☉✶☽ 8:10 am
☽△♆ 8:13 am
☉✶♆ 8:53 am
☽✶♇ 5:59 pm v/c
☿□♂ 6:44 pm

On the World Road

Bountiful One, guide us on the World Road.
When we are lost, bring us, please,
to the next step on our way to you.
When the road is obscured with fog,
shine your luminous *rayos* upon it.
Mother *Luminosa*, when life grows cold and harsh,
cover us with your starry mantle.
Black Madonna, burn away our terror
of the unknown twists ahead.
Tender Guardian, remind us to rest,
send rain to slake dry lips, hard hearts.
Merciful Madre, when we go astray,
lift us from the ditch of depression, set us again on the way.
Medicine Mother, when we lie on the road
injured and vulnerable, tend us.
Woman Who Mends, when we meet the injured of spirit,
put it in our hearts to see beyond
any posturing, any crimes.
Generous One, help us to bandage wounds
and give to the sad of heart
your soft word of encouragement.
Companion of the Traveler, walk with us when we feel abandoned.
Goddess Mother of the Crossroads, guide us on the World Road,
bring us home to one another.

© Susa Silvermarie 2019

♄♄♄ sábado

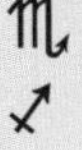

Saturday
9

☽→♐ 3:15 am
☽⚹☿ 6:15 am
☽⚹♄ 7:38 am
☽PrG 7:39 am
♀△♂ 7:53 am
☽⚹♃ 11:18 am
☿☌♄ 7:17 pm

☉☉☉ domingo

Sunday
10

☽□♆ 10:29 am v/c

Morning Walk

Time to be alone with my stories, the ones I've told myself for so long, held close, sewn into a shawl that wrapped tight around my heart. Many are old, tired, rubbed raw from the telling, fear dirtying everything.

Last night was long and full of doubt. Now I see two sides, how the past and present entwined, how there is no victim. The old story is not so powerful and dark. Fear caught in a pool of bright light.

Walking in this gentle morning, I feel like a warrior who has battled against herself in the inner wars, the ones that are bloodless, yet brutal. Like a soldier who knows she has been through the worst. A kind of weary invincibility cloaks me.

Suddenly I want to kick off my shoes to feel the rough gravel of the pavement with my bare feet, then let the morning put her warm arms around me.

© Elise Stuart 2014

Receiving Guidance ¤ *Shanti Bennett 2018*

II. SACRED PAUSE

Moon II: January 12–February 11

New Moon in ♑ Capricorn January 12; Sun in ♒ Aquarius Jan. 19; Full Moon in ♌ Leo Jan. 28

She Walks Two Worlds © *Amy L. Alley 2010*

January
yī yuè

☽☽☽ xīng qī yī

♐

♑

☽→♑ 5:30 am
☽△♂ 9:16 am
☿☌♃ 9:19 am
☿✶⚷ 9:23 am
♃✶⚷ 9:48 am
☽☌♀ 12:14 pm
☽△♅ 4:51 pm

Monday
11 felt Very Energetic in the evening

♂♂♂ xīng qī èr

☿□♅ 7:00 am
♀□⚷ 1:03 pm
☽✶♆ 1:17 pm
☉☌☽ 9:00 pm
☽☌♇ 11:22 pm v/c

Tuesday Period Started Overnight, No cramps!
12 Again felt the energy in the evening.

New Moon in ♑ Capricorn 9:00 pm PST

☿☿☿ xīng qī sān

♑

♒

♂□♄ 3:02 am
☽→♒ 8:44 am
☽☌♄ 2:11 pm
☽□♂ 2:29 pm
♀△♅ 4:22 pm
☽☌♃ 6:54 pm
☽□♅ 8:29 pm

Wednesday Today was a medium energy day, I
13 had coffee (alot) & powered through some work painlessly in the begining of the day, then was low energy the rest, bleeding heavily.

♃♃♃ xīng qī sì

♅D 12:36 am
☽☌☿ 1:28 am v/c
☉☌♇ 6:19 am

Thursday Today Was Super Productive! I got
14 alot done & was able to concentrate, no blood when I woke up but a light flow through out the day. Sore shoulders.

♀♀♀ xīng qī wǔ

♒

♓

☽→♓ 2:17 pm
☽✶♂ 10:29 pm

Friday had a headache all day today & But started
15 to get better near the end of the day, low energy and took a nap + slept in. I think a good night of rest will sort me out.

Point of Balance © Melissa Harris 2007

Centerpoint

Sometimes
at the ragged edges
of an unruly world
when life feels undone
there is a quiet
centerpoint
in which to dance
your unbound prayers.

© Molly Remer 2019

♄♄♄ xīng qī liù

♓

☽✶♅ 2:43 am
☽✶♀ 9:02 am
♇ApH 4:24 pm

Saturday
16

Energy Level was average, able to think & move/be productive well.

☉☉☉ lǐ bài rì

♓
♈

☽☌♆ 1:35 am
☽✶♇ 12:55 pm
♃□♅ 2:49 pm
☉✶☽ 7:44 pm v/c
☽→♈ 11:07 pm

Sunday
17

Today was a Super Emotional day, not that productive, not that restful. headache from crying

January

Poush

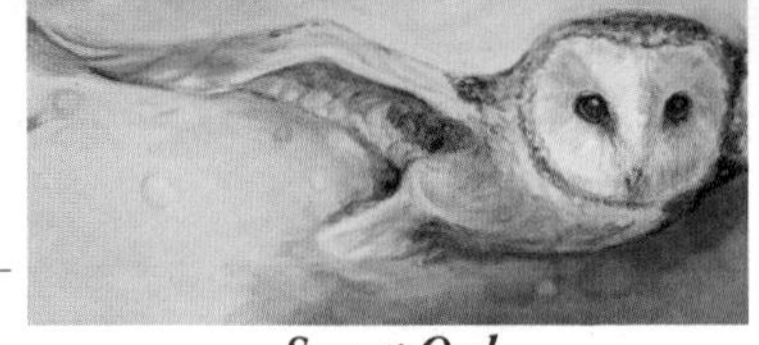

Sunset Owl

© Cary Wyninger Art N' Soul 2018

☽☽☽ sombar

Monday

18 Today was midline, feel bloated now felt hungry alot of the day.

☽✶♄ 6:19 am
☽✶♃ 12:45 pm

♂♂♂ mongolbar

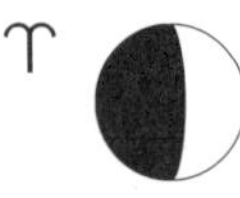

Tuesday

19 A good day, slow with lots of appointments, lots of coffee

☽□♀ 1:42 am
☽✶☿ 9:53 am
☉→♒ 12:40 pm

☉→♒

Sun in ♒ Aquarius 12:40 pm PST

☿☿☿ budhbar

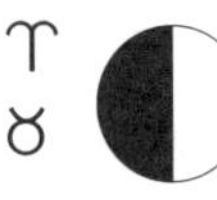

Wednesday

20

☽□♇ 12:29 am v/c
☽→♉ 10:56 am
♂☌♅ 12:38 pm
☉□☽ 1:01 pm
☽□♄ 7:00 pm

Waxing Half Moon in ♉ Taurus 1:01 pm PST

♃♃♃ brihospotibar

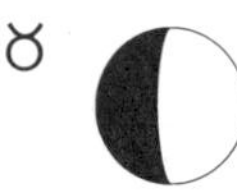

Thursday

21

☽☌♅ 12:36 am
☽☌♂ 1:08 am
☽□♃ 2:15 am
☽ApG 5:12 am
☽△♀ 9:28 pm

♀♀♀ sukrobar

♉ ♊

Friday

22

☽✶♆ 1:27 am
☽□☿ 5:59 am
☽△♇ 1:28 pm v/c
☽→♊ 11:43 pm
♂□♃ 11:49 pm

2021 Year at a Glance for ♒ Aquarius (Jan. 19–Feb. 18)

This year, there's no limit to what you can dream, and there's strong energy of support to make those dreams reality. Saturn and Jupiter are moving through your sign, Aquarius, and will create space for you to aspire to new heights of innovative thinking and vision. But there's an impatient streak inside you that could set a trap of self-doubt.

You have a gift for seeing a brighter future, but can procrastinate putting it into practice. Saturn can be a limiting force, but it's also the planet of mastery. Use its influence this year to come up with a plan—the weirder the better—and then work on upping your optimism game. Visualize your dreams every day, use affirmations, and participate in activities that encourage a feeling of flow, like tai chi, yoga, or walking meditation.

You are being reformed this year, so what form do you want to take? Clown, activist, innovator, political leader? Jupiter is expanding your sense of self to include the whole, wild universe while Saturn is showing you how to take your responsibilities more seriously. Use the winter to sit with the question of who you are ready to be, and allow yourself to emerge from the chrysalis when the spring arrives. There will be some obstacles to your creativity and vision in June and October, but view these as reminders that you don't yet know the full story. More will be revealed this year if you are willing to listen to others and to the messages from the universe.

Rhea Wolf © Mother Tongue Ink 2020

Light Carrier
© Janyt Piercy 2009

♄♄♄ sonibar

♊ ☾

Saturday
23 Medium Energy day,
More energy in the morning

☉△☽ 7:27 am
☽△♄ 8:19 am
♀⚹♆ 11:49 am

♄ApH 1:09 pm
☽△♃ 4:03 pm
☉☌♄ 7:01 pm

☉☉☉ robibar

♊ ☾

Sunday
24

☽□♆ 1:36 pm
☽△☿ 11:17 pm v/c

January
Mí Eanair

☽☽☽ Dé Luain

♊ ♋

Monday 25

☉⚹⚷ 2:29 am
☽→♋ 10:52 am
☽⚹♅ 11:49 pm

© Jakki Moore 2019

Turtle Dream

♂♂♂ Dé Máirt

♋

Tuesday 26

☉□♅ 4:48 am
☽⚹♂ 5:17 am
☽△♆ 10:57 pm

☿☿☿ Dé Céadaoin

♋ ♌

Wednesday 27

Very amorous feeling

☽☍♀ 7:36 am
☽☍♇ 9:55 am v/c
♃ApH 6:14 pm
☽→♌ 6:54 pm

♃♃♃ Dé Ardaoin

♌

Thursday 28

☽☍♄ 3:41 am
☽□♅ 7:11 am
♀☌♇ 8:18 am
☉☍☽ 11:16 am
☽☍♃ 11:39 am
☽□♂ 2:32 pm
☉☌♃ 5:39 pm

Full Moon in ♌ Leo 11:16 am PST

♀♀♀ Dé Haoine

♌

Friday 29

☽☍☿ 5:53 pm v/c

Arrival of the Goddess for the Emotionally Over-Dressed

Oh my, what a heavy overcoat of agitation.
You must be hot and bothered.
May I take that and hang it up over here?
Ah, now I see the hat, scarf, and gloves—
 the worries that scratch and itch
 and make it difficult
 to touch small things—
May I store them over here?
Still a little flushed, I see—
May I help you with the buttons
 on that angry sweater?
There, I bet that feels better—
Let's just put it over here.
Oh, that is expensive-looking jewelry
 of self-doubt,
Oh, and what a FEARFULLY large watch!
Still, without them,
 you look even more beautiful,
 and they won't be scratching
 the ones you embrace . . .
Let's go inside now and see what else
 you might remove,
 to feel more free.

© *Lisa S. Nelson 2017*

If the Shoe Fits
© Melonie Steffes 2018

♄♄♄ Dé Sathairn

♌ ♍

Saturday feeling very romantic + dreamy & also
30 very tired

☽→♍ 12:02 am
☿R 7:51 am
☽△♅ 11:52 am
☽△♂ 8:57 pm

☉☉☉ Dé Domhnaigh

♍

Sunday
31

☽☍♆ 9:09 am
☽△♇ 7:17 pm

February
febrero

☽☽☽ lunes

Monday
1

☉□♂ 2:34 am
☽△♀ 3:10 am v/c
☽→♎ 3:25 am
♀→♒ 6:05 am
☽△♄ 12:32 pm
☽△♃ 8:57 pm

Myriad
She is the pocket of time
between inhale and exhale.
We dwell within her mystery,
she dwells within our bones.
excerpt ¤ Rosemary Wright 2019

♂♂♂ martes

Tuesday
2

Imbolc

☉△☽ 2:49 am
☽□♇ 10:15 pm
☽△☿ 10:15 pm v/c

☿☿☿ miércoles

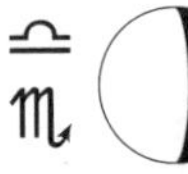

Wednesday
3

☽→♏ 6:14 am
☽□♀ 10:55 am
☽PrG 10:58 am
☽□♄ 3:47 pm
☽☍♅ 5:57 pm

♃♃♃ jueves

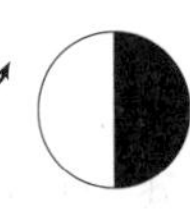

Thursday
4

☽□♃ 12:40 am
☽☍♂ 6:51 am
☉□☽ 9:37 am
☽△♆ 3:11 pm
☽□☿ 10:27 pm

Waning Half Moon in ♏ Scorpio 9:37 am PST

♀♀♀ viernes

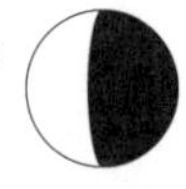

Friday
5

☽✶♇ 1:20 am v/c
☽→♐ 9:16 am
☽✶♀ 7:00 pm
☽✶♄ 7:20 pm
♀☌♄ 11:07 pm

Imbolc

Breathe into emptiness. Stir in the silence that winter gifted you. Touch new skin, the surprise aliveness, the contours winter revealed. There is an echoing silence that precedes every new thing.

Imbolc is the insistence of the spring waters, pushing up through cold earth. It is the restlessness of birdsong, the persistence of the sap. It is the dark that folds around all that is stirring, saying: *Pace yourself, love.*

Imbolc calls us to be simple. We have nothing but what winter left us. We have nothing but our own stirring heartbeats and desires. Nothing but the fire in our bellies that warmed us through the deepest darks. It is time to polish ourselves. To clear, clean, hone. To stand in the barest simplicity of our aliveness and promise ourselves to service, to spring.

Make a simple promise. To our wholeness, to becoming. Find the seed inside you, swollen with its own longing, that insists, with all the force of life, that it will sprout when the time is right. Simple, naked, clean, fiercely alive.

Maeanna Welti © Mother Tongue Ink 2020

Our Lady of 10,000 Names ◻ *Suzanne Grace Michell 2018*

Prayer for Sacred Pauses

Goddess of the sacred pause
please grant me the courage
to lay aside swiftness
and take up slowness,
to embrace limitations as learning,
silence as stabilizing,
waiting as worthy,
and sitting as divine.
Goddess of the sacred pause
help me to know stillness as strength,
patience as powerful,
and healing time
as holy necessity.

© Molly Remer 2019

Freeing Myself
© KT InfiniteArt 2019

Harvest As We Go

Patriarchy hobbles on one last standing foot
And we take its shoe,
Its balance lost long ago
One final wind, the beast collapses
This moment matters

The great search is over
We are here

Strong Woman, Powerful Woman
Stand with Me, I Stand with You
Together we find our ground

There is a central fire we gather around
Here in us, an ancestral fire

Quiet ourselves deeply
Enough to listen to our longing
Pay attention to what is emerging
Harvest as we go

¤ *Sophia Faria 2019*

ħħħ sábado

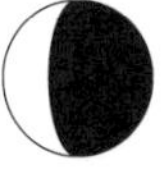

Saturday
6

♀✶⚷ 3:43 am
☽✶♃ 4:45 am
☉✶☽ 4:56 pm
☽□♆ 6:40 pm
♀□♅ 7:33 pm
☽✶☿ 10:16 pm v/c

☉☉☉ domingo

♐
♑

Sunday
7

☽→♑ 12:52 pm

February
èr yuè

☽☽☽ xīng qī yī

♑

Monday
8

☽△♅ 1:00 am
☉☌☿ 5:48 am
☽△♂ 6:21 pm
☽⚹♆ 10:55 pm

Atmosphere

© Ruby Singer 2019

♂♂♂ xīng qī èr

♑
♒

Tuesday
9

♄⚹⚷ 2:59 am
☽☌♇ 9:22 am v/c
☽→♒ 5:20 pm

☿☿☿ xīng qī sān

♒

Wednesday
10

☿□♂ 4:16 am
☽☌♄ 4:42 am
☽□♅ 5:51 am
☿PrH 6:21 am
☽☌♀ 2:11 pm
☽☌♃ 3:29 pm
☽☌☿ 11:22 pm

♃♃♃ xīng qī sì

♒
♓

Thursday
11

Lunar Imbolc

☽□♂ 1:55 am
♀☌♃ 6:59 am
☉☌☽ 11:06 am v/c
☽→♓ 11:23 pm

New Moon in ♒ Aquarius 11:06 am PST

♀♀♀ xīng qī wǔ

♓

Friday
12

Period! No cramps

☽⚹♅ 12:30 pm
☿☌♀ 11:48 pm

A Begging Presence

I sit, submerged in my electronic device
My heart beats responses to a superficial world
While nature begs me to be present with this one
She sends her rays
I feel one on my leg, then another, and another
The whole room fills up with the light of our mother
Painting my skin, smiling into my soul
Touching the edges of my leg hair
And like a house guest arriving
It's impolite to ignore her
I see her peering out from behind the clouds
And return my smile
My heart returns to a slow and rhythmic beat
Dancing in time to the tune of the wind
I am reminded of the gentle flow of her essence
The game, or text, or email that had my attention previously
Slips into the void
Irrelevant
For now I am captivated by her presence
And the gift of this present moment.

¤ *Kusuma Tiffany 2014*

♄♄♄ xīng qī liù

♓ 

Saturday
13 headache

☽✶♂ 11:55 am
☽☌♆ 12:11 pm
♂✶♆ 6:13 pm
☽✶♇ 11:28 pm v/c

☉☉☉ lǐ bài rì

Sunday Rest Day! Self care
14 tired! No other bad symptoms

☽→♈ 7:54 am
☿☌♃ 1:40 pm
☽✶♄ 9:23 pm

Dancing the Planet

The turmoil of our times
dances round the world,
stamping, frenzied, furious—
Kali destroying, Durga creating.
In the storm that tosses tiny earth,
let us cry and whirl with them.
Earth's equilibrium demands
that we dance the planet.

Lightning flashes all around us,
but even as we shudder,
we shall be the rods that ground it.
As we mediate the thresholds,
let us earth each other.
Though we shake and tremble,
we become conductors,
transmitters of the Change.
Let it turn us inside out
until protection disappears, until
we wear our hearts outside our shell.

Unleash it now, the oldest form of worship.
Bow and whirl, leap and dart,
Sway, gyrate, and quiver.
The turbulent disorder
of these times that we were made for,
calls for us to meld the parts of self
until the fusion powers us like stars!
Ride uncertainty and tumult.
Dance bedlam—into balance.

III. EARTH MUSE

Moon III: February 11–March 13

New Moon in ♒ Aquarius Feb. 11; Sun in ♓ Pisces Feb. 18; Full Moon in ♍ Virgo Feb. 27

Fancy Shawl Dancer
at Sac and Fox PowWow

February
Magh

☽☽☽ sombar

♈ 

Monday
15

Stardust © Christina Gage 2016

☽⚹☿ 8:50 am
☽⚹♃ 10:22 am
☽⚹♀ 7:40 pm

♂♂♂ mongolbar

♈
♉ 

Tuesday
16

☽□♇ 10:32 am
☉⚹☽ 4:17 pm v/c
☽→♉ 7:12 pm

☿☿☿ budhbar

♉ 

Wednesday
17

☽□♄ 9:47 am
☽☌♅ 9:48 am
♄□♅ 11:08 am
☽□☿ 6:32 pm
☽□♃ 11:51 pm

♃♃♃ brihospotibar

♉ 

Thursday
18

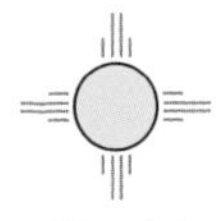
☉→♓

☽ApG 2:20 am
☉→♓ 2:44 am
☽⚹♆ 11:30 am
☽□♀ 3:21 pm
☽☌♂ 4:48 pm
☽△♇ 11:28 pm v/c

Sun in ♓ Pisces 2:44 am PST

♀♀♀ sukrobar

♉
♊ 

Friday
19

☽→♊ 8:03 am
☉□☽ 10:47 am
♀□♂ 3:04 pm
☽△♄ 11:15 pm

Waxing Half Moon in ♊ Gemini 10:47 am PST

2021 Year at a Glance for ♓ Pisces (Feb. 18–March 20)

You are no stranger to the depths of feeling, but this year will offer you an opportunity to find a sense of detachment from that intensity. Detachment is not apathy, but a way of viewing the world without expectations. At times, your powerful sensitivity can throw you off balance and lead to needless suffering. With Saturn's help, you can increase your capacity for compassion without falling into a pit of pain. Delve into intellectual realms to find support in building this new skill. Research theories of social change, study systems theory, or join a local organization that is doing work you believe in.

Playful curiosity can be a guide to re-imagining your home and communal life this year. A home base offers us solace and support for our outer world work. Take time in the early summer to consider whether your home is a place of inspiration. What interactive activities or places in your home can awaken a sense of wonder in you, such as crafts, books, puzzles, or altar-making?

Jupiter's influence calls you to spiritual adventure. You are being given fresh tools this year to add to your toolbox, and they may look strange to you. It would be a great year to explore your past sacred or psychological work in order to close a chapter. A door is opening to expand your sense of self into the transcendent through your mind rather than your heart. Study metaphysical practices, start a dream journal, or visit sanctuaries to learn about or volunteer with cultures different from your own.

Rhea Wolf © Mother Tongue Ink 2020

Water Star *© Paula Franco 2015*

ħħħ sonibar

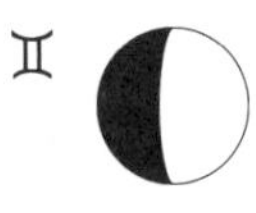

♊ Saturday 20

☽△☿ 6:20 am
☽△♃ 1:46 pm
☿D 4:52 pm

⊙⊙⊙ robibar

♊ ♋ Sunday 21

☽□♆ 12:10 am
☽△♀ 10:39 am v/c
☽→♋ 7:53 pm

February

Mí Feabhra

☽☽☽ Dé Luain

Transformation

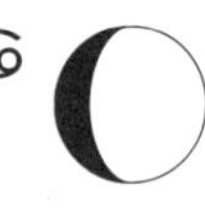

Monday 22

☉△☽ 3:47 am
☽✶♅ 10:09 am

♂♂♂ Dé Máirt

♋

Tuesday 23

☽△♆ 10:05 am
☽✶♂ 7:59 pm
☽☍♇ 8:54 pm v/c

☿☿☿ Dé Céadaoin

♋
♌

Wednesday 24

☽→♌ 4:23 am
☽□♅ 5:49 pm
♂△♇ 5:52 pm
☽☍♄ 6:52 pm

♃♃♃ Dé Ardaoin

♌

Thursday 25

☽☍☿ 1:56 am
♀→♓ 5:11 am
☽☍♃ 8:40 am
☉✶♅ 1:13 pm

♀♀♀ Dé Haoine

♌
♍
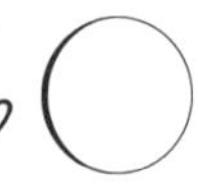

Friday 26

☽□♂ 3:32 am v/c
☽→♍ 9:07 am
☽☍♀ 11:50 am
☽△♅ 9:54 pm

ALL ASPECTS IN PACIFIC STANDARD TIME; ADD 3 HOURS FOR EST; ADD 8 HOURS FOR GMT

Our World, Our Time

O World
Sing to Us your sacred song
An eternal chant moving
across the altar of Our soul
with heart's beating
and every breath We take

As dawn comes We would to
delve the secrets
of your desert sands
rove your majestic mountains
gaze over the glistening shore
and welcome
the whispering winds
as a sweet lover might

A sublime sun stretches
saffron-gilded arms ever higher
embracing every corner
of creation
giving the Mother a gentle kiss
then continues traveling onward

In but a blink the day is gone
eventide falls revealing
a kaleidoscope of stars,
carpeting the sky in radiance
and the promise
of wishes fulfilled

O World
sing to Us your ancient song
it rumbles
low and long in Our souls
of peace and love,
of potential and possibilities
We are the sentinels
of your beauty and
Stewards of the future;
Our time has come

¤ *Patricia Telesco 2019*

♄♄♄ Dé Sathairn

♍ ○ Saturday
27

☉☍☽ 12:17 am
☽☍♆ 7:06 pm

☉☉☉ Dé Domhnaigh

Full Moon in ♍ Virgo 12:17 am PST

♍ ♎ Sunday
28

☽△♇ 4:42 am
☽△♂ 7:58 am v/c
☽→♎ 11:17 am

March

marzo

☽☽☽ lunes

Monday
1

☽△♄ 1:17 am
☽△☿ 11:27 am
☽△♃ 2:57 pm
☽PrG 9:12 pm

♂♂♂ martes

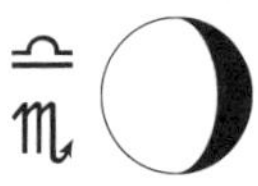

Tuesday
2

☽□♇ 6:09 am v/c
☽→♏ 12:38 pm

☿☿☿ miércoles

♏

Wednesday
3

☽△♀ 12:39 am
☽☍♅ 1:21 am
☽□♄ 3:05 am
♀⚹♅ 9:09 am
☉△☽ 10:52 am
☽□☿ 4:01 pm
☽□♃ 5:21 pm
♂→♊ 7:29 pm
☽△♆ 10:30 pm

♃♃♃ jueves

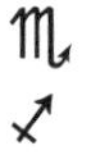

Thursday
4

☽⚹♇ 8:09 am v/c
☽→♐ 2:43 pm
☽☍♂ 3:32 pm
☿☌♃ 7:27 pm

♀♀♀ viernes

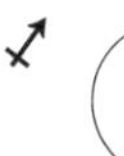

Friday
5

☽⚹♄ 5:56 am
☽□♀ 7:58 am
☉□☽ 5:30 pm
☽⚹♃ 9:07 pm
☽⚹☿ 10:35 pm

Waning Half Moon in ♐ Sagittarius 5:30 pm PST

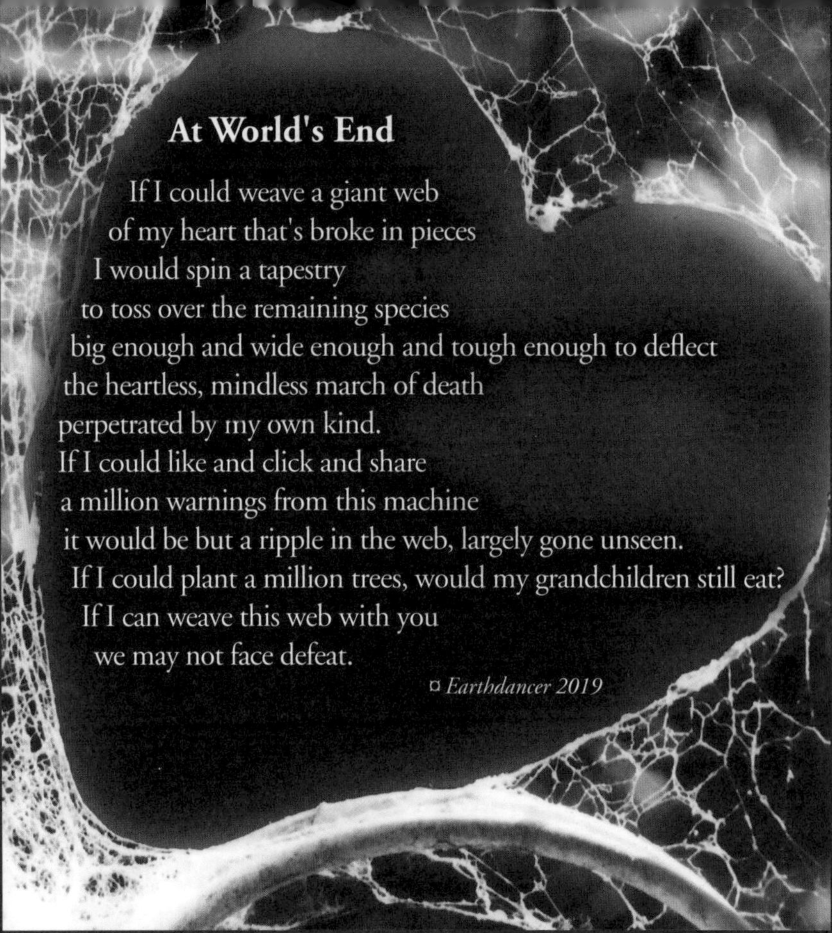

At World's End

If I could weave a giant web
of my heart that's broke in pieces
I would spin a tapestry
to toss over the remaining species
big enough and wide enough and tough enough to deflect
the heartless, mindless march of death
perpetrated by my own kind.
If I could like and click and share
a million warnings from this machine
it would be but a ripple in the web, largely gone unseen.
If I could plant a million trees, would my grandchildren still eat?
If I can weave this web with you
we may not face defeat.

¤ *Earthdancer 2019*

Grandmother Spider Weaves the World

♄♄♄ sábado

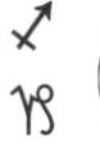
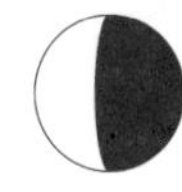

Saturday
6

☽□♆ 1:44 am v/c
☽→♑ 6:20 pm

☉☉☉ domingo

Sunday
7

☽△♅ 8:09 am
☽⚹♀ 5:29 pm

March
sān yuè

☽☽☽ xīng qī yī

♑ ♒

Monday
8

☉✶☽ 2:15 am
☽✶♆ 6:41 am
☽☌♇ 4:52 pm v/c
☽→♒ 11:41 pm

Starry Medicine Bowl ¤ *Beth Lenco 2019*

♂♂♂ xīng qī èr

♒

Tuesday
9

☽△♂ 5:23 am
☽□♅ 2:06 pm
☽☌♄ 4:45 pm

☿☿☿ xīng qī sān

♒

Wednesday
10

☽☌♃ 9:57 am
☉☌♆ 4:01 pm
☽☌☿ 7:32 pm v/c

♃♃♃ xīng qī sì

♒ ♓

Thursday
11

☽→♓ 6:44 am
♆ApH 12:53 pm
☽□♂ 3:16 pm
☽✶♅ 9:50 pm

♀♀♀ xīng qī wǔ

♓

Friday
12

☽☌♀ 7:29 pm
☽☌♆ 9:52 pm

Elemental Minuet *© Lindy Kehoe 2019*

♄♄♄ xīng qī liù

♓ ♈

Saturday 13

☉☌☽ 2:21 am
☽✶♇ 8:38 am v/c
☽→♈ 3:44 pm
♀☌♆ 8:07 pm

New Moon in ♓ Pisces 2:21 am PST

☉☉☉ lǐ bài rì

♈

Sunday 14

☽✶♂ 4:28 am
☽✶♄ 11:58 am

Daylight Saving Time Begins 2:00 am PST

When Women Lead

We're led by the holy darkness of the womb
By the urgent spark of earth's dreams.
When women lead, progress turns in on itself,
Spirals into a rose—
No more narrow arrow of Industry
No more unrelenting growth.
We know we feed each other with our lives.
We know that death and birth
Are both chords in this concert.
We know to take only what is offered,
To practice the honourable harvest,
That Earth understands consent,
Speaks in her own boundaried tongue.
We know she feels our feet as we walk,
That this kind of intimacy matters,
That our food is medicine,
That our death is also nourishment
For the soil that will feed our kin.
When women lead
We remember the great web
and we weave ourselves in.
When women lead
The world is repaired,
Thread by luminous thread.

¤ *Emily Kedar 2019*

IV. BORN TO LEAD

Moon IV: March 13–April 11

New Moon in ♓ Pisces Mar. 13; Sun in ♈ Aries March 20; Full Moon in ♎ LIbra Mar. 28

Unpretty ¤ *Destiney Powell 2017*

I cherish and honor
my sisters
May we lift each other up
to flourish and shine
In this often dark existence
And remind each other
to breathe

excerpt ¤ *Abril Garcia-Linn 2018*

March

Falgun

☽☽☽ sombar

♈ 

Monday 15

☽✶♃ 7:40 am
☿→♓ 3:26 pm
☽□♇ 8:40 pm v/c

Momentum

♂♂♂ mongolbar

♈ ♉ 

Tuesday 16

☽→♉ 3:56 am
☽✶☿ 5:31 am
☉✶♇ 11:26 am
☽☌♅ 8:37 pm

☿☿☿ budhbar

♉ 

Wednesday 17

☽□♄ 12:20 am
♂✶⚷ 8:35 pm
☽□♃ 9:14 pm
☽ApG 9:58 pm
☽✶♆ 10:15 pm

♃♃♃ brihospotibar

♉ ♊ 

Thursday 18

☽✶♀ 9:24 am
☽△♇ 9:30 am
♀✶♇ 10:20 am
☉✶☽ 1:40 pm v/c
☽→♊ 4:47 pm

♀♀♀ sukrobar

♊ 

Friday 19

☽□☿ 2:28 am
☽☌♂ 11:25 am
☽△♄ 1:49 pm

2021 Year at a Glance for ♈ Aries (March 20–April 19)

This is a year of collaboration for you, Aries. You like to do things on your own, take the lead, and make things happen. But 2021 will bring you fresh insights into how working with others can lead to opportunities that match your needs with the needs of the world. Take time this winter to reconnect with your hopes and dreams for the future. When spring comes, seek out others who may share those dreams with you. Join a group or enlist your chosen family to create a new chapter where your ideals become a reality. You may struggle with self-doubt and vulnerability as you share your aspirations with others, but collaboration holds the key to fruition.

New people will come into your life this year. Some of these new friendships will challenge you. They will be different from folks you usually hang out with. They will have wild ideas and eccentricities that may initially put you off. If you can handle the weird, these people will invigorate your own sense of self and inspire you to take risks in novel directions.

To help yourself integrate the innovative ideas and people moving into your life this year, you may want to take a class or engage in self-study in a subject that fascinates you. You don't need to go back to school necessarily, but you are learning to let your mental curiosity—instead of pure instinct—lead you. Enlivening your mind will allow you to take advantage of the opportunities for growth in your vocation or social justice work you may be called to.

Rhea Wolf © Mother Tongue Ink 2020

♄♄♄ sonibar

♊ Saturday 20 — Spring Equinox

☉→♈ 2:37 am
☽△♃ 11:14 am
☽□♆ 11:20 am

☉→♈

Sun in ♈ Aries 2:37 am PDT

☉☉☉ robibar

♊ ♋ Sunday 21

☽□♀ 5:04 am v/c
☽→♋ 5:17 am
♀→♈ 7:16 am
☉□☽ 7:40 am
☿✶♅ 4:35 pm
♂△♄ 7:35 pm
☽✶♅ 10:02 pm
☽△☿ 10:46 pm

Waxing Half Moon in ♋ Cancer 7:40 am PDT

Spring Equinox

There is a truth faster than any thought. More immediate than all our dearest visions of ourselves.

It is the thing that reaches, without thought, for love and comfort, to be soothed with tenderness, to be protected in fear. It is the thing that sends us out, questing recklessly, pushing the edges of comfort, safety and sense. It is the legacy of the animals we have always been, the cumulative wisdom of spring—new every time, ancient, timeless.

Hone your instincts. Pay attention to those truths that guide you, to the impulses that rule you beyond all your careful reckoning. This is the season of the wild. We are teeth bared, in need of both adventure and tenderness. Instinct is a whip, cutting through confusions and contortions both personal and collective.

Seek fluency instead of control. Hone skill and honesty instead of management. The wild will not be gainsayed. Its language needs to be remembered, spoken as easily as any tongue of cultivation and strategy, if we are to come back to the belly of the Earth.

Maeanna Welti © Mother Tongue Ink 2020

The Kissing Mountains © Bernice Davidson 2018

Chicory Dog © *LorrieArt 2019*

The Eve of Persephone

Three days, two, then the hour before she emerges again, too pale for a mother's liking. Demeter paces the softening Earth, just minutes until Equinox.

She knows the first moments will be awkward. Persephone blinking, blinded, disoriented by open sky. Demeter will temper her rush to hug, to blurt out plans for May and July. She will give her child time on the slow, unsteady path toward this half of home.

She will glance away from bruises, indigo tattoos of an underworld, attributing them to the trauma of re-birth. She won't ever ask about December. In a few minutes, her daughter will blossom. Demeter whistles to the old dog who has slept for six months at the foot of an empty bed. He sits expectant, ears pert, tail thumping the ground, hearing with his deeper ears, soil stirring.

The goddess in her vows not to let September overshadow spring. Any second, any second now pain will overwhelm her. A gush, a wail, the midwife wind announcing: "It's a girl."

March

Mí Márta

☽☽☽ Dé Luain

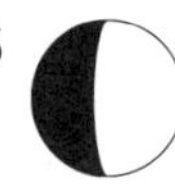

Monday 22

☽△♆ 10:14 pm

♂♂♂ Dé Máirt

Tuesday 23

☽☍♇ 8:26 am v/c
☽→♌ 2:56 pm
☿□♂ 8:26 pm
☽△♀ 8:49 pm
☉△☽ 9:54 pm

☿☿☿ Dé Céadaoin

♌

Wednesday 24

☽□♅ 6:45 am
☽☍♄ 10:38 am
☽✶♂ 1:08 pm

♃♃♃ Dé Ardaoin

♌
♍

Thursday 25

☽☍♃ 6:27 am v/c
☽→♍ 8:25 pm
☉☌♀ 11:58 pm

♀♀♀ Dé Haoine

♍

Friday 26

☽△♅ 11:16 am
☽□♂ 7:16 pm

Move out of my way, I'm changing the world. It may not be clear how or in exactly which way. I may not get credit and I don't care. Like rain today helps plants grow months down the line, it might look like nothing right now. Like one worker lays a part of a foundation for a structure that takes years to build and then stands for centuries. It might appear as a small job, unfinished. Like a forest fire burns away dead trees so new plants can grow, it might seem like utter devastation. Move out of my way . . . I'm changing the world.

¤ *Andrea Aragon 2017*

Goddess Sekhmet ¤ *Anna Lindberg Art 2018*

♄♄♄ Dé Sathairn

♍ ♎

Saturday 27

☽☍☿ 12:37 am
☽☍♆ 8:05 am
☽△♇ 4:48 pm v/c
☽→♎ 10:22 pm

☉☉☉ Dé Domhnaigh

♎

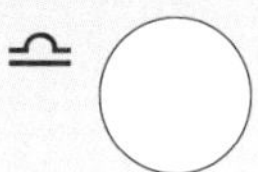

Sunday 28

♀☌⚷ 9:28 am
☉☍☽ 11:48 am
☽☍♀ 12:55 pm
☽△♄ 4:21 pm
☽△♂ 10:12 pm

Full Moon in ♎ Libra 11:48 am PDT

March / April

marzo / abril

☽☽☽ lunes

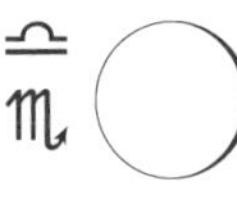

♎ ♏

Monday 29

☉☌⚷ 1:09 am
☽△♃ 11:01 am
☽□♇ 5:08 pm v/c
☿☌♆ 8:24 pm
☽→♏ 10:33 pm
☽PrG 11:09 pm
♀ApH 11:24 pm

Peek Experience

♂♂♂ martes

♏

Tuesday 30

⚷ApH 4:02 am
♀⚹♄ 8:47 am
☽☍♅ 12:54 pm
☽□♄ 4:39 pm

☿☿☿ miércoles

♏ ♐

Wednesday 31

☽△♆ 8:58 am
☽□♃ 11:52 am
☽△☿ 1:35 pm
☉⚹♄ 2:04 pm
☽⚹♇ 5:29 pm v/c
☽→♐ 10:59 pm

♃♃♃ jueves

♐

Thursday 1

April

☽⚹♄ 5:53 pm
☉△☽ 7:46 pm
☽△♀ 10:56 pm
☿⚹♇ 11:04 pm

♀♀♀ viernes

♐

Friday 2

☽☍♂ 3:40 am
☽□♆ 10:42 am
☽⚹♃ 2:17 pm
☽□☿ 10:23 pm v/c

The Next Ones

We can show the next ones fear,
Or we can teach them where to look for courage.
We can show them that wealth is made only of things,
Or we can try to nurture those riches that reach beyond.
We can show them a planet and Mother we abuse and fragment,
Or we can get creative with ways to heal this forgetfulness
—they came at a time where there's no other choice,
And they will have work to do.
We can raise them to heed, hush and fit in
Or let them show us they're not here for that,
And it seems to me we would do well to listen
And expand our containers
With all the patience and strength we can muster.
We will snap, we will shout, we will lose it again and again,
But the next ones must know
That there's a new way on the horizon:
A future remembering,
Where the songs and codes of Before and After
Ignite in change,
And bring us back home
To each other,
The earth
And the Mother
Of us all.

♄♄♄ sábado

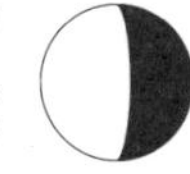

Saturday
3

☽→♑ 1:13 am
☽△♅ 5:05 pm
☿→♈ 8:41 pm

☉☉☉ domingo

♑

Sunday
4

☉□☽ 3:02 am
☽□♀ 7:33 am
☽⚹♆ 2:55 pm

Waning Half Moon in ♑ Capricorn 3:02 am PDT

April

sì yuè

Malala © Paula Franco 2018

☽☽☽ xīng qī yī

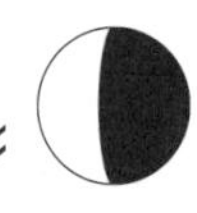

♒

Monday 5

☽☌♇ 12:05 am v/c
☽→♒ 6:03 am
☽✶☿ 11:19 am
☽□♅ 10:58 pm

♂♂♂ xīng qī èr

Tuesday 6

☽☌♄ 3:32 am
♀✶♂ 4:17 am
☉✶☽ 1:40 pm
☽△♂ 6:55 pm
☽✶♀ 7:43 pm

☿☿☿ xīng qī sān

♓

Wednesday 7

☽☌♃ 3:05 am v/c
☽→♓ 1:30 pm

♃♃♃ xīng qī sì

♓

Thursday 8

☽✶♅ 7:24 am

♀♀♀ xīng qī wǔ

♓

♈

Friday 9

☿☌⚷ 12:08 am
☽□♂ 6:49 am
☽☌♆ 7:04 am
♂□♆ 12:18 pm
☽✶♇ 4:48 pm v/c
☽→♈ 11:11 pm

Slow Motion Prayer

Get real quiet and listen in. Keep going.
You'll notice before long, some small tendril
of desire wrapped around the minerals that make you.
Feel it pull up through your core, like a river of blue opal

laced through boulder stone.
Let the breath lift and dance you
as bending grass dances with fragrant wind.
We know that longing can hurt. But realize it matters.

Your longing is slow motion prayer.
Remember that the world too is longing for you
to get out of your own holy way, so raise yourself up,
hands open and heart first.

We live on the wild edge of death and birth.
It's up to us to begin again.
Your belonging matters more than ever.
Every small dream of a thriving world

is one note in the new song,
one thread in the new story,
one cell in this earthbody—
pulsing toward vitality.

¤ *Emily Kedar 2019*

♄♄♄ xīng qī liù

♈ 

Saturday
10

☿✶♄ 8:09 am
♀✶♃ 11:53 am
☽✶♄ 11:00 pm

☉☉☉ lǐ bài rì

♈ 

Sunday
11

☽☌☿ 1:46 am
☉☌☽ 7:31 pm
♀□♇ 8:20 pm
☽✶♂ 8:59 pm

New Moon in ♈ Aries 7:31 pm PDT

a fragile bend of the heart

let us meet there
at a fragile bend of the heart
at a threshold of acceptance
where compassion and tenderness
utterly shift the world
utterly lift the world
from confusion to clarity
from darkness to light
from them to us
from us to everyone
let us meet there
at a fragile bend of the heart
where we are limited in all things
but our capacity to love
the weakness that will save us
utterly fragile love
utterly agile love
all our human venerabilities
merging there, invincible
at a fragile bend of the heart

¤ *Shelley Blooms 2019*

V. HEART SPRING

Moon V: April 11–May 11

New Moon in ♈ Aries April 11; Sun in ♉ Taurus April 19; Full Moon in ♏ Scorpio April 26

Three Cranes © *Lyndia Radice 2018*

Choitro

☽☽☽ sombar

Monday
12

☽✶♃ 1:24 am
☽□♇ 4:12 am
☽☌♀ 5:06 am v/c
☽→♉ 10:44 am

♂♂♂ mongolbar

♉

Tuesday
13

☽☌♅ 6:18 am
☽□♄ 11:30 am
☉✶♂ 4:09 pm

☿☿☿ budhbar

♉ ♊

Wednesday
14

☽✶♆ 7:03 am
☽ApG 10:45 am
♀→♉ 11:22 am
☽□♃ 3:02 pm
☽△♇ 5:00 pm v/c
☽→♊ 11:35 pm

♃♃♃ brihospotibar

♊

Thursday
15

☿ApH 7:08 am
☉✶♃ 9:58 am

♀♀♀ sukrobar

♊

Friday
16

☽△♄ 12:52 am
☉□♇ 6:27 am
☽□♆ 8:15 pm
♂△♃ 10:14 pm

Love Letter to the Cosmos

There you are! In all the ones who speak, sing, fly, dance, extend their roots! In the ones staying and the ones moving! I see you!

Sounds extending high-pitched and in deep vibration, rhythms, polyrhythms, splashes, cries, rustles, accelerating, slowing, linked and unlinked from what I see, I hear you!

Your jokes make me fall down, your light makes me stretch, your heat makes me curl up in comfort, your coolness refreshes me, your distances make me imagine!

I feel you!

© Lisa S. Nelson 2019

Women are Powerful ¤ *Destiney Powell 2019*

♄♄♄ sonibar

♊ ♋ Saturday 17

☽✶☿ 4:05 am
☽△♃ 4:53 am
☽☌♂ 5:08 am
☉✶☽ 8:03 am v/c
☿✶♃ 9:00 am
☿✶♂ 12:09 pm
☽→♋ 12:25 pm
☿□♇ 2:49 pm
☽✶♀ 8:49 pm
♂⊼♇ 9:26 pm

☉☉☉ robibar

♋ Sunday 18

☽✶♅ 8:18 am
☉☌☿ 6:49 pm

April
Mí Aibreán

☽☽☽ Dé Luain

♋ ♌

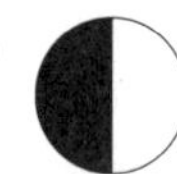

Monday 19

☿→♉ 3:29 am
☽△♆ 7:56 am
☉→♉ 1:33 pm
☽☍♇ 5:03 pm v/c
☽→♌ 11:10 pm
☉□☽ 11:59 pm

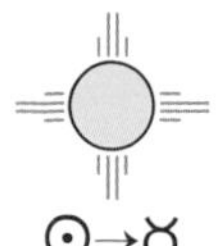

☉→♉

Sun in ♉ Taurus 1:33 pm PDT
Waxing Half Moon in ♌ Leo 11:59 pm PDT

♂♂♂ Dé Máirt

♌

Tuesday 20

☽□☿ 3:08 am
☽□♀ 1:21 pm
☽□♅ 6:11 pm
☽☍♄ 10:56 pm

☿☿☿ Dé Céadaoin

♌

Wednesday 21

No exact aspects

♃♃♃ Dé Ardaoin

♌ ♍

Thursday 22

☽☍♃ 12:54 am
☽✶♂ 5:05 am v/c
☽→♍ 6:08 am
☉△☽ 11:06 am
♀☌♅ 6:01 pm
☽△☿ 7:47 pm
☽△♅ 11:57 pm

♀♀♀ Dé Haoine

♍

Friday 23

☽△♀ 12:30 am
♂→♋ 4:49 am
☽☍♆ 8:10 pm
☿☌♅ 11:42 pm

2021 Year at a Glance for ♉ Taurus (April 19–May 20)

With Uranus making its seven-year journey through your sign, Taurus, you may be buzzing with energy and ideas. Channel this power into deepening your connections with the Earth, rejuvenating your body, and amplifying the pleasure in your life. Allow yourself to flow in new directions that break you out of those pesky habits you're so good at settling into. How much more beautiful could your life be if you finally let go of your fear of change? You'll never know unless you take the risk and say goodbye to who you think you are.

This renovated self will open the door to a fresh crop of possibilities related to your work life in the world. Even though you may like things stable overall, the time is right for a radical reinvention of what your trajectory looks like. Are you engaged in livelihood that is in line with your values? How could you (re)shape your work to fulfill your wildest dreams? Is it too weird to be realistic? Not so, say Saturn and Jupiter, who are conspiring to bring new hope with practical action into this area of your life. Sit with these questions and your visions through the winter, and make a plan to begin again. Use the bounty of energy you'll have in January through the beginning of March.

This fall, take care of yourself and reset your health routines. You may feel depleted from the activity of the summer. Perhaps a cleanse or different fitness routine is in order. Shower yourself with body care that invites a sensual, luxurious experience of healing. You're worth it.

Rhea Wolf © Mother Tongue Ink 2020

Blowing Bubbles © *Robin Urton 2016*

♄♄♄ Dé Sathairn

♍ ♎

Saturday
24

☽△♇ 3:50 am v/c
☽→♎ 9:06 am
☽□♂ 10:19 am
♀□♄ 9:21 pm

☉☉☉ Dé Domhnaigh

♎

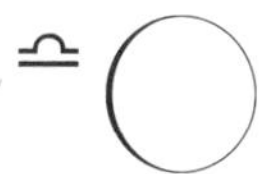

Sunday
25

☿□♄ 4:58 am
☽△♄ 6:02 am
☿☌♀ 3:19 pm

April
abril

DDD lunes

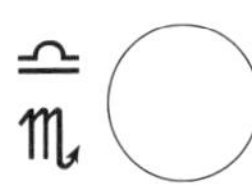

Monday 26

Lunar Beltane

☽□♇ 4:15 am
☽△♃ 5:39 am v/c
☽→♏ 9:18 am
☽△♂ 12:29 pm
☉☍☽ 8:31 pm

Full Moon in ♏ Scorpio 8:31 pm PDT

♂♂♂ martes

Tuesday 27

☽☍♅ 1:51 am
☽□♄ 5:47 am
☽PrG 8:27 am
☽☍♀ 10:35 am
♇R 1:03 pm
☽☍☿ 1:23 pm
☽△♆ 8:31 pm

☿☿☿ miércoles

Wednesday 28

☽✶♇ 3:38 am
☽□♃ 5:31 am v/c
☽→♐ 8:42 am

♃♃♃ jueves

Thursday 29

☽✶♄ 5:35 am
☿✶♆ 7:26 pm
☽□♆ 8:42 pm

♀♀♀ viernes

♐ ♑

Friday 30

☽✶♃ 6:27 am v/c
☽→♑ 9:16 am
☉☌♅ 12:54 pm
☽☍♂ 4:51 pm

Beltane

You strong one, your roots go deep. Remember this. Remember to glory in your roots, trace along them, let them drink and grow. You are one with the Earth.

Stretch from the ground you stand on. Grow from your oneness with what birthed you. That imperturbable, joyful, abundant fierce Earth. The legacy of the creatures we have always been.

At the heart of our wildness is a deep calm. Such an authentic reverence, the wonder of being exactly what we are. At the heart of all our beauty is something implacably committed, something born of the dance of earthquakes and shaken by nothing.

Love is the most radiant, transformative, intensive force that drives life. Life is asking us to truly fall in love, to show up with the unapologetic, fearsome tenderness of every formidable being that ever fought to nourish and protect what it cherishes—to become formidably loving, through earthquakes and tenderness.

What are the roots of your beauty? What is the foundation of your joy? What is the wellspring of your strength? How will you build your capacity for the love of this life and this world?

Maeanna Welti © Mother Tongue Ink 2020

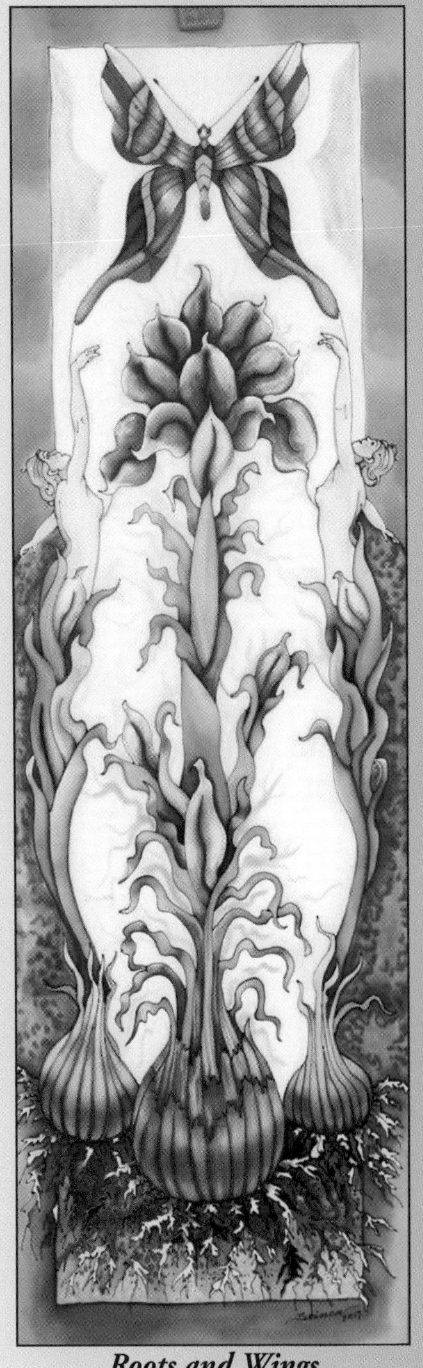

Roots and Wings

© Margriet Seinen 2016

Tree Lover

My juicy lover
Your long silhouette of elegance
Mirrors my own rhythmic dance
Sometimes bending furiously
Other times bending gently
Always in perfect balance
with your own inner tune

I see you, I feel you
Your wide veins exposed
Carrying the sacred fires of life
Your sturdy branches
Sheltering home for my soul

I feel your benevolent heart
Infinite welcome
In the softness of your moss next to my skin
Caressing me tenderly
Innocently

You and I
We are of the same kinship
One lifeblood, one family
Infinity of roots
Spreading riot through the world
Quickening its pulse

You and I
One breath—Rhythmic dance
Wayfarer
Cathedrals of hope
Entwined Sisters, lovers of hope

With first waking of the day
And sleep in my eyes
I inhale your moist fresh dew
Tasting aliveness and potency
My faithful companion
My juicy lover
My wild inspiration

Forgiveness ¤ Sundara Fawn 2011

ħħħ sábado

♑ Saturday 1

May
Beltane

♅ApH 12:04 am
☽△♅ 3:12 am
☉△☽ 4:12 am
☽△♀ 9:42 pm
☽✱♆ 11:16 pm

☉☉☉ domingo

Sunday 2

☿△♇ 2:19 am
☽☌♇ 6:54 am
☽△☿ 7:38 am v/c
☽→♒ 12:31 pm
♀✱♆ 3:38 pm

May
wu yuè

☽☽☽ xīng qī yī

Monday
3

☿□♃ 2:33 am
☉□♄ 3:01 am
☽□♅ 7:52 am
☽☌♄ 12:08 pm
☉□☽ 12:50 pm
☿→♊ 7:49 pm

Moonlit Love

Waning Half Moon in ♒ Aquarius 12:50 pm PDT

♂♂♂ xīng qī èr

♒ ♓
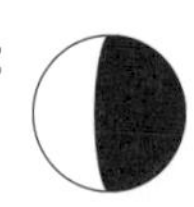

Tuesday
4

☽□♀ 8:59 am
☽☌♃ 5:05 pm v/c
☽→♓ 7:08 pm
☽□☿ 10:54 pm

☿☿☿ xīng qī sān

♓

Wednesday
5

☽△♂ 9:07 am
☽✶♅ 3:57 pm

♃♃♃ xīng qī sì

♓

Thursday
6

☉✶☽ 1:41 am
♀△♇ 4:24 am
☽☌♆ 2:17 pm
☽✶♇ 10:34 pm

♀♀♀ xīng qī wǔ

♓ ♈

Friday
7

☽✶♀ 12:36 am v/c
☽→♈ 4:52 am
☽✶☿ 6:00 pm
☽□♂ 10:35 pm

All aspects in Pacific Daylight Time; add 3 hours for EDT; add 7 hours for GMT

Complete Trust

Could we soften? Could we surrender? Say what we find edgy out loud? Could we have safe enough spaces? To keep exploring, to heal, to grow? To learn about our true purpose, our beauty, our gifts, our power?

If we had trust in one another, could we share more?

If we had trust in one another, could we know we are always held? That our voice matters too?

Could our bodies be softer?
Could our tensions be eased?
Could we see
the solutions we need
in our personal
and collective life?
And share them freely
without fear?

If we had
complete trust
in one another,
how would we walk
in the world?

¤ *Sophia Faria 2019*

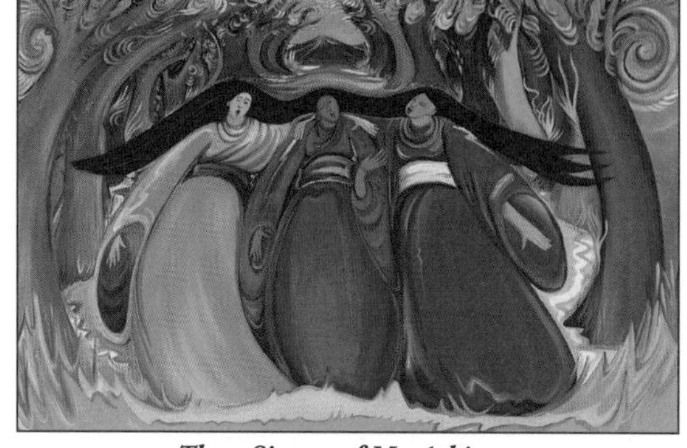

Three Singers of Mt. Ashigara
© Toni Truesdale 2008

♄♄♄ xīng qī liù

♈ 

Saturday 8

♀□♃ 6:38 am
☽✶♄ 7:18 am
♀→♊ 7:01 pm

☉☉☉ lǐ bài rì

♈
♉

Sunday 9

☽□♇ 10:16 am
☽✶♃ 3:50 pm v/c
☽→♉ 4:46 pm

second dancer

women. when you feel another woman trembling, see her hands start to sweat, the blood of her womb rising to color her cheeks. honestly, lookin' like she might vomit, or pass out . . .

women. when you sense another woman approaching the edge of just the "right-kind-of-madness," gearing up to say or do something that could change her life forever—and maybe even ripple back in time, healing generations of women before her . . .

women. when you see that look in her eyes, and she swallows hard—the moment when she digs, one more time.

digs. way. down. deep inside. reaching some primal reserve of wild courage she didn't yet know was there . . . and you are there when she ACTS on that wild courage, by SPEAKING her truth.

women. when you have the great blessing of witnessing another woman going out on THAT scary limb, taking the kind of risk she might have been trying to find the courage to take her whole life, knowing, in that moment, she moved against, and overcame, the weight and momentum of over 2,000 years of reasons why she shouldn't open her mouth.

ladies, women, sisters, witches and crones. yes, I'm talking to YOU. for Goddess' sake, BACK HER.

especially if you've ever been in her shoes. especially if you have privilege to offer up as collateral and to wield for right and good. especially if you've ever been on the receiving end of someone turning a blind eye.

be her second dancer. stand behind, or beside her, or wherever you can get your feet under you in the moment. it may be awkward, and it most certainly will be uncomfortable, both for her and for you. you might trip over yourself doing it. the articulate words of support you had waiting in the wings could fly completely away. everyone will stare at you. it very well might take you just as much courage to go second, as it took her to go first.

but PLEASE. STAND anyway. it will always be worth it. even when we were burned. it was still worth it.

¤ *Breyn Marr 2018*

VI. EMPOW-HER-MENT

Moon VI: May 11– June 10

New Moon in ♉ Taurus May 11; Sun in ♊ Gemini May 20; Full Moon in ♐ Sagittarius May 26

Women's Fire Circle

© Flame Bilyue' 2009

May
Boishakh

Desert Door, Two

☽☽☽ sombar

♉ 

Monday
10

☽✶♂ 2:12 pm
☽☌♅ 3:35 pm
☿✶⚷ 7:44 pm
☽□♄ 7:55 pm

♂♂♂ mongolbar

♉ 

Tuesday
11

☉☌☽ 12:00 pm
☽✶♆ 2:47 pm
☽ApG 2:49 pm
♂□⚷ 4:53 pm
♂✶♅ 7:48 pm
☽△♇ 11:07 pm

New Moon in ♉ Taurus 12:00 pm PDT

☿☿☿ budhbar

♉ ♊ 

Wednesday
12

☽□♃ 5:23 am v/c
☽→♊ 5:43 am
☿△♄ 11:34 am
☽☌♀ 3:20 pm
☉✶♆ 10:45 pm

♃♃♃ brihospotibar

♊ 

Thursday
13

☽△♄ 9:03 am
☽☌☿ 11:32 am
♃→♓ 3:36 pm

♀♀♀ sukrobar

♊ ♋ 

Friday
14

☽□♆ 3:51 am v/c
☽→♋ 6:30 pm
☽△♃ 6:45 pm

There Is A Mountain You Have To Climb

How it got in your back yard is impossible to tell, but there it is, throwing blankets of shadows over your suns, throwing slabs of darkness over your days. You try to ignore it, though it calls to the pit of your being. You can try to ignore it for years but it's always there, waiting for the day when you finally muster the courage to make an attempt. You can go around the world trying to avoid it but, as the taxi pulls away from the curb to take you to the airport, you see it trailing behind you in the rearview mirror. It will camp out in the backyard of your most exotic port of call, will follow you through lifetimes if need be, to begin the climb you've put off for years until it seems the attempt itself is the very thing that will kill you.

So you finally, finally shake off the self-doubt, self-disgust, self-hatred, put on your climbing boots and, what else? Start to climb. Sometimes you cannot see a place to put your foot next, and at times it doesn't feel like a mountain at all, more like a high hill, and you climb, one foot after another. Impossibly, the never-dreamed-of happens: you climb the mountain you have to climb and, at that dizzying height, you breathe relief as deeply as you have ever breathed in your life. You look out at all the life below you and see paths you have followed and feel your spirit put its arm around your shoulder. It says, "Now that wasn't so bad was it?" and you have to admit the anxiety and the dread were harder than the climb itself. And your spirit says, "Good! Rest here for a few minutes, give yourself a pat on the back and rest . . . I have a few more mountains for us to climb."

¤ *Shelley Blooms 2019*

♄♄♄ sonibar

♋

Saturday
15

♂⚻♄ 7:49 am
☽✶♅ 5:35 pm
☽☌♂ 10:06 pm

☉☉☉ robibar

♋ 

Sunday
16

☽△♆ 3:42 pm
☉✶☽ 11:05 pm
☽☍♇ 11:23 pm v/c

May

Mí Bealtaine

☽☽☽ Dé Luain

Apra Seed © *Mary Ruff-Gentle Doe 2011*

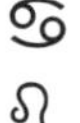
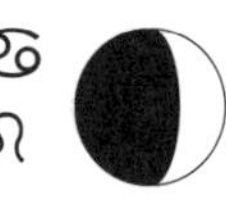

Monday 17

♋ ♌

☉△♇ 2:49 am
☽→♌ 5:44 am

♂♂♂ Dé Máirt

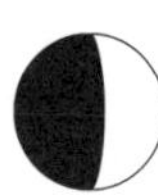

Tuesday 18

♌

☽⚹♀ 3:43 am
☽□♅ 4:04 am
♀⚹⚷ 4:44 am
☽☍♄ 7:29 am
☽⚹☿ 7:55 pm

☿☿☿ Dé Céadaoin

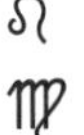

Wednesday 19

♌ ♍

☉□☽ 12:13 pm v/c
☽→♍ 1:59 pm
☽☍♃ 3:07 pm
♀△♄ 6:58 pm

Waxing Half Moon in ♌ Leo 12:13 pm PDT

♃♃♃ Dé Ardaoin

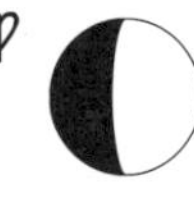

Thursday 20

♍

☽△♅ 11:08 am
☉→♊ 12:37 pm
☽□♀ 4:01 pm
☽⚹♂ 7:57 pm

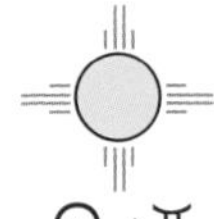
☉→♊

Sun in ♊ Gemini 12:37 pm PDT

♀♀♀ Dé Haoine

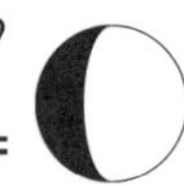

Friday 21

♍ ♎

☽□☿ 4:47 am
☽☍♆ 6:24 am
☉□♃ 8:03 am
☽△♇ 12:56 pm v/c
☽→♎ 6:35 pm
☉△☽ 8:46 pm

2021 Year at a Glance for ♊ Gemini (May 20–June 20)

You're full of ideas, Gemini. And that's why we love you. In 2021, the ideas that pop into your head will not be the usual variety. You may even get the urge to study a brand new subject. You are going through a transformation of mind, which will bring out radically different perspectives that challenge your worldview. For example, if you think the universe is centered in love, then perhaps you will begin to understand the chaos that is also present. If you've been cynical in the past, perhaps you will see reason to hope. Allow the contradictions to emerge and let them change the way you see yourself and the larger world.

In March and April, you will have an uptick in energy to put to use. You may feel more irritable, but you will also be able to get a lot more done than usual. Channel this abundance of energy into art projects that interest you, take a class, start or join a group working to restore our natural environment.

Your relationships are also changing this year. You are finally at a place to be able to let go of restlessness in regard to your significant others. As a natural-born wanderer, perhaps your relationships have been less than stable. This year, you can bring a sense of adventure to your love life without needing to abandon others in order to feel free. In the fall, reconsider your ideas about romance and see what you can do to fan the flames of desire.

Rhea Wolf © Mother Tongue Ink 2020

Panthera
© Kimberly Webber 2018

♄♄♄ Dé Sathairn

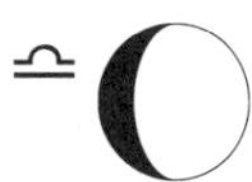

Saturday
22

☽△♄ 5:11 pm
☿□♆ 7:42 pm
☽△♀ 11:36 pm

☉☉☉ Dé Domhnaigh

Sunday
23

☽□♂ 12:51 am
♄R 2:19 am
☽△☿ 8:59 am
☽□♇ 2:36 pm v/c
☽→♏ 8:00 pm
☽△♃ 9:37 pm

May
mayo

☽☽☽ lunes

♏

Monday
24

☽☍♅ 3:15 pm
☽□♄ 5:35 pm

♂♂♂ martes

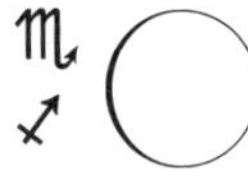

Tuesday
25

☽△♂ 3:01 am
☽△♆ 8:30 am
☽✶♇ 2:20 pm v/c
☽PrG 6:37 pm
☽→♐ 7:39 pm
☽□♃ 9:30 pm

☿☿☿ miércoles

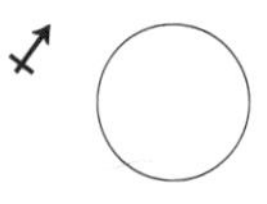

Wednesday
26

☉☍☽ 4:14 am
☽✶♄ 5:01 pm

Total Lunar Eclipse 4:18 am PDT*
Full Moon in ♐ Sagittarius 4:14 am PDT

♃♃♃ jueves

♐ ♑

Thursday
27

☽☍♀ 7:43 am
☽□♆ 8:06 am
☽☍☿ 10:35 am v/c
♀□♆ 12:25 pm
☽→♑ 7:23 pm
☽✶♃ 9:31 pm

♀♀♀ viernes

♑

Friday
28

☽△♅ 3:22 pm
☿☌♀ 10:13 pm

*Eclipse visible South and East Asia, Australia, the Pacific, and the Americas

Letter to my Moon Child

Rosas do Mar
© Karina Sulla 2010

Dear Heart,
You are so precious to me.
You are enough, whatever you do,
 or don't do.
I am with you, all-ways,
 side by side, hand in hand.
You are here to express
 your wildly unique self.
Be brave. Be seen.
Be proud
 of your beautiful honey skin.
Be bold,
 wear that afro,
for your curls are your strength.
You are safe to speak your truth, and shed your secrets.
The tears will stop. Trust.
Light will shine through the cracks of your broken heart.
For-give, Free yourself, and those to come, from ancestral burdens.
You Are Love. You are growing, There will always be time to play!
Stand up, speak out, own your Power.
Warrior Up, Gurl. Warrior Up!

© Mahada Thomas 2019

♄♄♄ sábado

♑ ♒

Saturday
29

☽☍♂ 7:36 am
☽⚹♆ 9:13 am
☽☌♇ 3:15 pm v/c
☿R 3:34 pm
☽→♒ 9:04 pm

☉☉☉ domingo

♒

Sunday
30

♀⚻♇ 10:47 am
☉△☽ 1:43 pm
☽□♅ 6:29 pm
☽☌♄ 8:25 pm
♂△♆ 10:15 pm

May / June

wǔ yuè / liù yuè

☽☽☽ xīng qī yī

Monday
31

☽△☿ 4:13 pm
☽△♀ 11:13 pm v/c

♂♂♂ xīng qī èr

Tuesday
1

June

☽→♓ 2:07 am
☽☌♃ 5:04 am

☿☿☿ xīng qī sān

Wednesday
2

☉□☽ 12:24 am
☽✶♅ 1:21 am
☉✶⚷ 4:23 am
♀→♋ 6:18 am
☽☌♆ 9:31 pm
☽□☿ 11:24 pm

Waning Half Moon in ♓ Pisces 12:24 am PDT

♃♃♃ xīng qī sì

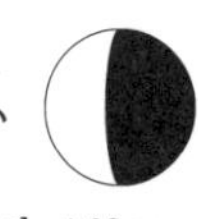

Thursday
3

☽△♂ 1:08 am
☽✶♇ 4:10 am v/c
☽→♈ 10:59 am
☉△♄ 12:05 pm
☽□♀ 2:09 pm
♀△♃ 4:33 pm

♀♀♀ xīng qī wǔ

Friday
4

☽✶♄ 1:24 pm
☉✶☽ 3:38 pm

Earth Prayer: Transformation © Kay Kemp Art 2012

Sister March

Tell me about our radiant Mother
How she led you into the street with your sisters.
United, determined, empowered.
Tell me about marching forward
How your voices rumbled around the lost world.

excerpt ¤ Angela Bigler 2017

♄♄♄ xīng qī liù

♈
♉

Saturday
5

☽✶☿ 8:56 am
☿□♆ 12:05 pm
♂☍♇ 12:45 pm

☽□♇ 3:37 pm
☽□♂ 3:47 pm v/c
☽→♉ 10:46 pm

☉☉☉ lǐ bài rì

♉

Sunday
6

☽✶♃ 2:32 am
☽✶♀ 8:57 am

June
Joishtho

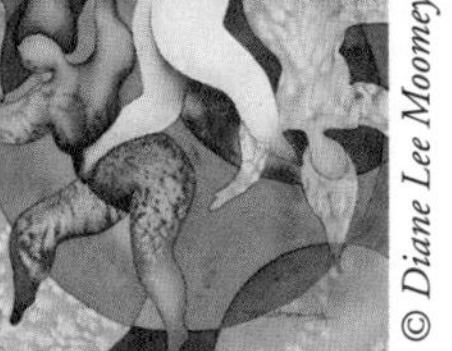

World by Night

☽☽☽ sombar

♉ 

Monday
7

☽☌♅ 12:39 am
☽□♄ 1:51 am
☽ApG 7:28 pm
☽✶♆ 9:46 pm

♂♂♂ mongolbar

♉ ♊ 

Tuesday
8

☽△♇ 4:30 am
☽✶♂ 8:07 am v/c
☽→♊ 11:47 am
☽□♃ 3:47 pm

☿☿☿ budhbar

♊ 

Wednesday
9

☽△♄ 2:44 pm

♃♃♃ brihospotibar

♊ 

Thursday
10

☉☌☽ 3:53 am
☿PrH 3:55 am
☽☌☿ 5:37 am
☽□♆ 10:37 am v/c
☉☌☿ 6:13 pm

Annular Solar Eclipse 3:41 am PDT*
New Moon in ♊ Gemini 3:53 am PDT

♀♀♀ sukrobar

♊ ♋ 

Friday
11

☽→♋ 12:22 am
☽△♃ 4:28 am
♂→♌ 6:34 am
☽☌♀ 11:59 pm

*Eclipse visible from North America, Europe and Asia

Some Big Loud Woman

I need some big loud woman to listen to
        Orangey red   Wild haired
Her voice like
                A waterfall of kettles
Her head back   eyes shut   back arched
To roar that music out

I need the brass and bramble   of her low notes
The trembling windows   of her highs
Bare feet planted on the floorboards
Green dress a summer canopy

The wail in one line
A scar on the air

I need to listen to a big loud woman
Heavy fists   pounding on my table
Her anger   fire in the hearth

I need the avalanche   of her laughter
    the flood   of her truth

I need to listen
    to some big loud woman

I need some big loud woman to listen to

♄♄♄ sonibar

♋

Saturday 12

☽✶♅ 2:10 am
♀□⚷ 11:28 am
☽△♆ 10:06 pm
♀✶♅ 10:38 pm

☉☉☉ robibar

♋
♌

Sunday 13

♀⚻♄ 1:15 am
☽☍♇ 4:16 am v/c
☽→♌ 11:22 am
☽☌♂ 2:07 pm
☉□♆ 4:39 pm

Too Awake

Be too awake.
Trust the trembling forest
place your hands on hot earth,
on cold stones,
in living streams.
Look for bridges into mystery
and thresholds into knowing
formed of leaning trees
and embracing roots.
Be too awake
and let wings of wonder
carry you into clouds of magic
winding wisps of pleasure
through your blood and bones.
Be too awake
and drink
all kinds of moonlight
curling yourself
into caves and grooves
alive with meaning.
Be too awake
for the world is full of birds
and you can feel the singing
in your soles and skin.
Be too awake
for there are lakes of longing
within you
and you know how to swim.
Let the greening earth
glow beneath you
let your buried power
rise and breathe,
for it is in being too awake
that you will know yourself
as whole and here.

Be too awake
even if it is the only thing
you have left to be.

Gratitude *© Rachael Amber 2018*

VII. LOVE OF NATURE

Moon VII: June 10–July 9

New Moon in ♊ Gemini June 10; Sun in ♋ Cancer June 20; Full Moon in ♑ Capricorn June 24

She Flourishes © *Gaia Orion 2017*

June

Mí Meitheamh

☽☽☽ Dé Luain

Green Darner Dragonfly

♌

Monday 14

☽□♅ 12:27 pm
☽☍♄ 12:28 pm
♄□♅ 3:01 pm
♂⚻♃ 5:39 pm
☽⚹☿ 9:58 pm

♂♂♂ Dé Máirt

♌
♍

Tuesday 15

☉⚹☽ 10:27 am v/c
☽→♍ 8:02 pm

☿☿☿ Dé Céadaoin

♍

Wednesday 16

☽☍♃ 12:00 am
☽△♅ 8:07 pm
☉⚻♇ 10:24 pm

♃♃♃ Dé Ardaoin

♍

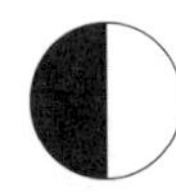

Thursday 17

☽□☿ 3:16 am
☽⚹♀ 5:07 am
☽☍♆ 1:54 pm
☽△♇ 7:18 pm
☉□☽ 8:54 pm v/c

Waxing Half Moon in ♍ Virgo 8:54 pm PDT

♀♀♀ Dé Haoine

♍
♎

Friday 18

☽→♎ 1:53 am
☽⚹♂ 9:32 am

2021 Year at a Glance for ♋ Cancer (June 20–July 22)

In 2021, you are being extended an invitation into the unknown. The gates of mystery are opening to teach you more about the hidden depths of yourself than ever before. Check in with your energetic boundaries and shore up any loose edges that leave you feeling depleted by the emotional needs of others. You tend to be a caring presence for the people in your life, but it's time to focus on your own shadows now.

Darkness can be a nurturing place where new life germinates and unfurls. In order to reap the benefits of the nourishing dark, you have to be willing to do some shadow work. That may mean recognizing the ways you diminish parts of you that are wild, eccentric, and just plain weird. You are learning how to be authentically you, even when that upsets the delicate balance you strive to create out of a desire to be accepted by others. Your dreams bring revelation about hidden aspects of yourself. Be willing to activate these secret gems.

The powerful emotional landscape of this year may have you feeling unmoored from the mundane world. This is a year for spiritual exploration rather than practical action. Use the surge of energy you'll feel in May and June to strengthen your connection with the divine, create world healing rituals, make sacred practice part of your routine. In the fall, you may feel the urge to rearrange your home to make it a true sanctuary for yourself and your clan—a place that reflects your inner landscape.

Rhea Wolf © Mother Tongue Ink 2020

♄♄♄ Dé Sathairn

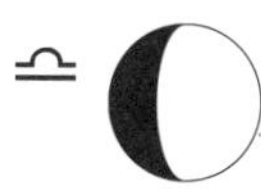

♎ Saturday 19

☽△♄ 12:15 am
☽△♅ 6:22 am
☽□♀ 2:07 pm
☽□♇ 10:37 pm

Jurema, Cabocla da Mata
© *Karina Sulla 2017*

☉☉☉ Dé Domhnaigh

♎ ♏ Sunday 20

☉△☽ 3:52 am v/c
☽→♏ 4:58 am
♃R 8:05 am
☽△♃ 8:35 am
☽□♂ 2:29 pm
☉→♋ 8:32 pm

Summer Solstice

☉→♋

Sun in ♋ Cancer 8:32 pm PDT

Summer Solstice

This is a wide open view. The wisdom and scope of the sea. This is the terrain the moon sees. The meeting of hard lines and softness.

Solstice will expand you—into hope, connection, revelation. It will draw you out with compassion, then demand the best your love has to give. Compassion is not all softness. It is fierce. It is unyielding, uncompromising in the love that feeds it. Centering love is no joke. No easy task.

It is for those who can stand in the hugeness of summer and look into what the light reveals. It is for those who soften into connection, melt into the tides, and also provide the definition of the shore. Centering love is for those with integrity. Not a moral code, per se, but the deep integration of beliefs with behaviors, commitments with actions, visions with knowledge of self and world.

We will not know the power of our love until we let it draw us out. Will not reveal our glory until summer strips us of our hiding. Until we seek to strengthen instead of defend.

Maeanna Welti © Mother Tongue Ink 2020

Alone in the Cosmos © *Sophia Rosenberg 2006*

Public Parking © Nancy Watterson 2019

Small Worlds of Hope and Healing

As I have re-connected with nature mid-life, I have been amazed at the everyday magic evident in every forest, marsh and urban park. I have seen Nurse Logs that appeared lifeless and filled with rot one week, birth an entire micro-forest the next. Dandelions bloom from solid asphalt; a frozen marsh thaws and pushes forth marigolds within days. Lifeless ponds lie dormant for months beneath a shawl of ice, then burst with bird and frog song. The Earth has not given up. She is not beaten, but merely recovering, and we can learn and gain strength from her resilience.

excerpt © Susan M. Warfield 2019

June
junio

☽☽☽ lunes

Monday
21

¤ *Natalie Gildersleeve 2019*

☽□♄ 2:08 am
☽☍♅ 3:02 am
♀△♆ 6:57 am
☽△♆ 6:57 pm
☽△♀ 8:01 pm
☽⚹♇ 11:43 pm v/c

♂♂♂ martes

Tuesday
22

☽→♐ 5:55 am
☽□♃ 9:26 am
☿D 3:00 pm
☽△♂ 5:16 pm

☿☿☿ miércoles

Wednesday
23

☽⚹♄ 2:25 am
☽PrG 2:52 am
☉△♃ 3:11 am
☽☍☿ 7:50 am
♀☍♇ 4:39 pm
☽□♆ 7:09 pm v/c
♄⚹⚷ 9:30 pm

♃♃♃ jueves

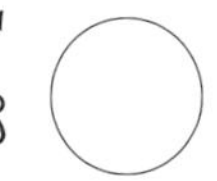

Thursday
24

☽→♑ 6:05 am
☽⚹♃ 9:33 am
☉☍☽ 11:40 am

Full Moon in ♑ Capricorn 11:40 am PDT

♀♀♀ viernes

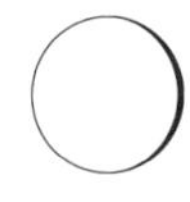

Friday
25

☽△♅ 4:04 am
♆R 12:21 pm
☽⚹♆ 7:51 pm

All aspects in Pacific Daylight Time; add 3 hours for EDT; add 7 hours for GMT

Nature of Me

I am no angel.
My feet are caked with dirt,
my thoughts like tainted snow,
my halo is askew
where my antlers want to grow.
That is the nature of me.

I am atoms and moondust
and laughter and tears,
sand, mud, and blood,
lightning, drought, and fears.
I am a force of nature.

With these freckles and wrinkles
and creaks, groans, and flaws
and magic and desires,
teeth, sneers, and claws;
with my history
and perspectives—
dogmas and views—
I swing from one tree branch
into another mood.
I am a freak of nature.

I am no angel,
just as nature meant for me.
My spirit outlined clearly
in impressions that I leave
as I step and I dance
and I spin and I sprawl,
as I write and I sing
and I stretch and I fall.
I am moss and the earth,
part root and part cone,
wings and some fur
and tendons and bone.

Though I know I'm no angel
I make snow-white wings
to soar my wild mind
where nature still sings.
That is the nature of me.

♄♄♄ sábado

♑ ♒

Saturday
26

☽☌♇ 12:35 am
☽☍♀ 5:49 am v/c
☽→♒ 7:08 am
♀→♌ 9:27 pm
☽☍♂ 11:29 pm

☉☉☉ domingo

♒

Sunday
27

☽☌♄ 4:23 am
☽□♅ 6:16 am
☽△☿ 12:08 pm v/c

June / July
liù yuè / qī yuè

☽☽☽ xīng qī yī

Tropical Wave

♒ ♓

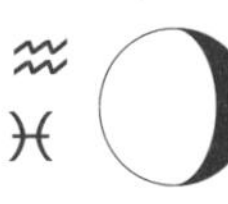

Monday
28

☽→♓ 10:51 am
♀⚻♃ 2:31 pm
☽☌♃ 2:33 pm

♂♂♂ xīng qī èr

♓

Tuesday
29

☉△☽ 12:53 am
☽⚹♅ 11:47 am
☽□☿ 7:59 pm

☿☿☿ xīng qī sān

♓ ♈

Wednesday
30

☽☌♆ 5:24 am
☽⚹♇ 10:39 am v/c
☽→♈ 6:21 pm

♃♃♃ xīng qī sì

♈

Thursday
1

July

☽△♀ 4:22 am
♂☍♄ 6:08 am
☉□☽ 2:11 pm
☽⚹♄ 6:15 pm
☽△♂ 6:58 pm

Waning Half Moon in ♈Aries 2:11 pm PDT

♀♀♀ xīng qī wǔ

♈

Friday
2

♂△⚷ 1:41 am
☽⚹☿ 9:12 am
☽□♇ 9:15 pm v/c

windspeak

go—go—
to the landscapes you drink
with your heart
where mystery is loved
for its shimmering touch
and death,
the sweet dessert
and the wind
speaks through you,
go—go—
to your home;
an ocean's eyelash
on the sand
where your village sings
at sunset
and in your place of rest
you can find
what is between your feet
and the ground
and you,
your words,
may land there

© patti sinclair 2012

Source Energy Protect (Wind Walk)
© Diane Norrie 2018

♄♄♄ xīng qī liù

♈
♉

Saturday 3

☽→♉ 5:28 am
☽⚹♃ 9:19 am
☉⚻♄ 3:51 pm
♂□♅ 6:40 pm
☽□♀ 10:44 pm

☉☉☉ lǐ bài rì

♉

Sunday 4

☽□♄ 6:06 am
☉⚹☽ 7:26 am
☉□⚷ 8:39 am
☽☌♅ 9:41 am
☽□♂ 10:28 am

July
Asharh

☽☽☽ sombar

♉
♊

Monday
5

☽⚹♆ 4:30 am
☽ApG 7:48 am
☽△♇ 9:57 am v/c
☉⚹♅ 12:14 pm
☽→♊ 6:24 pm
☽□♃ 10:03 pm

♂♂♂ mongolbar

♊

Tuesday
6

☿□♆ 12:39 am
☽⚹♀ 6:41 pm
☽△♄ 6:47 pm
♀☍♄ 7:36 pm

☿☿☿ budhbar

♊

Wednesday
7

☽⚹♂ 2:47 am
♀△⚷ 1:09 pm
☽□♆ 5:12 pm
☽☌☿ 9:20 pm v/c

♃♃♃ brihospotibar

♊
♋

Thursday
8

☽→♋ 6:51 am
☿⚻♇ 8:36 am
☽△♃ 10:09 am
♀□♅ 12:25 pm

♀♀♀ sukrobar

♋

Friday
9

☽⚹♅ 10:38 am
☉☌☽ 6:16 pm

New Moon in ♋ Cancer 6:16 pm PDT

All aspects in Pacific Daylight Time; add 3 hours for EDT; add 7 hours for GMT

Planted

In an attempt to escape the onslaught of tar and asphalt
In an attempt to make peace with this place I am in
I plant like a fiend
I find free plants, abandoned
by well-intentioned school projects brought to community gatherings
I take cuttings from curbsides, sweep up spilled seed on sidewalks
I create a buffer of life around me,
And I am calmed by it
I plant so I can feel planted
I plant so I won't flee again

¤ *Jules Bubacz 2019*

Grounded with Love © *Darlene Cook 2019*

♄♄♄ sonibar

♋
♌

Saturday
10

☽△♆ 4:10 am
☽☍♇ 9:10 am v/c
☽→♌ 5:20 pm

☉☉☉ robibar

♌

Sunday
11

☿→♋ 1:35 pm
☽☍♄ 3:32 pm
☽□♅ 8:10 pm

Vision Tree

In my dream I met an oak tree who saw everything.
The oldest mother in the endangered world.
She still felt the blood of life deep in the soil.
"There are things worth growing for," she said to me.
I saw the way her roots wove into the ground,
connected for miles to siblings and saplings.
"Open all your eyes," she said.
I saw the painted ducks floating in the stream,
a white-tailed deer and her daughter in the field.
I saw the mountain and its quiet breath,
the ocean full of colored songs—all these lives together.
Water in the earth, in the clouds, in my body, in the tree.
I thought of the people and how much we needed healing.
"What do we do?" I asked the tree, kneeling at her feet.
"Rise up," she said, "Come together—wail and love and fight."
"But how?"
"Stretch out your branches and call to your tribe,
they will reach out and find you, sisters united.
Go forth in action, your roots
joined as one."
"And what if we fail?" I worried.
She straightened her trunk
as she answered.
"Rise up again.
I did not grow this tall
in an instant."

¤ Angela Bigler 2018

Awaken
© Shannon Fitzgerald 2017

VIII. COME TOGETHER

Moon VIII: July 9–August 8

New Moon in ♋ Cancer July 9; Sun in ♌ Leo July 22; Full Moon in ♒ Aquarius July 23

The Tree of Life

July
Mí Iúil

☽☽☽ Dé Luain

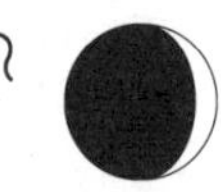

Monday
12

☽☌♀ 4:14 am
☽☌♂ 5:29 am v/c
☿△♃ 12:45 pm

Moon Sisters *© Jakki Moore 2016*

♂♂♂ Dé Máirt

♌
♍

Tuesday
13

☽→♍ 1:30 am
☽☍♃ 4:00 am
☽⚹☿ 6:05 am
♀☌♂ 6:33 am

☿☿☿ Dé Céadaoin

♍

Wednesday
14

☽△♅ 3:25 am
☉⚹☽ 6:46 pm
☽☍♆ 7:17 pm
☽△♇ 11:46 pm v/c

♃♃♃ Dé Ardaoin

♍
♎

Thursday
15

☉△♆ 1:49 am
♇PrH 3:16 am
☽→♎ 7:31 am
⚷R 7:50 am
☽□☿ 7:09 pm
♀⚻♆ 11:41 pm

♀♀♀ Dé Haoine

♎

Friday
16

☽△♄ 3:33 am
☽⚹♂ 10:04 pm

Cosmic Family Name

New World Women
© Elizabeth Diamond Gabriel 2010

Belonging's no goal, only
the state of everything.
Not a sense or feeling,
merely
what the stars do
in relation. Belonging
is the cosmic family name.

When false aloneness
sweeps through you, smile
at the misperception, bow
to the misunderstanding.
May the shaking hearts,
yours, mine,

grow as they quake.
Let belonging reveal
yearnings inside one other,
and a union unshakable.
Close your eyes. Find inside
the cauldron of belonging.

© Susa Silvermarie 2019

♄♄♄ Dé Sathairn

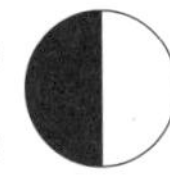

♎ ♏ **Saturday 17**

☽⚹♀	2:04 am	☽→♏	11:38 am
☉□☽	3:11 am	☽△♃	1:23 pm
☽□♇	4:03 am v/c	☉☍♇	3:46 pm

Waxing Half Moon in ♎ Libra 3:11 am PDT

☉☉☉ Dé Domhnaigh

♏ **Sunday 18**

♀⚻♇	12:48 am	☿⚻♄	10:13 am
☽△☿	6:13 am	♂⚻♆	11:21 am
☽□♄	6:45 am	☽☍♅	12:00 pm

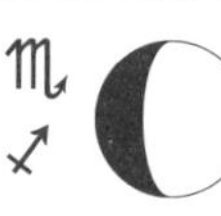

July
julio

Full Moon Tiger

☽☽☽ lunes

♏ ♐

Monday
19

☽△♆ 2:33 am
☽□♂ 3:15 am
☽✶♇ 6:40 am
☿□⚷ 7:52 am
☽□♀ 9:27 am
☉△☽ 9:30 am v/c
☽→♐ 2:08 pm
☽□♃ 3:32 pm

♂♂♂ martes

Tuesday
20

☿✶♅ 2:37 am
☽✶♄ 8:31 am

☿☿☿ miércoles

♐ ♑

Wednesday
21

☽PrG 3:22 am
☽□♆ 4:08 am
☽△♂ 7:06 am
☽△♀ 3:25 pm v/c
☽→♑ 3:36 pm
☽✶♃ 4:41 pm
♀→♍ 5:37 pm

♃♃♃ jueves

♑

Thursday
22

♀☍♃ 5:45 am
♂⚻♇ 7:08 am
☉→♌ 7:26 am
☽△♅ 3:25 pm
☉⚻♃ 9:10 pm

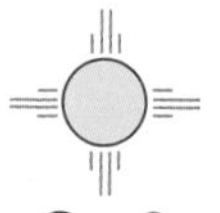

☉→♌

Sun in ♌ Leo 7:26 am PDT

♀♀♀ viernes

♑ ♒

Friday
23

Lunar Lammas

☽☍☿ 12:53 am
☽✶♆ 5:32 am
☽☌♇ 9:34 am v/c
☽→♒ 5:12 pm
☉☍☽ 7:37 pm

Full Moon in ♒ Aquarius 7:37 pm PDT

All aspects in Pacific Daylight Time; add 3 hours for EDT; add 7 hours for GMT

2021 Year at a Glance for ♌ Leo (July 22–Aug 22)

Leo has a reputation for being self-focused, but this year you will feel as if the self you've so carefully constructed is being unraveled. The people you feel closest to will offer you reflections about who you are, and the truth may bring about a shift of radical proportions. New people will come into your life to assist you in uncovering more of your uniqueness and even eccentricities. Allow yourself to become a wilder, stranger version of yourself.

With partners and close friends, there may be challenges as you learn more about what you need in order to feel loved. The key to success this year involves letting go of stubborn tendencies with regard to your significant others, and instead allowing more freedom and space between you and your beloveds. If you set love free, it could lead to even more security.

Take time in late spring and summer to reevaluate your own aspirations and dreams for your life. Is the universe urging you to take on more of a leadership role in your community? Are you striving to live up to ideals that are unrealistic? Are you too scattered to come up with a plan for the future? You are learning how to balance your desire for social stimulation with the need to make a lasting contribution to the world. Rather than over-relying on yourself, listen to your chosen family and the broader community to see how your creative gifts may be best utilized.

Rhea Wolf © Mother Tongue Ink 2020

Mary Walks in Peace #2
¤ *Virginia Maria Romero Art 2015*

♄♄♄ sábado

♒

Saturday
24

☿△♆ 9:35 am
☽☌♄ 11:25 am
☽□♅ 5:42 pm

☉☉☉ domingo

♒
♓

Sunday
25

☿☍♇ 1:15 pm
☽☍♂ 4:14 pm v/c
☽→♓ 8:30 pm
☽☌♃ 8:56 pm

July / August

qī yuè / bā yuè

☽☽☽ xīng qī yī

♓

Monday 26

☽☍♀ 6:04 am
☽✶♅ 10:28 pm

♂♂♂ xīng qī èr

♓

Tuesday 27

☽☌♆ 1:47 pm
☿→♌ 6:11 pm
☽✶♇ 6:13 pm v/c
☿⚻♃ 6:45 pm

☿☿☿ xīng qī sān

♓
♈

Wednesday 28

☽→♈ 2:58 am
☽△☿ 4:42 am
♃→♒ 5:42 am
☉△☽ 2:19 pm
☽✶♄ 10:53 pm

♃♃♃ xīng qī sì

♈

Thursday 29

♂☍♃ 8:50 am
♂→♍ 1:32 pm

♀♀♀ xīng qī wǔ

♈
♉

Friday 30

☽□♇ 3:44 am
♀⚻♄ 9:27 am
☽✶♃ 12:38 pm v/c
☽→♉ 1:08 pm
☽△♂ 2:26 pm

A Woman's Hallelujah

up drip drip   down scrub scrub   up drip drip   down scrub scrub

The women called to an ancient Goddess as they washed their laundry at this pond with the rhythm more ancient than their grandmothers' grandmother, more ancient than time. Silent, but for the breeze, yet ever so present.

gumf cuu   gumf cuu   a whisper from the bundle at her breast,
in rhythm with a little Goddess

ti ti ta . . . ti ti ta   a small sand-tinted bird added her syncopation

We knelt around the washing pond, these Somali women and I. A small vanishing pond in the midst of thorn bush country. Softly I began the only washing song I knew

This is the way we wash our cloths, Wash our clothes, wash our clothes

Try as I might, I couldn't quite get my little song to match the rhythm of theirs. No matter. I felt the smiles of the women as they nudged the rhythm of their washing to echo the rhythm of my little song. A lilting laughter slipped around us, drawing us closer.

A Somali woman began a new song, a call and response of joy. I clapped and swayed as the women's embrace swept me along.

This is the song of women

the slosh slosh drip drip of work
the gumf cuu of birth
the ti ti ta of our Mother Earth

This is our Hallelujah. This is our Joy.

♄♄♄ xīng qī liù

♉ Saturday 31

☽□☿ 3:24 am
☉□☽ 6:16 am
☽□♄ 9:47 am
☽△♀ 12:41 pm
☽☌♅ 6:34 pm

Waning Half Moon in ♉ Taurus 6:16 am PDT

☉☉☉ lǐ bài rì

♉ Sunday 1 August

☉☌☿ 7:07 am
♀⚻⚷ 10:16 am
☽⚹♆ 11:13 am
☿☍♄ 2:50 pm
☽△♇ 4:01 pm
☉☍♄ 11:14 pm

August
Srabon

☽☽☽ sombar

♉ ♊ 

Monday 2

Lammas

☽ApG 12:31 am
☽□♃ 12:41 am v/c
☽→♊ 1:46 am
♄PrH 4:02 am
☽□♂ 6:30 am
☿△⚷ 8:41 pm
☽△♄ 10:19 pm
♀△♅ 11:53 pm

♂♂♂ mongolbar

♊ 

Tuesday 3

☉⚹☽ 12:30 am
☽⚹☿ 5:12 am
☽□♀ 8:25 am
☿□♅ 6:57 pm
☽□♆ 11:55 pm

☿☿☿ budhbar

♊ ♋ 

Wednesday 4

☽△♃ 12:38 pm v/c
☽→♋ 2:17 pm
☉△⚷ 3:41 pm
☽⚹♂ 10:12 pm

♃♃♃ brihospotibar

♋ 

Thursday 5

☿ApH 5:12 am
☽⚹♅ 7:12 pm

♀♀♀ sukrobar

♋ 

Friday 6

☽⚹♀ 2:17 am
☽△♆ 10:43 am
☽☍♇ 3:11 pm v/c
☉□♅ 4:57 pm

Lammas

The world is full of pageantry. Of beauties in many forms. The world is made of shiny, outrageous gifts. They pour out of the Earth. Out in the fruits, the trees, in birdsong, in the fluidity of our queerness, in the genius of our hearts and minds, in the rewards for our diligence. The gifts move through our bodies, our laughter, the generosity of the breath we share.

There is no harvest without celebration.

We receive what we have been given, what we have worked for, and what has been shared with all the creative abundance we can muster. Generosity moves many ways. It is in the giving, yes. And also in reception. Also in the wonder that we share about what can exist. Also in the reflection we offer to each other, complex in all our parts, celebrating the wholeness of self and others.

Take pride in this abundance. Care for it by reveling in its strength and possibility. Be a love letter to generosity, exploring every inch of its beautiful ways. Come together in service and joy.

Maeanna Welti © Mother Tongue Ink 2020

Dance, Dance, Dance *© Bernice Davidson 2018*

WomanWorks at BK and Mary's

No news drones
on the radio. No radio
plays at all as I lift withered carcasses
of purple bush bean plants out of the damp earth.
Their organic bean babies long ago crunched by
hungry humans. The murmur of women's voices
softens the shriek of a passing crow as we
prune and dig in a yard. The yard is not ours. We did
not plant the beans nor eat them. We are not hired as a work
crew. We are women, friends helping friends. WomanWorks.
Door screen clicks open. Mary calls, "Tell Sara it's time to
come in and wash up. I've got her plate ready since
she needs to leave early." Boots crunch gravel;
Zelda tromps past to exchange clippers for loppers.
BK appears from the side of the house holding a rake and shovel.
"Who said they needed these?" she shouts in her raspy voice
that laughed in Cuba, and whispered while ducking bullets
in Nicaragua. "Schlootz," my trowel
opens a   dirt   womb
into which
I place a plump
bulb—purple
readiness for
the next cosmic
dance with cold,
darkness, warmth,
light. Now—only the
chirruping humming birds,
who fill the tree under which
we gather together in wonder.

(originally published in Sinister Wisdom)

Visiting Sunflowers © Leah Marie Dorion 2018

♄♄♄ sonibar

♋

♌

Saturday
7

☽→♌ 12:31 am
☽☍♄ 6:50 pm
☿⚻♆ 7:24 pm

☉☉☉ robibar

♌

Sunday
8

☽□♅ 4:04 am
☉☌☽ 6:50 am
☽☌☿ 10:45 pm

New Moon in ♌ Leo 6:50 am PDT

Time to Drum

If we're gonna ride
this surge toward a shimmering new world
to make life good for all the living
we gotta shake
out pain, out rage, off mind-shackles
that keep us scared and alone
we know about
burning stakes, historic lies, silencing
we been acting up, speaking out, spittin' mad
we gotta drum now
all our women ancestors drummed
when their drums were smashed
the unstoppable beats played on
we gotta raise them up
their hands are thumping on hide right now
cracking and toppling us, tumbling
and remaking us, driving us to the gates
we gonna ride their spirit-waves
beyond dead-ends and dread
to where the universe keeps Her answers
look in our own hands where they buried the keys
time to drum
all my many sisters in all our many worlds
time has come to fullness and spirit pipers
at the gates of dawn are asking for living coin
we didn't make this mess
but our ancestors saw it coming
at the curl of this surge buoying us into tomorrow
in their drumming live our answers.

IX. ANCESTRY

Moon IX: August 8–September 6

New Moon in ♌ Leo August 8; Full Moon in ♒ Aquarius August 22; Sun in ♍ Virgo August 22

The Women Are Drummin' © *Louie Laskowski 2019*

August
Mí Lúnasa

☽☽☽ Dé Luain

♌
♍

Monday
9

☿⊼♇ 12:02 am
☽☍♃ 5:22 am v/c
☽→♍ 7:55 am
♀☍♆ 5:20 pm
☽☌♂ 8:42 pm

♂♂♂ Dé Máirt

♍

Tuesday
10

☽△♅ 10:19 am
☿☍♃ 6:20 pm

☿☿☿ Dé Céadaoin

♍
♎

Wednesday
11

☽☍♆ 12:15 am
☽☌♀ 3:15 am
☽△♇ 4:22 am v/c
☽→♎ 1:08 pm
☿→♍ 2:57 pm
♀△♇ 3:45 pm

♃♃♃ Dé Ardaoin

♎

Thursday
12

☽△♄ 5:32 am

♀♀♀ Dé Haoine

♎
♏

Friday
13

☉✶☽ 1:13 am
☽□♇ 8:20 am
♂⊼♄ 9:27 am
☽△♃ 1:39 pm v/c
☽→♏ 5:01 pm

Grandma Poem

Elders passing through time,
ancestral wisdom gathered and bestowed
Crone women, wrinkled and wise,
pure love burns in their hearts and eyes.
Assuring us we are an essential design
in the threads of an elaborate tapestry

excerpt ¤ Mary Theresa Wertz 2016

Grandmother Moon © *Cara Gwizd 2018*

♄♄♄ Dé Sathairn

Saturday
14

☽✶☿ 12:33 am
♀⚻♃ 3:58 am
☽□♄ 8:54 am
☽✶♂ 10:08 am
☽☍♅ 6:18 pm
☉⚻♆ 9:13 pm

☉☉☉ Dé Domhnaigh

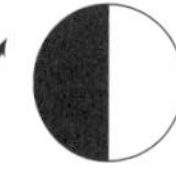

Sunday
15

☽△♆ 7:33 am
☉□☽ 8:19 am
☽✶♇ 11:32 am
☽□♃ 4:23 pm
☽✶♀ 8:05 pm v/c
☽→♐ 8:12 pm
♀→♎ 9:26 pm

Waxing Half Moon in ♏ Scorpio 8:19 am PDT

August
agosto

Completion
She recalls the past.
Receives impressions of the future
She remembers why she is needed.
The purpose of the journey.
For Humanity. The World.
excerpt © Zalayshia 2019

☽☽☽ lunes

Monday 16

☽□☿ 10:57 am
☽✶♄ 11:40 am
☽□♂ 3:31 pm
☿⊼♄ 4:35 pm

♂♂♂ martes

Tuesday 17

☽PrG 2:15 am
☉⊼♇ 6:31 am
☽□♆ 10:18 am
☉△☽ 2:51 pm
☽✶♃ 6:43 pm v/c
☽→♑ 10:58 pm

☿☿☿ miércoles

Wednesday 18

☽□♀ 3:27 am
♂⊼⚷ 7:09 am
☿⊼⚷ 3:19 pm
☿☌♂ 8:28 pm
☽△♂ 8:37 pm
☽△☿ 8:38 pm
☽△♅ 11:59 pm

♃♃♃ jueves

♑

Thursday 19

☽✶♆ 12:59 pm
☽☌♇ 4:59 pm v/c
☉☍♃ 5:28 pm
♅R 6:40 pm
♃PrH 10:22 pm

♀♀♀ viernes

♑
♒

Friday 20

☿△♅ 1:06 am
☽→♒ 1:49 am
☽△♀ 11:01 am
☽☌♄ 4:55 pm

2021 Year at a Glance for ♍ Virgo (August 22–Sept. 22)

In 2021, your carefully planned routines will be overthrown by our celestial friends Saturn and Jupiter. If you let your day-to-day life be overhauled, you will uncover a deeper, more authentic connection to yourself and the work you do in the world. This might be as simple as changing your healthcare regimen. The point is to spend some time pampering yourself, Virgo. Use affirmations to bolster your self-esteem. Recognize the gifts you bring to the world. Focus on yourself rather than others a bit more.

A major theme of this year is work/life balance. This may involve finding a new job, starting a creative project at home, broadening your connection with the world to decrease tendencies to burn-out. Do you need to take on more responsibilities at work, or is it time to back off and focus more on your private life? It's time to be sure your livelihood is synchronized with your personal values.

As you simmer on these changes, be ready to take action in August and September when a burst of energy will help you take advantage of opportunities to expand your sphere of influence.

In the Fall, it's time to evaluate how actions you took in previous months effect your financial and personal well-being. As the dust settles, you may realize a trade-off between having fewer physical resources but more time, or alternatively, that there are now more resources to contribute to your ideals. Listen for the harmony as you learn to balance material needs with ethics and aspirations.

Rhea Wolf © Mother Tongue Ink 2020

© Adrienne Simms 2019

♄♄♄ sábado

♒ ○ **Saturday 21**

☽□♅ 3:11 am
♂△♅ 11:38 pm

☉☉☉ domingo

♒ ♓ ○ **Sunday 22**

☽☌♃ 12:18 am
☉☍☽ 5:02 am v/c
☽→♓ 5:42 am
☉→♍ 2:35 pm

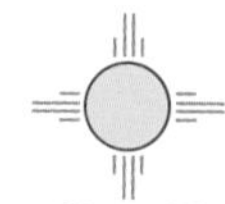

☉→♍

Full Moon in ♒ Aquarius 5:02 am PDT
Sun in ♍ Virgo 2:35 pm PDT

August
bā yuè

☽☽☽ xīng qī yī

♓

Monday
23

♀△♄ 5:48 am
☽⚹♅ 8:04 am
☽☍♂ 9:43 am
☽☍☿ 7:03 pm
☽☌♆ 9:50 pm

Reflection

♂♂♂ xīng qī èr

♓
♈

Tuesday
24

☽⚹♇ 2:12 am v/c
☽→♈ 11:57 am
☿☍♆ 6:14 pm

☿☿☿ xīng qī sān

♈

Wednesday
25

☽⚹♄ 3:58 am
☽☍♀ 8:57 am

♃♃♃ xīng qī sì

♈
♉

Thursday
26

♀☍⚷ 6:24 am
☿△♇ 7:23 am
☽□♇ 11:02 am
☽⚹♃ 2:14 pm v/c
☽→♉ 9:27 pm

♀♀♀ xīng qī wǔ

♉

Friday
27

☉△☽ 6:19 am
☿⚻♃ 8:05 am
☽□♄ 2:04 pm

Wounds of the Mother

They say I have my mother's eyes. They shine an English hazel when I rim them with Kohl in honour of my Turkish ancestors—strong women with strong arms, ready to pound dough into flat bread.

They say I have inherited her power of spirit, her quiet voice, her un-elegant way of expressing emotions. "You are just like her!" they cry in delight. And I smile. My wonderful, ever-giving mother is just like me. But nobody ever told me I had inherited her wounds—wounds like shards of broken glass, broken dreams, broken expectations that deflate the soul it in a way only disappointment can.

So, one clear day I surrendered and sat with them, loosened them from my belief that they were invaders of my spirit. I listened to them sing their wisdom, heavy, like cascading water off a mountainside:

"The river you cry is not yours alone. It is made from the tears of your mother's mother's mother's mother—it runs deep and far back."

I heard her message in her curves and the way she moved like velvet over all obstacles in her path. She said: "Every woman who heals herself, heals all the women who came before her and all the women who come after." And, at last, I understood.

So I stood up, open to changing my mind about the world and proclaimed that I didn't want the sadness of women to continue. I chanted over and over to the sky, to the Goddess, to myself, that I will heal, because I would never want my daughters to cry my tears.

In my healing, I reach out and heal with every woman who ever graced this Earth, and every woman yet to walk it.

excerpt ¤ *T.Y. Chambers 2016*

♄♄♄ xīng qī liù

♉

Saturday
28

☽☌♅ 2:51 am
♀⚻♅ 10:43 am
☽△♂ 11:14 am
☽⚹♆ 5:55 pm
☽△♇ 10:50 pm

☉☉☉ lǐ bài rì

♉
♊

Sunday
29

☽□♃ 1:36 am
☽△☿ 7:58 am v/c
☽→♊ 9:42 am
☽ApG 7:14 pm
☿→♎ 10:10 pm

Aug. / Sept.

Srabon / Bhadro

☽☽☽ sombar

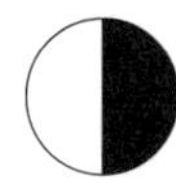

♊

Monday
30

☉□☽ 12:13 am
☽△♄ 2:26 am
☽△♀ 9:30 pm

Waning Half Moon in ♊ Gemini 12:13 am PDT

♂♂♂ mongolbar

♊
♋

Tuesday
31

☉⊼♄ 1:46 am
☽□♂ 3:36 am
☽□♆ 6:41 am
☽△♃ 1:48 pm v/c
☽→♋ 10:26 pm

☿☿☿ budhbar

♋

Wednesday
1

September

☽□☿ 4:46 am
☉⚹☽ 5:52 pm

♃♃♃ brihospotibar

♋

Thursday
2

☽⚹♅ 3:33 am
♂☍♆ 10:43 am
☽□♀ 3:24 pm
☽△♆ 5:52 pm
☽⚹♂ 6:16 pm
☽☍♇ 10:37 pm v/c

♀♀♀ sukrobar

♋
♌

Friday
3

☽→♌ 8:58 am
♀⊼♆ 5:13 pm
☽⚹☿ 9:45 pm
☉⊼⚷ 10:20 pm
☽☍♄ 11:54 pm

Roots

I am reluctant to leave my warm bed, but the words parade themselves across the billboard of my brow. My child must know this: There is an Indigenous face in the mirror. The eyes, the cheekbones, The forehead, the earlobes. Does your husband know of our people who will come through you?

The Woman who was my great great grandmother—the Apache woman—and her mother, your great great great grandmother, who knew the feel of buffalo hide, who knew the taste of buffalo liver, who watched for the subtle change of light across a darkening prairie. Her blood, my blood, your blood, runs in your child's veins.

My world view embraces sky and wind and water and fire. Smoke raises my prayers to God. My libation slakes my grandmother's thirst, and this tobacco is her gift. She, and all the grandmothers and the grandfathers, are with you. Always.

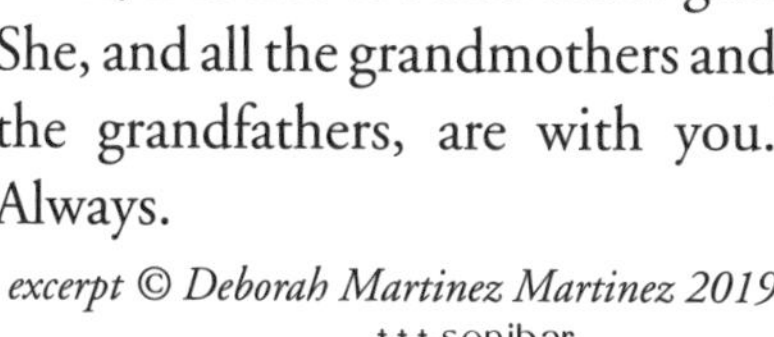

excerpt © Deborah Martinez Martinez 2019

Blessing ¤ *Carolyn Batten-Kimzey 2014*

♄♄♄ sonibar

♌

Saturday
4

☽□♅ 12:23 pm
☿△♄ 6:30 pm

☉☉☉ robibar

♌
♍

Sunday
5

☽⚹♀ 4:58 am
☽☍♃ 7:21 am v/c
☽→♍ 4:05 pm
♀□♇ 8:07 pm

A Call to Pens

Let our poems put stolen children
    back into the caring arms of their families
Melting the bars
    around the jailers
        and every policy-maker

    Let our poems plant honeysuckle
        and aster for the bees
            and let them ban the pesticides
                that makes us all sick

        Let our poems bust lies on the airwaves
                    and that fierce loyalty to power

            Let our poems be the revolution
                the turning towards the light
                    that includes every being

                Let our poems be antidotes
                    to the poisoned bombs
                        on parade down
                            Pennsylvania Avenue

                    And the madman standing
                        at salute

Careful Balance
© Danielle Helen Ray Dickson 2016

Let our poems
  be the doctor the therapist
  the priestess
      that melts away
      addiction and lies

Let our poems rip-off bandaids
  to expose ulcers to the air

Let them be the balm
  the aloe and calendula
  that will finally heal us
      to the bone

© Valerie A. Szarek 2019

X. INCITE JUSTICE

Moon X: September 6–October 6

New Moon in ♍ Virgo Sept. 6; Full Moon in ♓ Pisces Sept. 20; Sun in ♎ Libra Sept. 22

HeartSong *© Colleen Koziara 2014*

September

Mí Meán Fomhair

☽☽☽ Dé Luain

♍ 

Monday 6

♂△♇ 5:20 am
♀△♃ 6:05 am
☉☌☽ 5:52 pm
☽△♅ 5:54 pm
☉△♅ 6:29 pm
♂⊼♃ 8:50 pm

Taika ◻ *Destiney Powell 2017*

New Moon in ♍ Virgo 5:52 pm PDT

♂♂♂ Dé Máirt

♍ ♎ 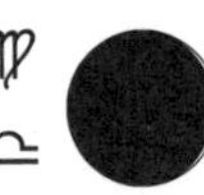

Tuesday 7

☽☍♆ 6:34 am
☽△♇ 10:56 am
☽☌♂ 12:23 pm v/c
☽→♎ 8:20 pm
☿☍⚷ 9:30 pm

☿☿☿ Dé Céadaoin

♎ 

Wednesday 8

☽△♄ 9:29 am
☽☌☿ 6:01 pm

♃♃♃ Dé Ardaoin

♎ ♏ 

Thursday 9

☽□♇ 1:48 pm
☽△♃ 2:03 pm
☽☌♀ 9:48 pm v/c
☽→♏ 11:05 pm

♀♀♀ Dé Haoine

♏ 

Friday 10

☿⊼♅ 9:17 am
☽□♄ 11:53 am
♀→♏ 1:39 pm
☽☍♅ 11:36 pm

Being Black

Before leaving the house, I look in the mirror, and take off items that make me seem more black—turban, big hoop earrings. Big hair gets tied back. "Wrong attitude" gets adjusted.

I enter the car, a potential tomb, pull out license and registration, preparing for the DWB experience: Driving While Black. I say a prayer, sending it out to all police. "Bless you and your family, may I be seen as human, as a member of your family."

I drive away, knowing I could disappear, become another one, a video in the Facebook feed, eliciting comments I will never hear.

Do they know me? Do they know this brown skin that sings at weddings and funerals? Helps healing? Otherness begets otherness, and separation places armor on my tired shoulders—armor I despise, for it makes me less human.

I drive exactly the speed limit when a white man in grumbling truck comes close to my bumper, anxious to pass. Impatient, he passes with a muffler growl. Another privilege he has that I do not: to speed, to follow impulse. For me, to even get pulled over could be the end of this precious life.

"Oh God, here comes one." My stomach feels shock waves, my hands tremble. I'm doing no wrong, but I've been stopped before for no other reason than curiosity. I utter my silent prayer: "Bless you and your family." He passes by, faster than the speed limit. I reach my destination. I take a deep breath.

It's okay to be myself again.

© Robin Diane Bruce 2016

♄♄♄ Dé Sathairn

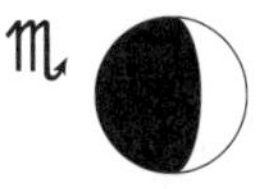

Saturday
11

☽PrG 3:03 am
☉✶☽ 7:08 am
☽△♆ 11:50 am
☽□♃ 4:08 pm
☽✶♇ 4:13 pm
☽✶♂ 10:33 pm v/c

☉☉☉ Dé Domhnaigh

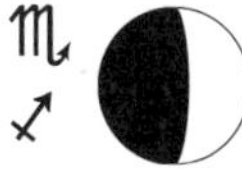

Sunday
12

☽→♐ 1:34 am
☽✶♄ 2:18 pm

September
septiembre

☽☽☽ lunes

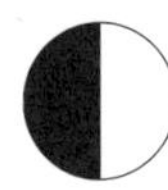

Monday
13

ΨPrH 5:30 am
☽✱☿ 7:31 am
☉□☽ 1:39 pm
☽□Ψ 2:33 pm
☽✱♃ 6:38 pm

Words Matter

I am conservative,
I conserve that which sustains life.
And there are no such things as
peace-keeping missiles.

excerpt ¤ Robin Rose Bennett 2019

Waxing Half Moon in ♐ Sagittarius 1:39 pm PDT

♂♂♂ martes

Tuesday
14

☉☍Ψ 2:21 am
☽□♂ 3:57 am v/c
☽→♑ 4:34 am
☽✱♀ 12:20 pm
♂→♎ 5:14 pm

☿☿☿ miércoles

Wednesday
15

☽△♅ 5:31 am
☽□☿ 2:41 pm
☽✱Ψ 6:01 pm
☉△☽ 9:07 pm
☽☌♇ 10:40 pm v/c

♃♃♃ jueves

♑
♒

Thursday
16

☉⚻♃ 7:18 am
☽→♒ 8:23 am
☽△♂ 10:19 am
☉△♇ 6:53 pm
☽□♀ 9:02 pm
☽☌♄ 9:14 pm
♀□♄ 11:14 pm

♀♀♀ viernes

♒

Friday
17

☽□♅ 9:45 am
☿⚻Ψ 9:18 pm
☽△☿ 10:36 pm

The Last Stand of Free Tribes of Earth ◘ *Akefa Azu 2011*

Wage Sanity

Imagine all of the world's guns,
melted into sculptures
and park benches

excerpt © Valerie A. Szarek 2018

♄♄♄ sábado

♒ ♓

Saturday
18

☽☌♃ 2:14 am v/c
☽→♓ 1:22 pm

☉☉☉ domingo

♓

Sunday
19

☽△♀ 7:26 am
☽⚹♅ 3:26 pm

Fall Equinox

Let it rest in your belly. Satisfaction, deep and delicious. Completion takes skill. It takes appreciation. When lovingly tended, the process of culmination will nest the magic down deep, filling every cranny of our lives with its wonder, with its wholeness.

Magic is in the details. It is in the way we infuse the simplest of acts with the depth and passion of our connections. It is in the way we imbue every little thing with our devotion to the sacred—the ways we feed community by looking into each other's faces, risking connection, bringing our humanity to each other's truths.

Speak life into your life. Speak life into all the threads we weave and tend. Speak to and hear the wisdom of the daily, the gold revealed in the small things. There is a beautiful coherence being woven from large to small and back again. Satisfaction will settle the gifts of your work into your bones and breathe life into what still needs your heart, focus and radical courage.

Breathe love into every skill this time demands of us; gather the harvest and delight in the work of the year.

Maeanna Welti © Mother Tongue Ink 2020

Back to Basics ¤ *Diana Denslow 2001*

Blue Moon © *Jeanette M. French 2018*

The Benevolence of This

Driving through the reservation
In anticipation of another calico
Sandstone formation, we click off
The station reporting on the unfaithful
Elation of those wanting to take another
Species off the endangered list to listen
To the benevolence of this: silence.

Everyone can say they want a revelation.
But in the borderlands (of both geography
And history) between the states of cruelty
And civilization, the lines keep changing
Like an earthquake, making indistinguishable
What we must embrace or resist or transcend.

A nocturnal storm will come later
To paint with spirits on dry land,
But even thunder here is not naughty,
Simply a bold declaration of the power
To affect what might be cleansed,
What might give birth or rebirth,
As what was crestfallen arises from a
Native hand. At sunrise: stillness.

excerpt ¤ *Cassie Premo Steele 2019*

September

jiǔ yuè

☽☽☽ xīng qī yī

♓ ♈

Monday 20

♂ApH 4:38 am
☽☌♆ 4:39 am
♀⊼⚷ 9:12 am
☽⚹♇ 9:45 am
☿△♃ 3:53 pm
☉☍☽ 4:55 pm v/c
☽→♈ 8:13 pm

Fox ¤ *Robin Lea Quinlivan 2016*

Full Moon in ♓ Pisces 4:55 pm PDT

♂♂♂ xīng qī èr

♈

Tuesday 21

☽☍♂ 4:02 am
☽⚹♄ 9:43 am

☿☿☿ xīng qī sān

♈

Wednesday 22

Fall Equinox

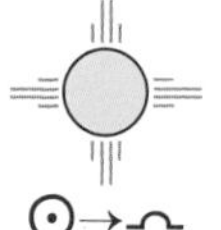

☿□♇ 6:12 am
☉→♎ 12:21 pm
☽⚹♃ 4:42 pm
☽□♇ 6:37 pm
☽☍☿ 7:05 pm v/c

Sun in ♎ Libra 12:21 pm PDT

♃♃♃ xīng qī sì

♈ ♉

Thursday 23

♀☍♅ 2:41 am
☽→♉ 5:38 am
☽□♄ 7:40 pm

♀♀♀ xīng qī wǔ

♉

Friday 24

☽☌♅ 9:56 am
☽☍♀ 1:15 pm

2021 Year at a Glance for ♎ Libra (Sept. 22–Oct. 22)

This year, the focus is on closing the door on negative self-talk and opening the door to seeing the beauty bubbling within you. You may face obstacles that keep you stuck in the realm of ideas rather than action. Expressing yourself creatively gets you out of your head and out of your own way. Take a risk through art-making, writing, music or community engagement.

On the romance front, you may be tempted by people you aren't normally attracted to. These unusual encounters can help you release sexual limitations and recover greater authenticity. If you have children in your life, they can be remarkable teachers of how to use your creativity as a force for social change —and of how to be creative just for fun.

In late Spring, you may feel inspired to broaden your knowledge of the world. Studying subjects like ethics, spirituality, or journalism might be especially suited for you during this time. Whatever the topic, it's time to break out of your usual ways of seeing the world and get educated on areas of life that are entirely new to you.

In the Fall, you will receive a boost of energy to put your dreams into action. This year is a lot about letting go of cynical tendencies and allowing the contradictions within you to breathe. While it's easy for you to get caught in either/or thinking, you are learning how opposites create more beauty and balance when they are blended together.

Rhea Wolf © Mother Tongue Ink 2020

Desert Magic
© Christina Gage 2017

♄♄♄ xīng qī liù

Saturday
25

☽⚹♆ 12:23 am
☽□♃ 3:48 am
☽△♇ 6:09 am v/c
♂△♄ 2:50 pm
☽→♊ 5:36 pm

⊙⊙⊙ lǐ bài rì

♊

Sunday
26

⊙△☽ 12:35 am
☽△♄ 7:56 am
☽△♂ 8:59 am
☽ApG 2:50 pm
☿R 10:10 pm

September / October

Bhadro / Ashshin

☽☽☽ sombar

Monday
27

☽□♆ 1:11 pm
☽△♃ 4:24 pm
☽△☿ 9:18 pm v/c

◘ *Hope Reborn 2019*

♂♂♂ mongolbar

♊
♋

Tuesday
28

☽→♋ 6:34 am
☉□☽ 6:57 pm

Waning Half Moon in ♋ Cancer 6:57 pm PDT

☿☿☿ budhbar

♋

Wednesday
29

☽□♂ 1:17 am
♀△♆ 9:14 am
☽⚹♅ 10:54 am
☉△♄ 3:19 pm

♃♃♃ brihospotibar

♋
♌
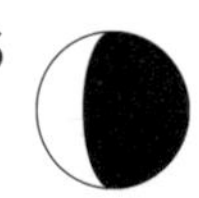

Thursday
30

☽△♆ 1:06 am
☽△♀ 2:44 am
☽☍♇ 6:54 am
☽□☿ 7:49 am v/c
♀□♃ 4:31 pm
☽→♌ 5:53 pm

♀♀♀ sukrobar

♌

Friday
1

October

♂☍⚷ 5:59 am
☽☍♄ 7:10 am
☿□♇ 7:27 am
☉⚹☽ 10:34 am
☽⚹♂ 2:46 pm
☽□♅ 8:31 pm

Overcoming

We've been hibernating below
the surface of the world
growing roots
dreaming of the sun
thirsting for rain

we sprout
crack concrete
overcome
the bullets and toxic exhale
of a machine built to kill

we rise
like sunshine
the shadows
our memory
of the struggle it took
to lift our heads
above drowning

we breathe
exhale this sky full of stars
pregnant with moon
trace the constellations
in the shape of
our revelation for tomorrow

this tomorrow has no name
but we are calling her forth
this tomorrow is not the same
as yesterday
but she is as ancient
as the world

we are ready for light
we are ready to live
ready to hold each other
against the rim of existence

cause they who build concrete
against the corners of our hearts
need to feel our resistance
like a million dandelions
cracking sidewalks apart

reminding your runaway child
there is no place
that love cannot find you

by Naima Penniman
reprinted from
CLIMBING POETREE, Whit Press 2015
Used by permission of the author, and Whit Press

♄♄♄ sonibar

♌  Saturday 2

♀✶♇ 12:47 am
☽☍♃ 12:28 pm
⚷PrH 1:49 pm
☽✶☿ 1:57 pm
☽□♀ 4:43 pm v/c

☉☉☉ robibar

♌
  Sunday 3

☽→♍ 1:37 am
☉☍⚷ 8:50 am
☿△♃ 5:05 pm

Her Name was Helen

Great Grandmother
We called her Ma
My secret inspiration
Her eyes twinkled with the magic of stars
She talked to the spirits
Offered connection to the living feeling left behind
Not fancy but perfect
Astrology, tarot, and messages from beyond
Her legacy lives on in my experience
She taught me to wonder, inspect, analyze
Her belief in the unseen
Is now my solid foundation
The outcast
We embraced her
The odd duck
With us
She belonged
Sitting on her throne of quiet acceptance
Spinning with the elements of the cosmos
With worms and fish and the lake
The outhouse and the compost
Laughter and love
Coming to me in my dreams
Teaching me
I was too young to understand
The Self had not yet recognized the Other
Questions left unanswered
Perceptions of lines continued to blur
Near and far
The desire of consciousness incarnate
The holy embodiment of matter
We called her Ma

XI. CHANNELING

Moon XI: October 6–November 4

New Moon in ♎ Libra Oct. 6; Full Moon in ♈ Aries Oct. 20; Sun in ♐ Scorpio Oct. 22

Kindness in the City *© Jakki Moore 2019*

October

Mí Deireadh Fomhair

☽☽☽ Dé Luain

Monday
4

☽△♅ 2:19 am
☽☍♆ 2:47 pm
☽△♇ 8:03 pm

♂♂♂ Dé Máirt

Tuesday
5

☽✶♀ 1:46 am v/c
☽→♎ 5:41 am
☿⚻♆ 6:53 am
☽△♄ 5:15 pm

☿☿☿ Dé Céadaoin

Wednesday
6

♂⚻♅ 2:26 am
☉☌☽ 4:05 am
☽☌♂ 5:04 am
♇D 11:29 am
☽☌☿ 2:40 pm
☉⚻♅ 4:11 pm
☽△♃ 7:08 pm
☽□♇ 10:03 pm v/c

New Moon in ♎ Libra 4:05 am PDT

♃♃♃ Dé Ardaoin

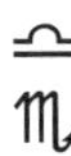

Thursday
7

♀→♐ 4:21 am
☽→♏ 7:22 am
☿PrH 2:14 pm
☽□♄ 6:37 pm
☉☌♂ 9:01 pm

♀♀♀ Dé Haoine

♏

Friday
8

☽☍♅ 6:00 am
☽PrG 10:35 am
☽△♆ 5:53 pm
☽□♃ 8:04 pm
☽✶♇ 11:05 pm v/c

Priestess Poem

It is my calling to be hollow and empty
like a bamboo reed.
The wind may blow through me,
or a song.
Or the breath and voice of one
on the other side of the veil.

I could be a messenger
or a vehicle for love.
I could be an echo in a canyon
or a hawker in the city.
I could be a puppet
or a whirling dervish.
I could be a clown
or a mourner.

My crown opens.
My feet are planted.
Whatever comes, comes.
I must take my desires
And my preferences
and stash them away.

Empty.
Hollow.
Come, goddess, come.

¤ *Maya Spector 2019*

Awakening © *Jenny Hahn 2008*

ħħħ Dé Sathairn

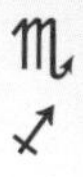

Saturday
9

☽→♐ 8:24 am
☉☌☿ 9:18 am
☽☌♀ 12:37 pm
☿☌♂ 3:48 pm
☽⚹ħ 7:43 pm

☉☉☉ Dé Domhnaigh

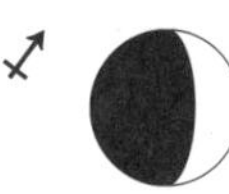

Sunday
10

☽⚹☿ 9:49 am
☽⚹♂ 12:12 pm
☉⚹☽ 1:45 pm
☽□♆ 7:17 pm
ħD 7:17 pm
☽⚹♃ 9:30 pm v/c

October
octubre

True Colors © *Darlene Cook 2017*

☽☽☽ lunes

♐
♑
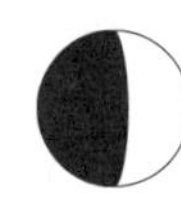

Monday
11

☽→♑ 10:15 am
☿⚻♅ 10:29 pm

♂♂♂ martes

♑

Tuesday
12

☽□☿ 8:50 am
☽△♅ 9:34 am
☽□♂ 5:27 pm
☉□☽ 8:25 pm
☽⚹♆ 10:10 pm

Waxing Half Moon in ♑ Capricorn 8:25 pm PDT

☿☿☿ miércoles

♑
♒

Wednesday
13

☽☌♇ 3:53 am v/c
♀⚹♄ 12:26 pm
☽→♒ 1:47 pm
☉⚻♆ 8:31 pm

♃♃♃ jueves

♒

Thursday
14

☽☌♄ 1:54 am
☽⚹♀ 3:03 am
☽△☿ 10:09 am
☽□♅ 1:52 pm

♀♀♀ viernes

♒
♓

Friday
15

☽△♂ 12:57 am
☉△♃ 4:46 am
☽☌♃ 5:29 am
☉△☽ 5:33 am v/c
☽→♓ 7:22 pm

The Dancing Species

We are the dancing species. Practice this sacred power.
We are shapeshifters, sheltering the common spark of all form
in the curling ribbon of changing breath.
Try on other skins, and move around in them.
Become spring rain, blood lusting tiger, watchful gazelle.
One beat to the next,
Become anything, all by falling through space and catching yourself,
Falling and catching, falling and catching,
Music carrying you beyond and through all form.

Practice this power. Let it ground you, feed you.
Shapeshifter, lean in
To the rhythm, fall through space,
Body melt into song's silent light,
Change, change, change,
Now water, now flame,
Now the big wave grief,
now the clear night of desire,
all woven into bodies
falling in time.
Oh dancer,
become the breath itself,
here you are Vanishing
And you've never
been more here.

¤ *Emily Kedar 2019*

cuidando lo fugaz © *Annika Gemlau 2018*

♄♄♄ sábado

♓ Saturday 16

♀△⚷ 11:49 am
☽□♀ 1:59 pm
♂⊼♆ 5:31 pm
☿✶♀ 6:23 pm
☽✶♅ 8:14 pm

☉☉☉ domingo

♓  Sunday 17

☉□♇ 5:12 am
☽☌♆ 10:00 am
☽✶♇ 4:24 pm v/c
♃D 10:30 pm

October

shí yuè

© Greta Boann Perry

Heart of the Matter

☽☽☽ xīng qī yī

♓ ♈

Monday 18

☽→♈ 3:04 am
☿D 8:17 am
☽✶♄ 4:15 pm
♂△♃ 7:36 pm
☽☍☿ 10:26 pm

♂♂♂ xīng qī èr

♈

Tuesday 19

☽△♀ 3:40 am
♀⚻♅ 4:15 pm
☽✶♃ 9:58 pm
☽☍♂ 11:28 pm

☿☿☿ xīng qī sān

♈ ♉

Wednesday 20

☽□♇ 1:55 am
☉☍☽ 7:57 am v/c
☽→♉ 12:59 pm

Full Moon in ♈Aries 7:57 am PDT

♃♃♃ xīng qī sì

♉

Thursday 21

☽□♄ 2:45 am
☽☌♅ 3:28 pm
♂□♇ 9:19 pm

♀♀♀ xīng qī wǔ

♉

Friday 22

☽✶♆ 6:26 am
☽□♃ 9:31 am
☽△♇ 1:35 pm v/c
☉→♏ 9:51 pm

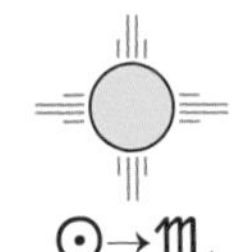

☉→♏

Sun in ♏ Scorpio 9:51 pm PDT

All aspects in Pacific Daylight Time; add 3 hours for EDT; add 7 hours for GMT

2021 Year at a Glance for ♏ Scorpio (Oct. 22–Nov. 21)

The beginning of 2021 will focus on radical shifts occurring in the most personal area of life—home and family. Scorpios can sometimes feel as though they don't really fit with their family of origin. This year, you will have opportunities to get in synch with your lineage. Study and connect with your ancestors. You may feel challenged by what you find, but diving into your roots will lead to acceptance and generosity about how you relate to your origins.

If you've been considering a move or change in the home front, this is the year to initiate your dreams. Perhaps it's just a matter of redecorating or rearranging, but maybe you've been in denial about how your home just isn't working for you right now. You might find yourself contemplating a big move that breaks you out of old patterns and allows you to innovate your personal space.

The Spring may bring a blast of emotional sensitivity that throws you off track. It's important that you find other people to share your feelings with, even if that feels risky. During this time, the universe is helping you build resiliency and intimacy.

In late Fall, use a surge of energy to get new projects and dreams off the ground. You may feel more agitated than usual—use these new activities to channel excess power into. Like screwing in a lightbulb, this time of year will yield brilliance if you create appropriate outlets to express yourself. The world needs your gifts now more than ever.

Rhea Wolf © Mother Tongue Ink 2020

Connection © *Paula Franco 2018*

♄♄♄ xīng qī liù

♉ ♊ Saturday 23

☽→♊ 12:57 am
☽△♄ 3:12 pm

☉☉☉ lǐ bài rì

♊ Sunday 24

☽△☿ 3:17 am
☽ApG 8:29 am
☿⊼♅ 10:45 am
☽☍♀ 2:42 pm
☽□♆ 7:14 pm
☽△♃ 10:33 pm

October
Ashshin

Tonight She howls, cackles, laments,
prays out loud while slapping her thigh
as she stirs a pot of metamorphosis
all night long.
excerpt © Jennifer Lothrigel 2019

☽☽☽ sombar

♊ ♋

Monday 25

☽△♂ 7:11 am v/c
☽→♋ 2:00 pm
☉△☽ 7:54 pm

♂♂♂ mongolbar

♋

Tuesday 26

☽⚹♅ 4:37 pm
♀□♆ 6:06 pm
☽□☿ 10:10 pm

☿☿☿ budhbar

♋

Wednesday 27

☽△♆ 7:47 am
☽☍♇ 3:08 pm
☽□♂ 11:02 pm v/c

♃♃♃ brihospotibar

♋ ♌

Thursday 28

☽→♌ 2:07 am
♀⚹♃ 12:15 pm
☉□☽ 1:05 pm
☽☍♄ 4:03 pm

Waning Half Moon in ♌ Leo 1:05 pm PDT

♀♀♀ sukrobar

♌

Friday 29

☽□♅ 3:25 am
☽⚹☿ 3:32 pm
☽☍♃ 9:23 pm

All aspects in Pacific Daylight Time; add 3 hours for EDT; add 7 hours for GMT

Samhain

This is the breath of change, the demand of surrender, the relief of letting go. Relish it. It will whisper to you, unrelenting, gazing into your wholeness and asking for payment.

In the veins of the crone's hands flow the stories of every river. In the cloudiness of the crone's eye is the gate to mystery. In the richness of her laughter and the nearness of her death are the bountiful gifts of life. In her voice, our humanity.

We are none of us exempt from any cycle. The laws of the Earth are for everyone.

The laws of this time are for everyone, and it is time to let go. To release the old, relinquish fruits to the transformation of the soil, everything that we birthed in the fullness of the year to the stripping down of the dark.

Savor your wholeness, that when pared down, reveals more abundance. Melt into the call for surrender. Relish the tang of change, roll it around in your mouth. A kiss and a prayer.

Maeanna Welti © Mother Tongue Ink 2020

After Sunrise *© Marissa Arterberry 2018*

Resurrection by Vulture

Imagine a world whose creation myth begins not with Light, nor even with Darkness, but with a vulture picking clean the bones of a dream we finally admitted was dead. Our own magic destroyed us in the end. Humanity couldn't rule after all; our own bodies betrayed us. But for the vulture with her naked head, her naked face, the comforting tent of her black wings discreetly enfolding our dying, there is no shame in a body, no shame in our mistakes. Every sinew, every organ, is sacred in its undoing. She scented out our grief. She traveled down from the highest pinnacles of the sky to alight upon our bare, helpless bones. Her body is a crucible that destroys every foul pathogen; she comes to cleanse the earth of its suffering. She comes to ingest our unfinished stories, the sweet intentions in our lies, the meat of our devouring, the wounds of our losses, our shapes that once cast shadows. She comes to recycle them into muscle and wing, and remind us they belong to the universe.

Yes, this is our time of belonging.

Imagine a world whose creation myth begins with letting go. Letting the ugly vulture unbind our beauty, letting the form unwind, letting her prepare us to become the earth. From her nest on the highest cliffs, she digests us and watches the release of our remains now available for new nourishment. She's going to live a long, long time, as vultures do, because they eat truth every day. And for all the thousand ways we resurrect into new lives, new worlds, out of the green heedless fronds of the earth, we are also living up there in her wings, forever, in the absolute stillness of her flight on the skies of forgiveness.

¤ *Mindi Meltz 2019*

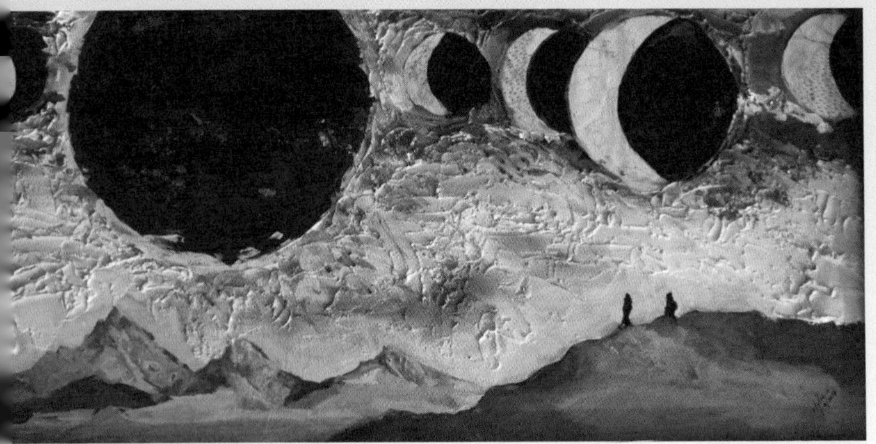

Sense of Wonder © *Sue Tyler Design 2017*

Destruction is a Form of Creation © *Danielle Helen Ray Dickson 2016*

♄♄♄ sonibar

♌  Saturday

♍ 30

☽△♀ 12:05 am v/c
☉□♄ 2:53 am
♂→♏ 7:21 am
☽→♍ 11:09 am
☽✶♂ 11:22 am
☿⚻♆ 12:40 pm

☉☉☉ robibar

♍  Sunday

31

Samhain

☉✶☽ 1:57 am
☽△♅ 10:33 am
☿△♃ 9:18 pm

November

Mí na Samhna

A Spell is like a Prayer
so be not afraid
and cast Loud and Wild
The world needs
our Healing Spells.
excerpt © KamalaDevi Venus 2019

☽☽☽ Dé Luain

Monday
1

☽☍♆ 12:04 am
☽△♇ 6:42 am
☉⚻⚷ 8:20 am
☽□♀ 10:00 am v/c
☽→♎ 4:11 pm

♂♂♂ Dé Máirt

Tuesday
2

☿□♇ 2:39 am
☽△♄ 4:31 am

☿☿☿ Dé Céadaoin

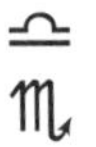

Wednesday
3

☽△♃ 6:08 am
☽□♇ 8:57 am
☽☌☿ 12:27 pm
☽✶♀ 3:32 pm v/c
☽→♏ 5:52 pm
☽☌♂ 10:55 pm

♃♃♃ Dé Ardaoin

♏

Thursday
4

Lunar Samhain

☽□♄ 5:46 am
♅PrH 8:01 am
☉☌☽ 2:14 pm
☽☍♅ 2:26 pm
☉☍♅ 4:58 pm

♀♀♀ Dé Haoine

New Moon in ♏ Scorpio 2:14 pm PDT

♏
♐

Friday
5

☽△♆ 2:53 am
♀→♑ 3:44 am
☽□♃ 6:33 am
☽✶♇ 9:10 am v/c
☽PrG 3:31 pm
☿→♏ 3:35 pm
☽→♐ 5:52 pm

All aspects in Pacific Daylight Time; add 3 hours for EDT; add 7 hours for GMT

If you are waiting for Kali
or Mary or the Moon
to speak to you before
your holy life can begin
before you know certainly
there is magic here

if you are waiting for your body
to look like yoga journal and
your third eye to beam rainbows
the thousand-petal lotus in your
crown to start channeling wisdom
before you can love like a saint

just open your ordinary hands
and look at what is written there

excerpt ¤ Stephanie A. Sellers 2016

Modern Witch
© Aralia Diana Rose 2013

♄♄♄ Dé Sathairn

Saturday
6

☽✶♄ 5:46 am
☿✶♀ 8:59 am

☉☉☉ Dé Domhnaigh

Sunday
7

☽□♆ 2:46 am
☽✶♃ 5:44 am v/c
☽→♑ 5:03 pm
☽☌♀ 9:18 pm
☽✶☿ 11:13 pm

Daylight Saving Time Ends 2:00 am PDT

Letter to the World

This is my letter to the world,
that writes to me, to all of us,
in the language of sea-foam and sunlight,
tornadoes, typhoons, tsunamis,
Nature's tongue that can be gentle and loving, like a mother animal,
or harsh and hurting when we do not respect her skin,
her heartbeat, her children.

This is my dream for the world—
let us learn before it is too late
that love is the force that greens and grows us all,
molecule to mollusk to human,
connecting our flowing current,
keeping us whole,
restoring our broken-ness.

These are our hopes for the world—
hear our cries,
teach us to cry before it is too late,
before fire, flood, and ice consume us.
Let us shed the old snake-skins of greed and hatred,
reborn in new and silken welcome,
shining with abundance and new light.

I am the world, writing in response,
hoping against hope
for more light, fresher air, water,
clean and clear as starlight.
I have whispered to you in flowers and fruits,
thundered and wept in tornados and hurricanes,
scorched in drought and fire,
opened my heart to rebirth.
I want to save my children, not swallow them up.
Will you listen?

XII. ON THE BRINK

Moon XII: November 4–December 3

New Moon in ♏ Scorpio Nov. 4; Full Moon in ♉ Taurus Nov. 19; Sun in ♐ Sagittarius Nov. 21

Mami Wata *© Zena Carlota 2013*

November
noviembre

3 Goldfish

☽☽☽ lunes

♑ 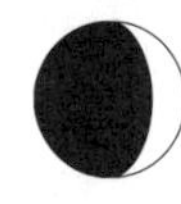

Monday
8

☽⚹♂ 2:48 am
☽△♅ 1:48 pm
☉⚹☽ 9:06 pm

♂♂♂ martes

♑ ♒ 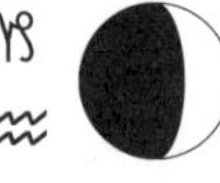

Tuesday
9

☽⚹♆ 3:01 am
☽☌♇ 9:51 am v/c
☽→♒ 7:03 pm

☿☿☿ miércoles

Wednesday
10

☿☌♂ 4:56 am
☽□♂ 7:54 am
☽□☿ 8:08 am
☽☌♄ 8:14 am
☿□♄ 9:04 am
♂□♄ 3:14 pm
☽□♅ 4:45 pm

♃♃♃ jueves

♒ ♓ 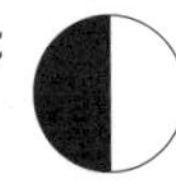

Thursday
11

☉□☽ 4:46 am
☿⚻⚷ 6:06 am
☽☌♃ 11:52 am v/c
☽→♓ 11:53 pm

Waxing Half Moon in ♒ Aquarius 4:46 am PST

♀♀♀ viernes

♓ 

Friday
12

☉△♆ 8:23 am
☽⚹♀ 12:18 pm
♂⚻⚷ 3:19 pm
☽△♂ 4:28 pm
☽△☿ 9:23 pm
☽⚹♅ 10:43 pm

All aspects in Pacific Standard Time; add 3 hours for EST; add 8 hours for GMT

The Meadow Does Not Know

about the stock market.
Today she is worth
exactly what she was worth
yesterday, a year ago, at creation.
I don't mean property value,
taxable assets. I mean
milkweed and copper moths
honeybees, cow vetch,
king snakes. Meadow life
is not money. What rises
and falls here are stems
and flowers, leaves and fruit.
No zigzag line of profit and panic
but the great wheel turning.
Here God gives of her
extravagance and here, like
flicker, viceroy, dragonfly
we come into our inheritance.

© George Ella Lyon 2008

♄♄♄ sábado

♓ ☽ **Saturday 13**

☿☍♅ 7:57 am
☽☌♆ 1:46 pm
☉△☽ 4:18 pm
☽⚹♇ 9:40 pm v/c

☉☉☉ domingo

♓ ♈ ☽ **Sunday 14**

☽→♈ 7:48 am
☽⚹♄ 10:59 pm

November
shí yī yuè

☽☽☽ xīng qī yī

Sacred Intention
Today be like the eagle
Fly where your dreams are
excerpt © Joy Brady 2019

♈

Monday
15

♀□⚷ 12:07 am
☽□♀ 1:06 am
☉□♃ 11:58 am

♂♂♂ xīng qī èr

♈
♉

Tuesday
16

☽✶♃ 5:55 am
☽□♇ 7:51 am v/c
☉✶♇ 1:01 pm
☽→♉ 6:18 pm

☿☿☿ xīng qī sān

♉

Wednesday
17

♂☍♅ 9:23 am
☽□♄ 10:19 am
☽△♀ 4:39 pm
☽☌♅ 6:44 pm
☽☍♂ 7:20 pm

♃♃♃ xīng qī sì

♉

Thursday
18

☿△♆ 7:38 am
☽✶♆ 11:14 am
☽☍☿ 11:47 am
☽□♃ 6:22 pm
☽△♇ 7:57 pm
♀△♅ 10:08 pm

♀♀♀ xīng qī wǔ

♉
♊

Friday
19

☉☍☽ 12:57 am v/c
☽→♊ 6:33 am
☽△♄ 11:12 pm

Full Moon in ♉ Taurus 12:57 am PST
Partial Lunar Eclipse 1:02 am PST*

* Eclipse visible from Americas, N. Europe, E. Asia, Australia, and the Pacific.

2021 Year at a Glance for ♐ Sagittarius (Nov. 21–Dec. 21)

In 2021, big changes are afoot in how you see yourself and your significant relationships. For yourself, you are learning a new definition of freedom that includes being centered rather than scattered. It may be time to let go of philosophies or spiritual practices that are trapping you in the past.

Your relationships will undergo radical shifts this year, as you are challenged to listen to those closest to you in order to clearly comprehend their needs. Don't assume you know what a loved one is saying; keep asking questions until you are sure you understand. The late Spring will be an especially tumultuous time, but if you remember to take a deep breath, be curious, and listen, you will gain valuable insights into creating more authentic partnerships.

A key to this year is in staying closer to home. While you are a wanderer by nature, there is plenty to explore in the world around you without going to the four corners of the Earth. You will be challenged to master your understanding of the immediate environment—the nature park you drive by every day, the community center down the street, your local animal shelter. It is in everyday experiences that the news of the universe will be heralded. If you allow yourself to explore places like this, you will be rewarded with new vision for how to use your unique skills to make the world a better place.

Rhea Wolf © Mother Tongue Ink 2020

The Poet's Journey: Cover Illustration
© Kat Beyer 2007

ħħħ xīng qī liù

♊ Saturday 20

☿□♃ 3:43 pm
☽ApG 6:14 pm

⊙⊙⊙ lǐ bài rì

♊ ♋ Sunday 21

☽□♆ 12:05 am
☿⚹♇ 1:14 am
☽△♃ 7:52 am v/c
⊙→♐ 6:34 pm
☽→♋ 7:33 pm

⊙→♐

Sun in ♐ Sagittarius 6:34 pm PST

November
Kartik

☽☽☽ sombar

♋ 

Monday 22

☽✶♅ 7:59 pm

Medicine Bear

♂♂♂ mongolbar

♋ 

Tuesday 23

☽☍♀ 2:49 am
☽△♂ 4:24 am
☽△♆ 12:50 pm
☽☍♇ 9:46 pm v/c

☿☿☿ budhbar

♋ ♌ 

Wednesday 24

☿→♐ 7:36 am
☽→♌ 7:58 am
☽△☿ 8:02 am
☉△☽ 1:34 pm

♃♃♃ brihospotibar

♌ 

Thursday 25

☽☍♄ 12:51 am
☽□♅ 7:32 am
☽□♂ 7:19 pm

♀♀♀ sukrobar

♌ ♍ 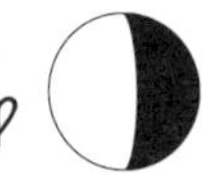

Friday 26

☽☍♃ 8:24 am v/c
♄✶⚷ 5:03 pm
☽→♍ 6:12 pm

All aspects in Pacific Standard Time; add 3 hours for EST; add 8 hours for GMT

Winter the Womb

Didn't we want endless Summer? Endless abundance? Isn't that what Progress was for? But it's too much of everything. Hot-bleached seas are dying while up north a white, rippling giant, with a head like an arrow and paw prints like prehistoric art, drowns somewhere we can't imagine—because imagination happens between snow flakes on a slow afternoon when we have time. And we don't have time.

Send out the warriors. Change it by chemicals, wrestle the weather back by newer technology. Demand it from the leaders.

But she said, *you cannot win the Winter back by battle.* Then what will you do for it? *Nothing,* she said. *I'm just going to listen.* To whom? asked the warriors. *To Bear,* she said. *The oldest, fiercest warrior, who in Winter goes into the darkness, and just rests.*

She goes quiet—a thing Winter used to do, long ago. She dreams of the curves snow makes over every ugly thing, turning it soft like the body of a woman. The way fireside stories remade us with wonder, the way food tasted when we needed food to live—Remember?

Dream, says Bear, *of these things that were lost when you lost the Winter. Your world is burning right out. But Winter is the time for stopping to remember. You're going to need to know how to tell your grandchildren a story, about what a polar bear is. What a forest is. What it feels like, to have things in this world that are grander than you.*

In the warm furred cave of her body, in the cold eternal cave of Winter dark, where Bear's children first suckle, in this womb of stillness—this is the only place from which a world can ever be reborn.

¤ *Mindi Meltz 2019*

♄♄♄ sonibar

♍

Saturday
27

☽□☿ 2:27 am
☉□☽ 4:28 am
☽△♅ 4:18 pm

Waning Half Moon in ♍ Virgo 4:28 am PST

☉☉☉ robibar

Sunday
28

☽△♀ 5:14 am
☽✶♂ 6:36 am
☽☍♆ 7:50 am
☽△♇ 4:02 pm v/c
☉☌☿ 8:39 pm

Nov. / Dec.

Mí na Samhna / Mí na Nollag

☽☽☽ Dé Luain

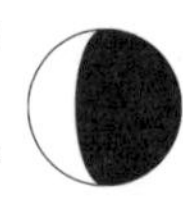

Monday
29

☽→♎ 12:55 am
♂△♆ 6:10 am
☉⚹☽ 2:44 pm
☽⚹☿ 3:33 pm
☽△♄ 4:24 pm
☿△⚷ 6:41 pm
☿⚹♄ 11:19 pm

End of Days

♂♂♂ Dé Máirt

Tuesday
30

☉△⚷ 6:38 am
☿ApH 6:54 am
☽□♀ 11:56 am
♀⚹♆ 12:46 pm
☉⚹♄ 3:14 pm
☽□♇ 7:43 pm
☽△♃ 8:19 pm v/c

☿☿☿ Dé Céadaoin

♎ ♏

Wednesday
1

December

☽→♏ 3:55 am
♆D 5:22 am
☿⚻♅ 6:15 pm
☽□♄ 6:43 pm
☽☍♅ 11:01 pm

♃♃♃ Dé Ardaoin

♏

Thursday
2

☽△♆ 12:58 pm
☽⚹♀ 2:52 pm
☽☌♂ 4:45 pm
☽⚹♇ 8:26 pm
☽□♃ 9:22 pm v/c

♀♀♀ Dé Haoine

♏ ♐

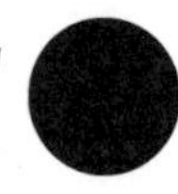

Friday
3

☽→♐ 4:12 am
☉⚻♅ 7:14 am
☽⚹♄ 6:45 pm
☉☌☽ 11:43 pm

Total Solar Eclipse 11:33 pm PST*
New Moon in ♐ Sagittarius 11:43 pm PST

* Eclipse visible from Antartica, S. Africa, S. Atlantic

Sea Turtle © *Tamara Phillips 2014*

Borrowed Earth

To continue the story,
we must decide
our allegiance to you, Mother.
To honor your strength
is to also see your fragility

excerpt ¤ Liza Wolff-Francis 2019

♄♄♄ Dé Sathairn

Saturday
4

☽PrG 2:01 am
☽☌☿ 4:43 am
☽□♆ 12:22 pm
☽✶♃ 9:08 pm v/c

☉☉☉ Dé Domhnaigh

Sunday
5

☽→♑ 3:31 am
☽△♅ 9:56 pm

A Love Poem to Global Sisters

Sisters
Far away, deep in my heart,
I call out your names in joy
I carry your stories and how we have met
This is a new ecstasy.
Now that this ancient dream is coming true
This dream that we carried
Before we were born—
We are finally,
Finally meeting each other
In this lifetime.
Now I have met you
Where you are, who you are
I have read what you have to say
I have read from you what we can do
Across barriers of time and distance
In which we have always known
That each other was there
And now stories and photos
of your beautiful faces
And the faces of all those girls and women
That you are gathering in your loving arms
Your voices carry across the oceans
I call out your names,
I hear you singing
and dancing together
"Until every woman is heard,
Until every woman is heard"*
And we sing back
and drum and dance from here
The same ancient dance
We are here to do this,
and in this life time
We are finally,
Finally meeting each other.

¤ *Tamarack Verrall 2014*

* *Sung by the Power Women Group, Kenya*

Love poem written when I found our global community, World Pulse.

Sunset
© Jakki Moore 2019

XIII. ONE WORLD

Moon XIII: December 3–Jan 2, 2022

New Moon in ♐ Sagittarius Dec. 3; Full Moon in ♊ Gemini Dec. 18; Sun in ♑ Capricorn Dec. 21

Seven Sisters of the Moon

¤ *Diana Denslow 1991*

All We Ever Are

Each corner of this perfect globe
has its arts, its languages,
its people ingrained in the life of that place,
seeds sprouting in native soil.
Yes, we were born for this!

excerpt © Annelinde Metzner 2016

December
diciembre

☽☽☽ lunes

♑

Monday
6

♂⚹♇ 3:41 am
☽⚹♆ 12:09 pm
☽☌♀ 5:21 pm
☽☌♇ 7:55 pm
☽⚹♂ 8:42 pm v/c

Maria Milagros

♂♂♂ martes

♑
♒

Tuesday
7

☽→♒ 3:48 am
☿□♆ 7:16 am
☽☌♄ 7:43 pm
♂□♃ 10:21 pm
☽□♅ 11:01 pm

☿☿☿ miércoles

♒

Wednesday
8

☉⚹☽ 7:56 am
☽⚹☿ 6:07 pm

♃♃♃ jueves

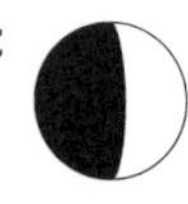

♒
♓

Thursday
9

☽☌♃ 12:53 am
☽□♂ 1:59 am v/c
☽→♓ 6:53 am

♀♀♀ viernes

♓

Friday
10

☽⚹♅ 3:22 am
☉□☽ 5:35 pm
☽☌♆ 7:50 pm

Waxing Half Moon in ♓ Pisces 5:35 pm PST

Nomadic Spirit

I am living on a temporary body which has limitations. I was born into this world a world citizen—landless, country-less, fatherless, moneyless—a nomadic spirit warrior of the past, present and future.

I am living on a temporary place, brown roots violated by white dominance, oppression, complex systemic sins. Why do I care for it so much? Resistance, resilience, pure nurturing love and connection—beacause this is a non-permanent, uncomfortable, magical space.

I am living on a temporary status, never the same, always in movement. As tiring as these journeys are, my daily ritual has been my practice of letting go of what kills me and letting grow of what transforms me. Static, I am not, even if the empire says so. Pay me for the emotional labor that requires this storytelling. I am tired of being defined by my country of origin.

I am living on a temporary apartment with coffee, chocolate and love I've made with help from strong spirits, accepting visits from my mother's soul, crying out painful realities of persecutions, bloodshed.

I am living on a temporary job, enslaved by capitalism, student loans unpaid. No time for idealism, though money isn't what matters most—community, solidarity. Let's reclaim space, be brave to speak up.

I am living on a temporary mindset, constantly changing, hopeful ideas emerging, at the same time that self-doubt threatens to break me to pieces—Bruja Sanadora soy!

I am living on a temporary life, socialized to perform in ways that felt always wrong, longing to belong, flying with imagination to other possible worlds in which my nomadic spirit can coexist with us all.

♄♄♄ sábado

♓ ♈

Saturday
11

☽✶♀ 4:52 am
☽✶♇ 4:56 am
☽□☿ 7:33 am
♀☌♇ 8:29 am
☿✶♃ 11:24 am
☽△♂ 11:40 am v/c
☽→♈ 1:46 pm
☉□♆ 10:21 pm

☉☉☉ domingo

♈

Sunday
12

☽✶♄ 8:50 am

December
shí èr yuè

☽☽☽ xīng qī yī

Monday
13

♂→♐ 1:53 am
☉△☽ 8:03 am
☿→♑ 9:52 am
☽□♇ 3:00 pm
☽□♀ 4:02 pm
☽⚹♃ 6:52 pm v/c

Living Impartially

♂♂♂ xīng qī èr

♈ ♉

Tuesday
14

☽→♉ 12:11 am
☽△☿ 2:20 am
☽□♄ 8:36 pm
☽☌♅ 10:51 pm

☿☿☿ xīng qī sān

♉

Wednesday
15

☽⚹♆ 5:21 pm

♃♃♃ xīng qī sì

♉ ♊

Thursday
16

☽△♇ 3:28 am
☽△♀ 5:14 am
☽□♃ 8:08 am v/c
☽→♊ 12:43 pm
☽☍♂ 5:56 pm

♀♀♀ xīng qī wǔ

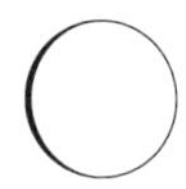

Friday
17

☽△♄ 9:57 am
☽ApG 6:20 pm

The Political Exercise of Mapping

has us questioning, what is ours
and what is theirs, on what side
of a line do you belong?
On what side of food and water,
of education and opportunity
do we deserve to be?
Un-mapping, erasing
lines not dictated by earth
is to practice the phonetics
of speaking in tongues,
but we must persist.
Each of our languages and beliefs
twisted in our mouths
as we struggle year after year
to try to understand each other.
Drawing new lines, new roads
to justice, as we try to come together
for the good of the whole.

¤ *Liza Wolff-Francis 2019*

ħħħ xīng qī liù

♊ Saturday 18

☽□♆ 6:24 am
☿□⛢ 6:35 pm
☉☍☽ 8:35 pm
☽△♃ 10:02 pm v/c

Full Moon in ♊ Gemini 8:35 pm PST

☉☉☉ lǐ bài rì

♊ ♋ Sunday 19

☽→♋ 1:42 am
♀R 2:36 am
⛢D 7:03 am
☉⚹♃ 4:31 pm
☽☍☿ 10:25 pm

Winter Solstice

The night breathes slow, deep, long. The breath of the Earth moves up to meet the stars.

Slow down, dear one. Slow down. Breathe.

The dark has its own music. The dark has its own spell. The dark is the breath that unclenches, bringing sweetness to our deeps.

Be as the sleeping mountains. In the rhythm of your patience, the world will be revealed. In the drum beat of our hearts, all the lessons of the year will tell their stories. Winter is stillness. It is deep calm. It is huge.

Carry your candle, yes. But do not let it blind you to the radiance of the dark. Do not let it crowd out the silence. Do not let it deafen the music of heartbeat, breath, starlight, humanity.

We turn the wheel of the year. We are time unfolding, seasons following seasons flowing through us, bodies, hearts, minds. We walk through the grace of the year, and our wholeness is revealed. We walk through the wisdom of the seasons and learn ever more how to love what we love.

Maeanna Welti © Mother Tongue Ink 2020

Super Nova Night *© Serena Supplee 2002*

Blessing for Hibisca

Sweet baby Hibisca
I hold you up to the Universe
so the stars and planets
may shine into your soul
and Mother Moon lead you
through all the seasons
of woman, circling, circling.
I show you to Sun
to receive her bounty of fire
and fierceness,
light that gives us life.

Sweet Hibisca
I hold you out to all
the great oceans, the wells
and rivers and lakes
so you are one with the tides
that sweep through us all,
all the changes, sweet water
and storms; the mirror of time.
I hold you up to the whole Earth
our home, so you can adore it all
tree and flower and hill
all your creaturely kin, blue horse
and grey wolf, raven and snake.

Look North,
love the land of ice
the long whiteness.
Look South
love spice and flowers,
soft warmth.

Reclamation *© Cara Gwizd 2018*

Look East,
love deserts and jungles.
Look West,
to love the ancient land
of your birth.
All is Beauty.

Sweet Hibisca,
Child of the World,
I hold you up to the Universe
so you may love it all as Family.
You are blessed
to be here in this time
and you are welcome,
welcome,
welcome.

¤ *Rose Flint 2019*

December

Ogrohaeon

☽☽☽ sombar

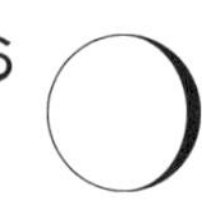

Monday 20

☽✶♅ 12:16 am
☿△♅ 12:18 pm
☽△♆ 7:00 pm

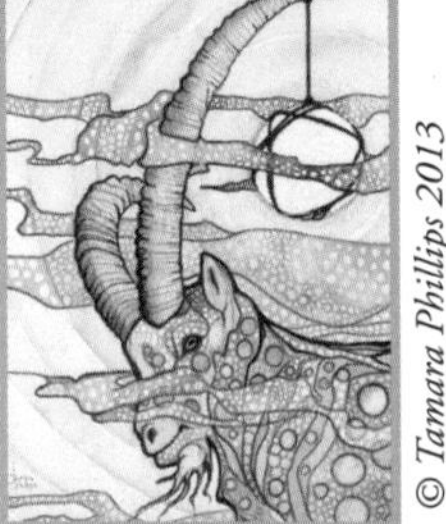

© Tamara Phillips 2013

Lamplighter

♂♂♂ mongolbar

Tuesday 21

☽☍♇ 5:10 am
☽☍♀ 6:44 am v/c
☉→♑ 7:59 am
☽→♌ 1:53 pm

Winter Solstice

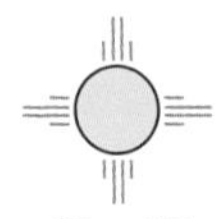

☉→♑

Sun in ♑ Capricorn 7:59 am PST

☿☿☿ budhbar

♌

Wednesday 22

☽△♂ 2:24 am
☽☍♄ 11:28 am
☽□♅ 11:50 am

♃♃♃ brihospotibar

Thursday 23

☽☍♃ 10:39 pm v/c
♄□♅ 11:17 pm

♀♀♀ sukrobar

Friday 24

☽→♍ 12:24 am
☉△☽ 6:05 am
☽□♂ 3:52 pm
☽△♅ 9:24 pm

2021 Year at a Glance for ♑ Capricorn (Dec. 21–Jan. 19)

The past few years have been a cycle of death and renewal for you, Capricorn. With all the deep changes that have been churning inside of you, you may not recognize the self that is starting to emerge. Look to the outer world's powerful transformations in order to understand more about what is happening within you. When there is turmoil in the world, what can it tell you about your inner state? When there is news of a breakthrough or cause for hope, where does that same feeling live in your body? Remember the old hermetic proverb, "As above, so below; as within, so without."

Your values and resources are in a state of flux this year, as you reprioritize your time and how you use your money. Don't make any big moves at the beginning of the year if you can help it. Wait until the spring, and then pay attention to the opportunities to generate material gains in ways that bring more of your unique strengths to the table.

This reorganization of values—what you hold dear, what you want to cultivate in the world—requires some discipline from you to follow through. Using some of your Capricorn super-powers, make yourself a calendar, a to-do list, a plan of action to manifest those values in the real world. You will notice a shift in early summer, as you complete one cycle and begin a new one that brings you more hope for building a life in line with your dreams and revolutionary aspirations.

Rhea Wolf © Mother Tongue Ink 2020

Forest Guardian
© Lindy Kehoe 2015

♄♄♄ sonibar

♍ 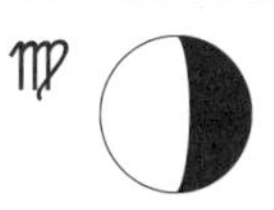

Saturday
25

♂△⚷ 2:37 am
♀☌♇ 4:02 am
☽△☿ 12:08 pm
☽☍♆ 3:07 pm

☉☉☉ robibar

♍ ♎ 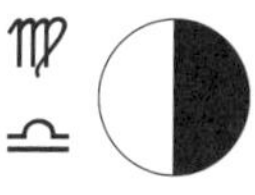

Sunday
26

☽△♀ 12:12 am
☽△♇ 12:39 am v/c
☽→♎ 8:24 am
☿✶♆ 1:29 pm
☉□☽ 6:24 pm

Waning Half Moon in ♎ Libra 6:24 pm PST

Dec. / Jan. 2022

Mí na Nollag / Mí Eanair

☽☽☽ Dé Luain

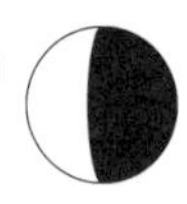

Monday 27

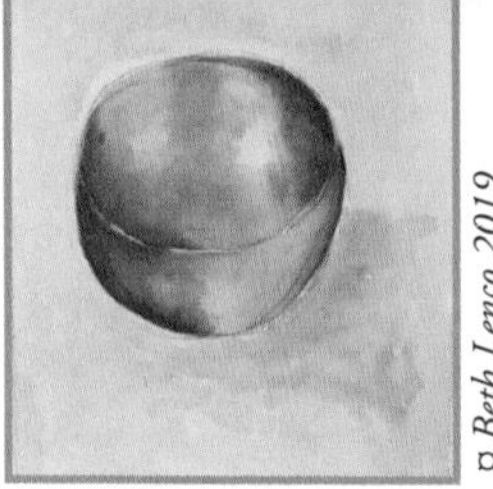

Singing Bowl

☽✶♂ 2:07 am
☽△♄ 4:55 am

♂♂♂ Dé Máirt

♎ ♏

Tuesday 28

☽□☿ 12:56 am
☽□♀ 4:19 am
☽□♇ 6:06 am
☽△♃ 1:10 pm v/c
☽→♏ 1:16 pm
♂⚻♅ 5:04 pm
♃→♓ 8:09 pm

☿☿☿ Dé Céadaoin

♏

Wednesday 29

☿☌♀ 2:27 am
☉✶☽ 2:42 am
☽☍♅ 7:51 am
☽□♄ 8:58 am
☉□⚷ 3:53 pm
♂✶♄ 4:22 pm
☽△♆ 11:51 pm

♃♃♃ Dé Ardaoin

♏ ♐

Thursday 30

☿☌♇ 1:53 am
☽✶♀ 5:18 am
☽✶♇ 8:27 am
☽✶☿ 9:10 am v/c
☽→♐ 3:08 pm
☽□♃ 3:42 pm

♀♀♀ Dé Haoine

♐

Friday 31

☽✶♄ 10:15 am
☽☌♂ 12:01 pm

I Have Seen One World

I have travelled an earth with no borders,
a round place where women
*never birth enemy faces,**
and flowers can never be foreign.
In countries not my own, the trees
are clearly kin to trees everywhere.
Mountains and waving grains
from one land to another
differ only as close cousins.
In all the countries, water
is our same generous Mother.
Everywhere birds sing, goats
and sheep ring their bells.
I have seen one world,
an earth without maplines where
flowers belong where they bloom.
We are everywhere the same
short-lived creatures, longing
for nourishment, love and beauty—
one world, oh so clearly, one world.

© Susa Silvermarie 2019

**from* Rites of Ancient Ripening *by Meridel Le Sueur*

When the World Was Young *© Emily Casper 2017*

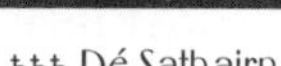
♄♄♄ Dé Sathairn

♐ ♑

Saturday **January**

1

☽□♆ 12:16 am v/c
☉△♅ 1:50 am
☽→♑ 3:02 pm
☽PrG 3:08 pm
☽⚹♃ 4:13 pm
☿→♒ 11:09 pm

☉☉☉ Dé Domhnaigh

♑

Sunday

2

☽△♅ 8:19 am
☉☌☽ 10:33 am
☽⚹♆ 11:52 pm

New Moon in ♑ Capricorn 10:33 am PST

We'Moon Evolution: A Community Endeavor

We'Moon is rooted in womyn's community. The datebook was originally planted as a seed in Europe where it sprouted on women's lands in the early 1980s. Transplanted to Oregon in the late '80s, it flourished as a cottage industry on We'Moon Land near Portland in the '90s and early 2000s, and now thrives in rural Southern Oregon.

The first We'Moon was created as a handwritten, pocket-size diary and handbook in Gaia Rhythms, translated into five languages, by womyn living together on land in France. It was self-published as a volunteer "labor of love" for years, mostly publicized by word-of-mouth and distributed by backpack over national borders. When We'Moon relocated to the US, it changed to a larger, more user-friendly format as we entered the computer age. Through all the technological changes of the times, we learned by doing, step by step, without much formal training. We grew into the business of publishing by the seat of our pants, starting with a little seed money that we recycled each year into printing the next year's edition. By the early '90s, when we finally sold enough copies to be able to pay for our labor, Mother Tongue Ink was incorporated as We'Moon Company, and it has grown abundantly with colorful new fruits: a datebook in full color, a wall calendar, greeting cards, a children's book, an Anthology of We'Moon Art and Writing, a Goddess-poetry book.

Whew! It was always exciting, and always a lot more work than anyone ever thought it would be! We learned how to do what was needed. We met and overcame major hurdles along the way that brought us to a new level each time. Now, the publishing industry has transformed: independent distributors, women's bookstores and print-based publications have declined. Nonetheless, We'Moon's loyal and growing customer base continues to support our unique womyn-created products, including the Anthology and the new We'Moon translation en Español! This home-grown publishing company is staffed by a steady and highly skilled multi-generational team—embedded in women's community—who inspire, create, produce and distribute We'Moon year in and year out.

Every year, We'Moon is created by a vast web of womyn. Our Call for Contributions goes out to thousands of women, inviting art and writing on that year's theme (see p. 236). The material is initially reviewed in Selection Circles, where local area women give feedback. The We'Moon Creatrix then collectively selects, designs, edits, and weaves the material together in the warp and woof of natural cycles through the thirteen Moons of the year. In final production, we fine-tune through several rounds of contributor correspondence, editing and proofing. Approximately nine months after the Call goes out, the final electronic copy is sent to the printer. All the activity that goes into creating We'Moon is the inbreath; everything else we do to get it out into the world to you is the outbreath in our annual cycle. To learn more about the herstory of We'Moon, the growing circle of contributors, and the art and writing that have graced its pages over the past three and a half decades of women's empowerment, check out the anthology In the Spirit of We'Moon (see page 234).

Sister Organizations

We'Moon Land, the original home of the We'Moon datebook in Oregon, has been held by and for womyn since 1973. One of the first intentional womyn's land communities in Oregon, it has continued to evolve organically towards a sustainable women's community and retreat center, on 52 acres, one hour from Portland. Founded on feminist values, ecological practices and earth-based women's spirituality, we envision growing into a diverse, generationally interwoven community of women-loving-women, friends and family, sharing a vision of creative spirit-centered life on the land. We host individual and group retreats, visitors, camping, workshops, events, periodic holyday circles, lunar/solar/astrological cycles and land workdays. Contact us FFI: wemoonland@gmail.com

We'Mooniversity is a 501c3 tax-exempt organization created by We'Moon Land residents for outreach to the larger women's community. WMU co-sponsors occasional events and projects on the land and aspires to become a hub—online and on land—for women's land communities, women's spirituality, herstory, culture, consciousness—and for We'Moon-related publications, classes, and networking resources. www.wemoonland.org, www.wemooniversity.org, www.wemoon.ws

Musawa ¤ Mother Tongue Ink 2020

Wild Card
© Jakki Moore 2013

The We'Moon Tarot is Out!

The *We'Moon Tarot* has just been released, along with *We'Moon 2021*, in Celebration of the 40th edition of We'Moon! Both are inspired by the final Major Arcana card in Tarot: XXI. The World. As the 21st year of the 21st century, 2021 is an auspicious year, completing a full cycle in our individual and collective evolution through We'Moon themes and corresponding Tarot archetypes. As a We'Moon-centered version of Tarot, it changes the dominant paradigm to a more matrilineal life-affirming world view: in Her image.

The images on the We'Moon Tarot cards are drawn exclusively from art published in We'Moon, spanning two decades on each side of the turn of this century. This new Tarot deck provides a spectacular view of an extraordinary period in our personal and planetary lives—from the unique, diverse feminist perspective of We'Moon creative culture and earth-based women's spirituality. Having been part of creating the We'Moon datebook from the beginning, I am grateful to be able to draw from the full spectrum of original We'Moon art as my pallet for creating a We'Moon Tarot deck: in the Mother Tongue.

Tarot is a time-honored divinatory tool for seeking guidance: a map of consciousness for tracking the trajectory of your life's path, artistically rendered to spark your intuition into revealing hidden meanings relevant to the question at hand. The structural design rests on the universal patterns of Nature—and human nature—as represented by the four ('mater-real') elements in the Minor Arcana suits:

⊕ **Earth** (physical/body)
☽ **Water** (emotional/heart)
✙ **Fire** (energetic/action)
✳ **Air** (mental/mind)

The Major Arcana consists of a fifth suit, the ('ether-real') element of Spirit. And the numbers on the cards mark your progression in the ongoing life cycles you are living through.

Whether you are new to Tarot, or an experienced Tarot card reader, the booklet that comes with the boxed set of 78 cards provides invaluable keys for interpreting the cards. This exquisite collection of We'Moon art introduces you to a whole Council of We'Moon familiars, empowered spirit'real we'moon you can converse with, in consulting your inner guidance.

Musawa ¤ Mother Tongue Ink 2020

Staff Appreciation

At the time of this writing, the We'Moon office is abustle with energy. A late Fall chill is in the air, but our home office is warm and cheery. Dana and Susie are in the shipping department, bundling up We'Moon goodies to send along to you lovelies, chatting and laughing all the while. In the living room, Bethroot stokes the fire, with quill in hand. She's putting her keen editing skills to task, as she hones and refines the words here. To my right, Leah dashes from kitchen table to office and back again, balancing the group work of crafting this treasured datebook, with answering the phone. Each call is a surprise: Need help with your order? Calling to rave about how much We'Moon means to you? Phoning in a question about an astrological anomaly? She gets to hear it all! During this extra-festive time, Sue joins us from our northern office, catching up with our progress, and excitedly helping choose the art for our cards and wall calendar. All the while, she's keeping the shipping department hopping with bookstore orders, and doing the work that keeps the We'Moon financial boat afloat. Resist as we might, it's hard to not peer over Sequoia's shoulder as she magically puts this mistresspiece together on screen. She's our Graphic Designer Extraordinaire. Want to know her super power? She has an uncanny ability to reach into our treasure trove of graphic submissions, and pull out the most perfect piece of art for a placement that had, until then, stumped us. All the while, Musawa, We'Moon founder, has been inside of the deep work of creating a We'Moon Tarot Deck! Her ability to weave multiple systems and ideas into one grand tapestry, sharply refined over these 40 years of We'Moon publications. With Eagle by her side, the two make a dynamic duo: Eagle truly has an Eagle Eye when it comes to the many small but oh-so-important details, and we rely on her to help perfect each We'Moon.

Later on, in the evening, after cleaning dinner dishes, we'll gather around our Altar of Conjuring. Candles will be lit, a sacred song will be sung, and we will ask the Goddess for guidance. We are pulling together threads of the future. We are braiding what is, with what will be, with what the Spirit of We'Moon wishes to become. We are conduits for Her wisdom-gifts that want to come through.

Being part of this group touches my heart, and I extend my deepest gratitude to these lovely women for journeying so well together, and to the Spirit of We'Moon for cradling us in this sacred container.

Barbara Dickinson

From left to right: Barb, Eagle, Bethroot, Musawa, Sue, Leah. Sequoia, Dana, Susie & Stella the dog.

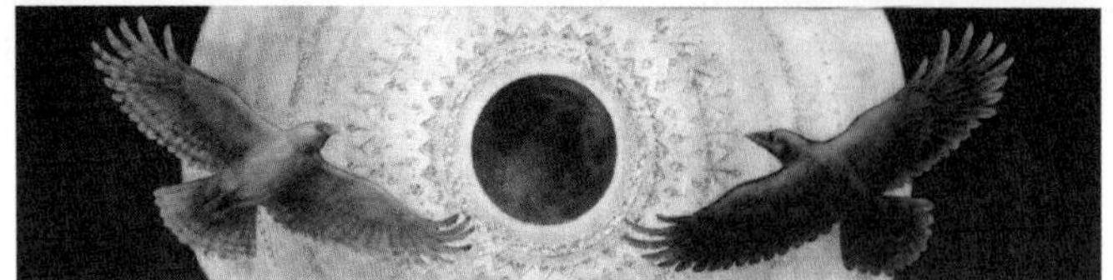

Harmony © *Autumn Skye 2019*

We'Moon Ancestors

We honor wemoon who have gone between the worlds of life and death recently, beloved contributors to wemoon culture who continue to bless us from the other side. We appreciate receiving notice of their passing.

Agnes Baker Pilgrim/Grandma Aggie (1924-2019) was a Native American spiritual elder in Southern Oregon, the oldest living member of the Takelma tribe. Her life was devoted to preserving indigenous culture and to protecting the woods, waters and wildlife of the region. Her influence spread wide; she was an honored speaker and ceremonialist, an ambassador for Native awareness and spiritual values. Grandma Aggie graduated from university at 61, in a time before "continuing education" became normalized. She co-founded a short-term university residential program for Native American youth, and was a co-founder of the International Council of 13 Indigenous Grandmothers, dedicated to protection of earth and indigenous cultures.

Barbara Hammer (1939-2019) was a lesbian filmmaker whose work spanned a 50-year career. She brought lesbian image and story to the screen, with a determined commitment to put lesbian sexuality into films. Her first work (1974) was a short experimental piece called "Dyketactics," claiming space for lesbian sex depicted by lesbian film artists themselves."Nitrite Kisses" (1992) was a feature film narrating the history of lesbian and gay life from the 1920s through the 1990s.She was prolific, creating over 100 films and receiving many awards and grants. In 2017 she established an annual filmmaking grant for lesbian experimental filmmakers. Toward the end of her life, she became an outspoken advocate for death with dignity.

Jean Mountaingrove (1925-2019) held a historic place in American feminism and within the Oregon women's land community. Guided by her roots in Quaker practice and by reverence for the natural world, she brought together the streams of feminist spirituality and country dyke culture evolving in the 1970s. She co-founded WomanSpirit (1974-84),a quarterly magazine homespun in country cabins with, quickly, scores of women contributing writing and art as Goddess consciousness was emerging.

At Rootworks, a small rugged foresthome, Jean and her then-partner Ruth Mountaingrove gathered women for workshops and "ovulars," art projects and writing groups, Dyke Art Camp, and for building sheds and cabins. In her later years, Jean continued to change lives as she sat at her kitchen table with women visitors, offering her sometimes off-beat wisdom. She was beloved by many—Gone away now, but as Jean famously said, "There is no Away."

Marie Summerwood (1949-2019) was a singer, artist, activist, writer, herbalist and Dianic witch in the Wild Woman Tradition. She was based in Syracuse, NY, and gave devoted service to progressive community projects for decades. Marie taught workshops on chanting, grief, sacred sexuality, and other women's spirituality subjects. Her musical work includes three CDs of women's sacred chanting. She wrote and produced a play, "In Praise of She the Muse." For three years, Marie directed Women Circles, a guided retreat for women in MA, and she was a long-time presenter at Where Womyn Gather, a women's spirituality festival in Pennsylvania.

Ruth Gates (1962-2018) was an eminent marine biologist working hard to save the world's endangered coral reefs. In her early research, she discovered links between climate change and the bleaching and dying of warm water coral reefs. She eventually created her own lab at the University of Hawaii, and became the first woman elected president of the International Society for Reef Studies. She was featured in the award-winning 2017 documentary "Chasing Coral." She was a fascinating and charismatic speaker, passionate about coral reefs and persistently optimistic about saving them. Her most recent research focused on breeding hardier varieties of coral.

Toni Morrison (1931-2019) was an extraordinary, indeed revolutionary presence in American culture and in the world of literature. Her novels catapulted her to a prominence that no other African-American woman had attained.The Bluest Eye (1970) was her first novel, and by the time of Song of Solomon (1977), honors and awards were bringing her national attention. Her masterwork Beloved won the Pulitzer Prize for Fiction in 1987 and was made into a film in 1998. She was awarded the Presidential Medal of Freedom in 2012, and was awarded the Nobel Prize for Literature in 1993.

Toni taught and lectured at several prestigious colleges; and in her editing career, she fostered a new generation of African-American writers, bringing black literature into the mainstream. Toni's work explored black identity in America with imagination and pathos, bringing forth characters whose soul-power was profound and enduring.

Vicki Gabriner (1942–2018) was an activist extraordinaire, on the cutting edge of social justice movements in mid-century America. She was among the many young New Leftists who went to the south in the 1960s and worked with Local African-Americans on civil rights. She was involved in gathering materials and records from local activist groups—which became the second largest collection of 1960s civil rights documents. Then there was anti-war organizing, then feminist and lesbian activism. In 1971, Vicki published *Sleeping Beauty: a Lesbian Fairy Tale*, openly discussing incest, encouraging other women to speak out. She wrote prolifically for the gay and lesbian press; for three years, she published Sojourner: The women's Forum and was director of the Sojourner Feminist Institute.

In her later life, Vicki drew on her Jewish Roots, writing to commemorate struggles in the early 1990s for workers' rights.

© Copyrights and Contacting Contributors

Copyrights for most of the work published in We'Moon belong to each individual contributor. Please honor the copyrights: ©: do not reproduce without the express permission of the artist, author, publisher or Mother Tongue Ink, depending on whose name follows the copyright sign. Some wemoon prefer to free the copyright on their work: ¤: this work may be passed on among women who wish to reprint it "in the spirit of We'Moon." In all cases, give credit to the author/artist and to We'Moon, and send each a copy. If the artist has given permission, We'Moon may release contact information. Contact mothertongue@wemoon.ws or contact contributors directly.

Contributor Bylines and Index

See page 236 for info about how YOU can become a We'Moon contributor!

Abril Garcia-Linn (San Antonio, TX) is a writer and artist. She believes everyone has a story to tell and that every story matters. She creates art to connect with people and build community. **p. 63**

Adrienne Simms (San Francisco, CA) The artwork is part of a series called *Witches, Cats, and Kimonos*. You can find out more on her website: adriennesimms.com and on Instagram @adriennesimmsart. **p. 127**

Akefa Azu (Slocan, BC) is a mixed race, conscious visual and performing artist. She lives in the Kootenays on her hobby farm with her husband, mother, and beast-friends. Join her on-line community @ akefamusic.com to see her up-coming passion projects. **p. 33, 137**

Alexandra Kisitu (Saint Paul, MN) is a home-birth mother of two young children, a writer, a creator, a bellydancer, and a PhD candidate at the University of Hawaii at Mánoa. Her research focuses on deinstitutionalized birth in Hawaii as well as medical sociology. **p. 35**

Amy Alana Ehn (Eugene, OR) Healing Arts Practitioner, helicopter pilot, animal wellness advocate, traveler and lifetime lover of words. She is inspiring blissful balance, playing with magical manifestation, and breathing in creation. Exquisitehealing.com **p. 144**

Amy L. Alley (Greenwood, SC) is a mother, artist, writer, poet, avid knitter, yarn-bomber, and lover of nature who lives, plays, paints, writes and knits with her son in beautiful upstate SC. See her work at panpanstudios.blogspot.com/ or etsy at PanPanStudios **p. 39**

Andrea Aragon (Portland, OR) is a native Oregonian. She is a mother, counselor, daughter, partner, friend, sister, runner, artist, human, empath of the planet earth. propelled by love, fueled by visions, wielder of compassion. She is. **p. 69**

Angela Bigler (Lancaster, PA) is a writer of poetry, fiction and memoir, who seeks to uplift and heal others with her strong talk. Dreambigwords.wordpress.com, angelabigler42@gmail.com **p. 95, 110**

Anna Lindberg Art (Stockholm, Sweden) has been drawing and painting for most of her life, always determined to make art, using it to reflect and make sense of the world as she knows it. Website: annalindbergart.com, Instagram: @anna.lindberg.art **p. 69**

Annelinde Metzner (Black Mountain, NC) My life's mission as composer and poet has been to open a gateway for the reemergence of the Goddess. I welcome Her in all Her forms! Contact me at annelinde@hotmail.com and see annelindesworld.blogspot.com **p. 169**

Annika Gemlau (Essen, Germany) Artist, Illustrator and Cultural Anthropologist. My paintings invite to undertake the journey to your inner home via the strange landscapes. Prints & originals can be ordered via annikagemlau@gmail.com asombrasdelsur.wordpress.com **p. 149**

Aralia Diana Rose (El Prado, NM) creates art which reflects the spiritual journey unique to women. Her work can be viewed and purchased at magdahliahstudios.com or Facebook.com/magdahliastudios. **p. 157**

Autumn Skye (Powell River, BC) I offer my artwork as a mirror, as an intimate personal reflection and a grand archetypical revelation. Within these visions, may you recognize your own sacred heart, your cosmic divinity, and the innate grace that dwells within. Autumnskyeart.com **p. 24, 184**

Barbara Dickinson (Sunny Valley, OR) practices magical arts in the most mundane of ways, so subtle as to go unnoticed by most. She's a home-steader, home-maker and home-builder. **p. 4, 183**

Barbara Landis (San Francisco, CA) is a fine art photographer creating images locally and abroad. Practicing Nichiren Shoshu Buddhism since 1968, she belongs to Myoshinju Temple in Pinole, CA. Please visit barbara-landis.com **p. 53**

Beate Metz (Berlin, Germany) was an astrologer, feminist, translator & mainstay of We'Moon's German edition & the European astrological community. **p. 207**

Bernice Davidson (Summertown, TN) Bernice is a civil rights artist who creates murals and public works in small southern towns which point to heroes of the heart. She also keeps sketch diaries of dreams and mystical musings. bernicedavidsonart.com **p. 20, 66, 119**

Beth Lenco (Hubbards, Nova Scotia) is a visual artist, teacher and witch shaman. She leads retreats for women and paints for joy. bethlenco.com, Ancientpracticesforwomen.com **p. 60, 178**

Bethroot Gwynn (Myrtle Creek, OR) 25 years as WeMoon's Special Editor & 45 at Fly Away Home women's land, growing food, theater & ritual. For info about spiritual gatherings, summertime visits send SASE to POB 593, Myrtle Creek, OR 97457. For info about her new book of poetry and plays, *PreacherWoman for the Goddess*, see p. 233. **p. 28, 29**

Breyn Marr (La Pine, OR) Devotee. Changemaker. Activist. Heart-follower. Dreamer. Believer. Breyn's studies and work have taken her around the country and globe, all in the name of contributing to reawakening Wild Feminine Soul and creating vibrant, possibility-oriented community. Thank you Mother and We'Moon for this remarkable opportunity! **p. 86**

Cara Gwizd (Ilderton, ON) is an award winning graphite artist whose work reflects her journey as a woman while aiming to encompass both the simplicity and complexity of motherhood, pregnancy, birth and loss. To learn more about Cara visit caragwizd.com **p. 125, 175**

Carmen R. Sonnes (Phoenix, OR) creates paintings to bring beauty, healing and balance to our planet. By acknowledging culture, the feminine and spirit in each work, she fulfills her purpose. Visit carmenrsonnes.com; carmenrsonnes@yahoo.com **p. 107**

Carolyn Batten-Kimzey (Grants Pass, OR) Storyteller, imagineer, multimedia artist creating women's ritual through music, dance, masks—passionate-humorist envisioning healthy higher vibrations for Mother Earth. Gardener, lover of wildcrafting medicinal plants wherever I am led. **p. 131**

Cary Wyninger Art N' Soul (Trempealeau, WI) is an artist from the midwest who paints from her soul. She's inspired by nature, colors, and the images she sees during meditation and healing sessions. She has an immense love of life, her children, grandchildren, sisterhood, brotherhood and animals that bless her life. carywyninger@yahoo.com, carywyninger.com **p. 42**

Cassie Premo Steele (Columbia, SC) is the author of 16 books and audio programs about intergenerational trauma, intersectional feminism, and empowerment through experiences with the natural world. She lives with her wife in South Carolina. cassiepremosteele.com **p. 139**

Cathy McClelland (Kings Beach, CA) paints from her heart and imagination. Her love for nature, cross-cultural mythical subjects, magical, sacred places and symbols fuel her creative spirit. Cathymcclelland.com **p. 24, 114**

Christina Gage (New Mexico) creates soulful fine art inspired by the sacred feminine. Each painting carries the transmission of love and luminosity, a non-verbal prayer: Experience her online art gallery at christinagage.com **p. 54, 141**

Colleen Koziara (Itasca, IL) I lived my most formative years immersed in nature and filled with wonder. I strive to make each of my works a doorway. I hope the viewer sees through that doorway, the deeper magic within the image being mirrored back within themselves. Mysticalwillow.com **p. 8, 133**

Cynthia Kennedy (Santa Barbara, CA) is a sculptor, painter, and photographer who seeks to capture beauty and metamorphosis in her art. She loves glimpses into small openings where experience shifts and says her best work creates itself. She lives in Santa Barbara with her 2 children. CynthiaKennedy.com, ArtemisStudios.com **p. 59**

Danielle Helen Ray Dickson (Nanaimo, BC) considers art to have the power to heal people, change lives and shed light on the world in a new way. She infuses this into her work with each intentional brush stroke. Danielledickson.com **p. 132, 155**

Darlene Cook (Townsend, GA) It is a dream come true to share my Intuitive Art. My paintings develop in a personal way, but I believe that they are meant to touch many. Find me on Facebook: healingartspacebydarlenecook or Instagram @ healing_artspace **p. 109, 148**

Deborah Martinez Martinez (Pueblo, CO) is a writer and publishing facilitator with a deep regard for ancestral herstory. Living on borrowed lungs after a double lung transplant, she hopes to give back to the world with activism. Vanishinghorizons1@me.com **p. 131**

Destiney Powell (Murfreesboro, TN) poeticallyillustrated.net **p. 63, 77, 134**

Diana Denslow (Poulsbo, WA) mother, artist, crone, big fan of We'Moon and cats, is happily and thankfully seeking her destiny under big old cedar trees in a modest and diverse neighborhood. **p. 138, 169**

Diane Lee Moomey (Half Moon Bay, CA) paints in watercolor and writes poetry. Visit her at dianeleemoomeyart.com. If you write to her, she will write back! **p. 88, 96**

Diane Norrie (Coquitlam, BC) I live on the banks of the Fraser River in Coquitlam "Little Pinkfish" British Columbia. My art is strongly influenced by a spiritual connection. I love art; it is a constant calling. **p. 107**

Dorrie Joy (Devon, UK) is an intuitive artist working in many mediums in celebration of our shared indigeny as people of Earth. Originals, prints, commissions of all kinds at dorriejoy.co.uk **p. 29**

Durdica M. (Surrey, UK) Becoming worn out by life, she received a call in 2008. It guided her into depths of her underworld. She recognized it as a catalyst to begin reclaiming her authentic feminine power and true voice which she longs to share with other women. **p. 82**

Earthdancer (Golconda, IL) is a weaver of words and worlds, a mother, a farmer and magical multi-tasker, co-creating Interwoven Permaculture in the Shawnee Forest of SOIL, at the crossroads of eclipses. Interwovenpermaculture.com **p. 59**

Elise Stuart (Silver City, NM) lives in the southwest corner of New Mexico, where Light takes you on a journey and Sound brings you home. elisestuart16@gmail.com **p. 38**

Elizabeth Diamond Gabriel (St. Paul, MN) is a professional artist, illustrator, writer and teacher-in-practice since 1975. She loves animals, nature, a good veggie burrito and long listening walks among her beloved Minnesota woods and lake waters. **p. 17, 113**

Ellen S. Jaffe (Toronto, ON) is a poet, teacher and healer, living in a multicultural Toronto neighborhood with her partner. Contact her at ellen-s-jaffe.com **p. 158**

Elspeth McLean (Pender Island, BC) creates vivid, vibrant paintings completely out of dots. Each dot is like a star in the universe. Elspeth hopes her art connects people with their inner child. Elspethmclean.com **p. 15**

Emily Casper (Berkley, CA) It is an honor to listen to and engage with the Elemental Realms. My artistic pieces reflect the wild beauty I feel and see daily. So much gratitude to Earth and Kin for their creative support and joyful, profound presence. **p. 179**

Emily Kedar (Toronto, ON) is a therapist, writer and dancer living and working in Toronto, Canada and Salt Spring Island, BC. She works to support reconnection between humans and the living world through her clinical work and her writing. Connect with her at emilykedar.com **p. 30, 62, 73, 149**

Erika Sanadora (Ypsilanti, MI) is an independent storyteller, facilitator, organizer and educator. Erika earned a master of social work from the University of Michigan. Contact her at sanadora.nomadicspirit@gmail.com or emurica@umich.edu **p. 171**

Flame Bilyue' (Charlottesville, VA) is a shamanic healer, bodyworker and creator of jewelry, paintings, masks and mirrors. "I am inspired by visionary art that evokes strength, reverence and wonder." Intuitive Readings and commissioned art. Flame@ flamebilyue.com Flamebilyue.com **p. 87**

Frencene Hart (Honaunau, HI)is an internationally recognized visionary artist whose work utilizes the wisdom and symbolic imagery of sacred geometry, reverence for the Natural Environment and interconectedness between all things. francenehart.com **p. 25**

Gaia Orion (Sebright, ON) is a successful international artist. She is an art career and creativity coach for individuals and organizations. She is also the host of Gaia's Art Podcast, a platform that discusses art for a peaceful and flourishing world. Gaiaorion.com **p. 99**

George Ella Lyon (Lexington, KY) I write by listening, and teach the same way, helping people find and free their voices. An activist for social and environmental justice, I recently served as Kentucky's Poet Laureate (2015–2016). georgeellalyon. com **p. 97, 161**

Gretchen Lawlor (back from Mexico to Whidbey Island, WA) We'Moon oracle, now mentor to new oracles & astrologers. Astrology is my great passion—the stars my friends, my loves, my allies. Let me help connect you to these wise guides. Readings in person, skype or zoom. 206-698-3741 (call or text) light@whidbey.com; gretchenlawlor.com **p. 14, 22**

Greta Boann Perry (Oakland CA) since childhood, has been deeply connected with Mother Earth. Ocean sailor, country Artist Potter, tree planter, forest protector, meditation teacher and Painter. About which, Healers, shaman say, "your paintings are full of life energy, healing power" HealingSpiritScapes.com **p. 150**

Heather L. Crowley (East Kingston, NH) is a mother, wife, sister, daughter, visual artist, poet, mindfulness meditation teacher, and MD. Willow Road Watercolors & The Circle Studio, LCC. "Art exploring the beauty and mystery of nature and spirit." willowroadwc.com **p. 3**

Heather McElwain (Sandpoint, ID) is a freelance writer and editor whose passions are words and wandering about, within and beyond. Find her at Facebook: bardontheroam. **p. 105**

Heather Roan Robbins (Ronan, MT) ceremonialist, spiritual counselor, & astrologer for 40 years, author of *Moon Wisdom, Everyday Palmistry* & several children's books, writes weekly Starcodes columns for We'Moon & The Santa Fe New Mexican, works by phone & Zoom, practices in Montana, with working visits to Santa Fe, NM, MN, & NYC. roanrobbins.com **p. 8, 11, 204, 205**

Helena Arturaleza (Noord-Holland, The Netherlands) "Mi corazón va a donde quiera que fluya el arte" le gusta expresar amor, alegría y armonía a través de varias formas de expresión: arte, poesía, música y danza. Sus pinturas son como espejos, que reflejan la visión y el despertar espiritual. La vida, el color, la naturaleza y las personas inspiran el trabajo de Helena. Las visiones son un recordatorio de lo hermosa que es realmente la vida. arturaleza.art **back cover**

Hope Reborn (San Jose, CA) Aloha! I am an emerging creatress, exploring and expressing the journey of the soul through art and song. instagram@rebornhope **p. 142**

Jakki Moore (Oslo, Norway) is an artist, illustrator and storyteller currently living in three places: Norway, Ireland and Bulgaria. Her books can be found on Amazon. com jakkiart.com **p. 19, 44, 112, 145, 168, 182**

Jan Pellizzer (Grass Valley, CA) Living and creating in the Sierra Nevada Mtn. foothills, my inspiration surrounds me—creative spirits, art. Find me on Facebook: pellizzerjan **p. 166**

Jana Parkes (Grants Pass, OR) Art created through my heart. I never know beforehand what I will paint. I simply ask with an open heart for the highest good. My hope is that others find art as healing and inspiring as I do. Janaparkesart.com, etsy.com/shop/janaparkesart **p. 23**

Janis Dyck (Golden, BC) has been making things since she can remember and feels grateful that she still has the privilege of making art. She lives with her husband and two teenage sons and practices art therapy and art making. To her, creativity is an ever-evolving process that she gets to tap into through her work. Janisdyck. com **p. 161**

Janyt Piercy (Courtenay, BC) I am an artist, knitter, teacher and grandmother, living and creating on beautiful Vancouver Island. **p. 43**

Jeanette M. French (Gresham, OR) inspiring relationship with Spirit and Mother Earth through portals of light, love, joy, beauty, compassion, hope and gratitude. Jeanette-french.artistwebsites.com **p. 106, 139, 160**

Jennifer Lothrigel (Lafayette, CA) is an intuitive healer, poet and artist in the San Francisco Bay area. Connect with her online at jenniferlothrigel.com **p. 152**

Jenny Hahn (Kansas City, MO) captures the inward journey with artwork that celebrates nature, spiritual awakening and the Divine Feminine. She travels with workshops teaching painting as a tool for mindfulness and self-discovery. Prints and more available at jennyhahn.com **p. 147**

Joanne M. Clarkson (Fort Townsend, WA) Joanne's 5th poetry collection, *The Fates*, won Bright Hell Press' contest and was published in 2017. She has read palms and Tarot for 50 years. Her poetry website is joanneclarkson.com Her psychic URL is Joannethepsychic.com **p. 67**

Joy Brady (San Francisco, CA) an elder, uses art, poetry for expression of her second half of life experiences. She has a practice in symbolic consultation in San Francisco. sacredintention@gmail.com **p. 162**

Jules Bubacz (Portland, OR) I live in my garden, and less often in my house, with my partner and my cat. The garden is my muse, spurring acts of writing, photography, painting and collage from time to time. **p. 109**

KamalaDevi Venus (Lakewood, OH) My creations are transmissions of healing love from/thru the Goddess. Contact her at kdvenus12@gmail.com **p. 156**

Karina Sulla (Honoka'a, HI) Visionary artist, spiritual practitioner, gardener of sacred plants, family and community; supporter of cultural rights, protector of sacred sites, student of Earth consciousness and total consciousness. Karinasulla.com **p. 93, 101**

Kat Beyer (Madison, WI) is an artist and writer who earned her strength by recovering from a hard injury. She loves her work and the family and forests it comes from. Katspaw.com **p. 163**

Kate Langlois (San Francisco, CA) My images reflect a resonance with social justice and deep listening to the interwoven connections from one's heart to the world. katelangloisart.com **p. 64**

Kay Kemp Art (Bastrop, TX) delights in creating heart-centered art that honors and inspires the power of the feminine spirit. She is the founder of Spirit Works 4 U, where she seeks to amplify a message of love and respect around the world. Spiritworks4u.com and kaykemp.com **p. 25, 95, 172**

Kimberly Webber (Taos, NM) Priestess of painting, alchemy and bees. Advocate for the Divine Feminine, personal freedom, youth, pollinators, biodiversity, animals, oceans, forests. Planter of flowers and corn. Pollinator of empowerment. Amplifier of hope. Kimberlywebber.com **p. 91**

KT InfiniteArt (Freeport, NY) Creatrix, artist, writer inspired by sensuality and spirit. Instagram @KTInfiniteArt Check out more artwork. Prints available: InfiniteArtWorld.com **p. 48**

Kusuma Tiffany (Victoria, BC) serves the birthing community as a social worker and doula. This poem was written while living in the forest in Alberta. Kusuma navigates this life through meditating daily, appreciating nature, building community and reading her We'Moon by sunlight in warm baths. kusumatiffany@gmail.com soldoula.com **p. 51**

Leah Marie Dorion (Prince Albert, SK) is an indigenous artist from Prince Albert, Saskatechewan, Canada. Leahdorion.ca **p. 11, 121**

Leah Markman (Eugene, OR) A Tarot enthusiast, astrology lover and leather craftswoman. She spends her time in the sunshine with her dog, horse and VW Bus. Visit her etsy for more writings and leatherwork! Etsy.com/DreamtenderLeather Leahdmarkman@gmail.com **p. 21**

Lindsay Carron (Los Angeles, CA) Her work lies at the crossroads of indigenous voice and environmental activism. She illustrated three children's books recounting Tlingit oral tradition tales. Lindsay's work represents the potential for humanity to realize a healthy future for the planet. Lindsaycarron.com, instagram: @lacarron **p. 31**

Lindy Kehoe (Gold Hill, OR) I am so grateful to be a creative participant in this time of the Human Heart Awakening. My intention is to create works that amplify the love frequency, through the innocence of wonder and imagination, along with the deeply rooted mystical understanding of the Earth and its Ancestors and Wisdom Keepers. lindykehoe.com **p. 61, 177**

Lisa S. Nelson (Ashland, OR) has a novel, *Growing the River Tao*, and two poetry chapbooks: *An Offering of Confetti*, and *With a Third Glance*. She and her daughter share the website, elatedodyssey.com **p. 45, 77**

Liza Wolff-Francis (Albuquerque, NM) is a literary artist with an MFA in Creative Writing from Goddard College. She has a poetry chapbook out called, *Language of Crossing* (SWEPress), and loves language, re-imagining the world, and dark chocolate. **p. 167, 173**

LorrieArt (Cleveland, OH) I am in my crone phase of life. I love animals, and you can see them often in my artwork. I am healing from trauma and fight my own mental illness battles with chronic depression, social anxiety and agoraphobia. These aspects of my life contribute to my unique tapestry and unite me with so many other women maybe even you. Instagram: @ lattesmith05, email lattesmith@ yahoo.com **p. 67**

Louie Laskowski (Brookston, IN) Artist, drummer and priestess of the Reformed Congregation of the Goddess; living and working in a small town. louielaskowski. com **p. 123**

Lupen Grainne (Sebastopol, CA) artist and illustrator inspired by the natural world and expressions of the feminine spirit. Currently illustrating a tarot deck. Find me on Instagram @clary.sage.moon **p. 26**

Lyndia Radice (Magdalena, NM) I live in rural NM, and I paint and portray the natural world around me. Lyndiaradice.myportfolio.com **p. 75**

Lynette Yetter (Portland, OR) is a PushCart Prize nominated poet, and award-winning filmmaker and musician. Lynette makes music, movies, books and art to touch your soul and make you think. LynetteYetter.com **p. 120**

Maeanna Welti (Portland, OR—unceded Chinook land) is a writer, astrologer and witch. She is the author of the *Healing Wheel Samhain to Samhain* workbook. Maeanna offers readings, coaching, support for ancestral and personal healing, and teaches astrology and the fundamentals of witchcraft. maeannawelti.com on Instagram @queenmaeanna **p. 26, 47, 66, 81, 102, 119, 138, 153, 174**

Mahada Thomas (Okanagan Falls, BC) Healing artist, writer, dreamer and Soul singer. I share my healing journey to inspire others. I recognize that healing for one, is healing for the whole. Contact: mahadathomas@yahoo.ca **p. 93**

Mandalamy Arts (Topeka, KS) Amy is an artist, mother, life learner, a nature lover and former psychologist. Her mandalas and paintings primarily have themes of connection and growth, often depicted in celestial scenes. Find her on Facebook and Instagram. **p. 202**

Margriet Seinen (Redway, CA) discovered silk painting in the early 80s. She painted scarves, pillow covers and then moved into fine art, including images of mermaids, nature devas, scenery and mandalas. She also teaches mandala classes where students learn silk paint. Seinensilk.com **p. 81**

Marissa Arterberry (Oakland, CA) I paint and draw the visions my ancestors and spirit guides share with me. I am a dreamkeeper, dancer, gardener and proud mama to Sage and Phoenix! Instagram: @marissaarterberry, email: MarissaArterberry@gmail.com Marissaarterberry.tumblr.com **p. 153**

Mary Ruff-Gentle Doe (Longview, TX) an artist and therapeutic massage therapist, she practiced the art of blended vision in her work and life. **p. 90**

Mary Theresa Wertz (Grants Pass, OR) Living life and loving it here in beautiful Southern Oregon. **p. 125**

MaryAnn Shank (Ashland, OR) Sometime author. See recent piece at mysticallandofmyrrh.com. Also the caregiver for two mystical cats. **p. 117**

Maya Spector (Oakland, CA) is a storyteller, poet, ritualist, retired children's librarian and certified SoulCollage facilitator. Her book of poems, *The Persephone Cycle* is available at: barryandmayaspector.com. She blogs at hangingoutwithhecate.blogspot.com **p. 36, 147**

Melissa Harris (West Hurley, NY) Artist, author, and intuitive. Join me at Art & Spirit Retreats in exotic locations. Author of *99 Keys to a Creative Life, Anything is Possible* card deck and artist of *Goddess on the Go* affirmation cards. Melissaharris.com **p. 41**

Melissa Kae Mason, "MoonCat!" (Florida, Montana, Texas) Traveling Astrologer, Artist, Radio DJ, Photographer, Jewelry Creator, PostCard Sender, Goddess Card Inventor, Seer of Patterns, Traveler and Adventurer. See LifeMapAstrology.com and MoonCat67.Etsy.com Contact: LifeMapAstrology@gmail.com **p. 206**

Melissa Winter (Bellingham, WA) Prints and original paintings may be found at Melissa's website, HoneyBArt.com. For commissions, please contact Melissa at mwinter1103@gmail.com **p. 33**

Melonie Steffes (Thompsonville, MI) lives in the woods of Northern Michigan, U.S.A. Melonie's work in visual and performing arts seeks release, nurture, and balance—guarding the raw wilderness of the internal landscape, without getting in the way of it's natural expression. More info at meloniesteffes.com **p. 45**

Mindi Meltz (Hendersonville, NC) is the author of two novels, *Beauty* and *Lonely in the Heart of the World*, and an upcoming fairy-tale trilogy. She creates personal Animal Wisdom Card decks customized for individuals' power animals and life journeys. mindimeltz.com **p. 154, 165**

Molly Remer (Rolla, MO) MSW, MDiv., D.Min, writes about theology, nature, practical priestessing, and the Goddess. Molly and her husband, Mark, co-create Story Goddess at brigidsgrove.etsy.com and Molly is the author of *Womanrunes, Earthprayer* and *She Lives Her* poems. brigidsgrove.com **p. 41, 48, 98**

Mosa Baczewska (Friday Harbor, WA) is in love with fractals and all geometry. As a math-magician, she creates images that are 'food for the quickening', brining wonder, joy and inspiration to the eye. You can see more of her work on her newly launched website mosazone.com **p. 24, 25**

Musawa (Estacada, OR & Tesuque, NM) I have been hatching the We'Moon Tarot deck for ages, it seems—re-living every stage in my own Fool's journey, in the process—so I'm glad it's now finally out! I am looking forward to starting a whole new creative cycle personally, and in We'Moon . . . as in the World at large: we can only hope! **p. 6, 24, 180, 182, 198**

Naima Penniman (Brooklyn, NY) Co-founder & steward of WILDSEED Community Farm & Healing Village, performance activist through ClimbingPoeTree, food-justice educator at Soul Fire Farm, & healing practitioner at Harriet's Apothecary, Naima cultivates collaborations that elevate the healing of our earth, ourselves, and our communities, lineages & descendants. Climbingpoetree.com **p. 143**

Nancy Watterson (Oakland, OR) is an artist, a mother and a grandmother. She lives and works along the Umpqua River in Oregon, where she finds an unlimited source for inspiration and balance. See more of her work at nwattersonscharf.com **p. 100, 103**

Natalie Gildersleeve (Portland, OR) Lifestyle, family and portrait photographer. nataliegildersleeve.com or find her on Instagram @nataliegildersleeve **p. 104**

Natasza Zurek (Pentiction, BC) Art is an expression of her appreciation of nature, as well as the mundane and mystical human experiences. It is her soul purpose to use the visual language as a tool of communication bridging the inner world with the outer world, thus making a positive contribution to our shared experience. natka@posteo.de, nataszasurekart.com **p. 70**

Patricia Telesco (Amherst, NY) Wordsmith, researcher, & poet of 25+ years, publishing full-length books, magazine articles and online features. She specializes in self-help, spirituality, metaphysics and culinary topics. Facebook: trish. telesco **p. 57**

patti sinclair (Edmonton, AB) believes it is Time to fully tap into our spiritual reservoir for healing. A poet of a certain season, patti has found home in composing and performing poetry. To see more or to listen, visit: poet-at-large.blogspirit.com **p. 107**

Paula Franco (Ciudad de Buenos Aires, Republica Argentina) Italo-Argentine Artist Shaman woman, visual and visionary illustrator, teacher in sacred art, writer and poet, astrologer, tarot reader, creator of goddess cards and coloring book: *The Ancestral Goddess and Heaven and Earth*. Ladiosaancestral.com **p. 55, 72, 111, 151**

Rachael Amber (Philadelphia, PA) is a nature-focused illustrator & designer who raises environmental awareness, social justice & radical self-care through her artwork. She is the creatrix behind *Cycles Journal*: an illustrated guide to tracking lunar & menstrual cycles. Find her online: rachaelamber.com or cyclesjournal.com, or on Instagram @rachael.amber or @cyclesjournal. **p. 98**

Rev. Dr. Judy DeRosa (Oakhurst, CA) As a visionary artist my work, beautifully expresses the spiritual yearnings of this age. The artful storytelling is used to remind the observer of their own deep innermost thoughts. To remember that humanity is never alone on our cosmic journey. jderosaart@yahoo.com **p. 128**

Rhea Wolf (Portland, OR) works to tear down the racist patriarchy through words, witchcraft, & workshops. The author of *The Light That Changes: The Moon in Astrology, Stories, and Time* and *Which is Witch* zines, Rhea is also a prison activist, mother, and teaches at the Portland School of Astrology. Keep in touch & visit RheaWolf.com **p. 15, 43, 55, 65, 79, 91, 101, 115, 127, 141, 151, 163, 177**

Robin Diane Bruce (Boulder, CO) artist, healer, teacher, human. Robindbruce.com **p. 135**

Robin Lea Quinlivan (Thomas, WV) lives in the beautiful Appalachian Mountains of West Virginia, where she co-owns an art gallery. She is inspired by love for the natural world, as well as the mutable nature and interconnectedness of all things. Robinquinlivan.etsy.com **p. 140**

Robin Rose Bennett (Hewitt, NJ) is an herbalist, writer, and educator, and the author of *Healing Magic: A Green Witch Guidebook to Conscious Living* and *The Gift of Healing Herbs: Plant Medicines and Home Remedies for a Vibrantly Healthy Life*. Her website is robinrosebennett.com **p. 136**

Robin Urton (Kansas City, MO) creates combines a reverence for nature with personal themes. She credits her dreams for leading her on a path to creating art. Themes include birds, trees, flowers, women and dreaming Buddhas. She also create commissioned art. DreambirdArt.com **p. 79**

Rose Flint (Wiltshire, UK) was Poet-Priestess to the Goddess Conference, Glastonbury for 20+ years. Her new collection of poetry, the award winning *Mapping the Borders* is a selection of 30 years of environmental writing. **p. 175**

Rosella (London, UK) Mandalas for meditation and self-empowerment. The Mandalas are hand drawn and painted in iridescent watercolours. rosella-creations.co.uk **p. 13**

Rosemary Wright (Ocean Grove, NJ) is a professional storyteller. She shares stories from many cultures including stories of goddesses. **p. 46**

Ruby Singer (East Montpelier, VT) is a junior in high school in Vermont. She plans to study graphic design after she graduates. **p. 50**

Sandra Pastorius (Ashland, OR) has been a practicing Astrologer since 1979, and a Featured Writer for We'Moon since 1990. Look for her collected We'Moon essays, "Galactic Musings" under Resources at wemoon.ws. With Sun in Gemini she delights in blending the playful and the profound. Sandra offers individual and couples charts, readings and transit updates in person or by phone. Email her about astrology classes at: sandrapastorius@gmail.com. Read more articles here: wemoon.ws/blogs/sandras-cosmic-trip. Peace Be! **p. 16, 18, 208**

Schar Cbear Freeman (Ele'ele, HI) a Native American artist, photographer, poet, hula dancer, living her dream on the beautiful island of Kauai. Find her art on Island at Banana Patch Studio, Hanapepe, Kilaeua HI. scharart.etsy.com, scharart.blogspot.com **p. 84**

Serena Supplee (Moah, UT) has been "Artist on the Colorado Plateau" since 1980. An oil painter, watercolorist and sculptor, she welcomes you to visit her website serenasupplee.com **p. 1, 174**

Shannon Fitzgerald (Hillsborough, NC) is an intuitive artist, author, SoulCollage Facilitator, at Bold Moves Studio: boldmovestudio.com. Follow her on Facebook, Twitter or Instagram @boldmovesstdio **p. 110**

Shanti Bennett (Gresham, WI) is a mixed media artist known for her work depicting women, with an emphasis on the face to evoke feelings and connection. Her work is described as whimsical, spiritual, colorful, thought provoking, and versatile. Artbyshanti.com **p. 38**

Shauna Crandall (Victor, ID) Creative; music, visual arts, written word. Seeker and artistic interpreter of the mystical, and the ordinary female experience. shaunacrandallart.com. **front cover**

Shelley Blooms (Cleveland, OH) is a Spirit Pilgrim, ever on the trail of cosmic breadcrumbs by which the muses choose to amuse the noodle, through picture, poem, kit and caboodle. **p. 74, 89**

Sophia Faria (Salt Spring Island, BC) is a sex educator, retreat facilitator and writer. Her private practice and home are on Salt Spring Island. She supports individuals and couples on their sexual healing journeys and co-creates nature based retreats for women. soulfoodsex.com **p. 49, 85**

Sophia Rosenberg (Lasqueti Island, BC) Thanks, We'Moon, for forty years of supporting women writers and artists and building alternative culture! Sophiarosenberg.com, Bluebeatle Studio on Etsy. **p. 102**

Stephanie A. Sellers (Fayetteville, PA) lives on a homestead in the mountains and is inspired by all the wemoon doing their beautiful healing work all over this beautiful world! Thanks to all and glad to be a part of the movement! XOXO sednasdaughters.com **p. 122, 157**

Sudie Rakusin (Hillsborough, NC) is a visual artist, sculptor, and children's book author and illustrator for established authors Mary Daly and Carolyn Gage. She lives in the woods with her dogs, on the edge of a meadow, surrounded by her gardens. Sudierakusin.com **p. 21**

Sue Burns (Portland, OR) is a feminist, witch, writer, herbalist, teacher, mother. She is renewed in bodies of water, puts salt in her coffee, and looks for magick everywhere. **p. 20**

Sue Tyler Design (Tetonia, ID) Western artist, teacher and Earth advocate, Sue has lived in the West her entire life. Her experiences in the mountains and with animals fuel her inspiration. She has spent 30 years exploring, teaching and sharing inspiration with others. Suetyler.com **p. 154**

Sundara Fawn (Oglesby, IL) MFA, Yogini, Visionary Artist, Kriyaban and disciple of Paramahansa Yogananda. Founder of *Reawakening the Soul*, a revolutionary transformational program. She created soul oracle wisdom cards, spiritual exploration books for self-discovery, and an online soul portal with guided meditations and transcendental videos for others to journey into their soul. sundarafawn.com **p. 56, 74, 83**

Susa Silvermarie (Ajijic, Mexico) I live and create joyfully in Ajijic Mexico. In 2021 I turn 74, and every year it gets better, my purpose clearer, my heart lighter. Please visit me at susasilvermarie.com or email me at ssilvermarie@gmail.com **p. 37, 52, 113, 179**

Susan Baylies (Durham, NC) sells her lunar phases as cards, larger print charts and posters at snakeandsnake.com Email her at sbaylies@gmail.com **p. 228**

Susan Levitt (San Francisco, CA) is an astrologer, tarot card reader, and feng shui consultant. Her publications include *Taoist Astrology* and *The Complete Tarot Kit*. Follow her astrology blog for new moon and full moon updates at susanlevitt.com **p. 19, 199**

Susan M. Warfield (Roseville, MN) Late blooming artist who returned to photography and nature after a long hiatus. **p. 103**

Suzanne Grace Michell (Sacramento, CA) I am passionate about, and delighted by, the interplay between spirit, humanity, the natural world, and creativity. These connections inspire my life and art. It is my joy to share it with you. SuzanneGraceStudios.com **p. 47**

T.Y. Chambers (London, UK) is the poetess behind *Don't You Dare Teach My Daughter To Fear The Forest & Other Poems of Remembrance for Women*. You can find her work at:.tychambers.co.uk **p. 129**

Tamara Phillips (Vancouver, BC) Tamara's art is inspired by the raw beauty of the natural world. Her watercolour paintings are woven together in earth tones, and she explores the connection between myth, dreams, intuition and reality. See more of her work here: tamaraphillips.ca **p. 34, 164, 167, 176**

Tamarack Verrall (Montreal, QC) Originally written for worldpulse.com, a network of 64,000 from 190 countries raising women's voices for change. Also self published in *Love Poems for Daring Women 2018*. **p. 168**

Toni Truesdale (Biddeford, ME) Artist, muralist, teacher and illustrator, Toni celebrates women, the natural environment and the diversity of the world's cultures. Contact her at tonitruesdale@gmail.com Prints and cards available through tonitruesdale.com **p. 85**

Valerie A. Szarek (Louisville, CO) is a performance poet & Native American Flute player, a leather artisan & shamanic practitioner. She resides in Louisville, CO with her magical cat Felix. Valerieszarek.com **p. 132, 137**

Virginia Maria Romero Art (Las Cruces, NM) As an artist who is deeply concerned about protecting wildlife, I strive to make sure that my art helps to educate and motivate people to protect nature. Virginiamariaromero.com **p. 115**

Wild Rose (Sebastopol, CA) is a weaver, magician, healer, teacher, poet, performance artist/actress, playwright, and dancer—doing her part to destroy internalized and externalized patriarchy and empower what is FEMALE . . . every Witch way. sebastopolrose@gmail.com **p. 59**

Wilma Hoffman (Klamath, CA) Native born into the northern California coastal tribes of Tolowa and Yurok, Wilma currently resides in the Pacific Northwest Coastal area producing original artwork and spending time with family. **p. 232**

Xochi Balfour (Somerset, UK) is an author and creatrix living in Somerset, UK, where she resides with her family, diving ever deeper into the sacred path of the feminine. Contact: xochibalfour.com **p. 71**

Zalayshia (Portland, OR) I walk with women on their ascension journey into motherhood. I also create wall hangings and healing tools inspired by nature, women and the mystery of life. zalayshia@imintuit.com imintuit.com **p. 126**

Zena Carlota (Raleigh, NC) is a musician, storyteller and visual artist working at the intersections of ritual and psychotherapy. As future arts therapist, she weaves movement, sound and visual arts into ceremony inspired by folkloric traditions of the African Diaspora. Zenacarlota.com **p. 4, 159**

Errors/Corrections

In *We'Moon 2020*, our astro data did not include indicators marking times when the moon is void-of-course. We have a blog post here: wemoon.ws/blogs/wemoon-tidbits/2020-moon-void-of-course-data with all of the v/c dates and times. Also, there is a printable PDF linked within that post.

We appreciate all feedback that comes in, and continually strive to get closer to perfection. Please let us know if you find anything amiss, and check our website near the beginning of the year for any posted corrections for this edition of We'Moon.

We'Moon Sky Talk

Gaia Rhythms: We show the natural cycles of the Moon, Sun, planets and stars as they relate to Earth. By recording our own activities side by side with those of other heavenly bodies, we may notice what connection, if any, there is for us. The Earth revolves around her axis in one day; the Moon orbits around the Earth in one month ($29^1/_2$ days); the Earth orbits around the Sun in one year. We experience each of these cycles in the alternating rhythms of day and night, waxing and waning, summer and winter. The Earth/Moon/Sun are our inner circle of kin in the universe. We know where we are in relation to them at all times by the dance of light and shadow as they circle around one another.

The Eyes of Heaven: As seen from Earth, the Moon and the Sun are equal in size: "the left and right eye of heaven," according to Hindu (Eastern) astrology. Unlike the solar-dominated calendars of Christian (Western) patriarchy, We'Moon looks at our experience through both eyes at once. The **lunar eye of heaven** is seen each day in the phases of the Moon, as she is both reflector and shadow, traveling her $29^1/_2$-day path around the Earth in a "Moon" Month (from each new moon to the next, 13 times in a lunar year). Because Earth is orbiting the Sun at the same time, it takes the Moon $27^1/_3$ days to go through all the signs of the Zodiac—a sidereal month. The **solar eye of heaven** is apparent at the turning points in the Sun's cycle. The year begins with Winter Solstice (in the Northern Hemisphere), the dark renewal time, and journeys through the full cycle of seasons and balance points (solstices, equinoxes and the cross-quarter days in between). The **third eye** of heaven may be seen in the stars. Astrology measures the cycles by relating the Sun, Moon and all other planets in our universe through the backdrop of star signs (the zodiac), helping us to tell time in the larger cycles of the universe.

Measuring Time and Space: Imagine a clock with many hands. The Earth is the center from which we view our universe. The Sun, Moon and planets are like the hands of the clock. Each one has its own rate of movement through the cycle. The ecliptic, a 17° band of sky around the Earth within which all planets have their orbits, is the outer band of the clock where the numbers are. Stars along the ecliptic are grouped into constellations forming the signs of the zodiac—the twelve star signs are like the twelve numbers of the clock. They mark the movements of the planets through the 360° circle of the sky, the clock of time and space.

Whole Earth Perspective: It is important to note that all natural cycles have a mirror image from a whole Earth perspective—seasons occur at opposite times in the Northern and Southern Hemispheres, and day and night are at opposite times on opposite sides of the Earth as well. Even the Moon plays this game—a waxing crescent moon

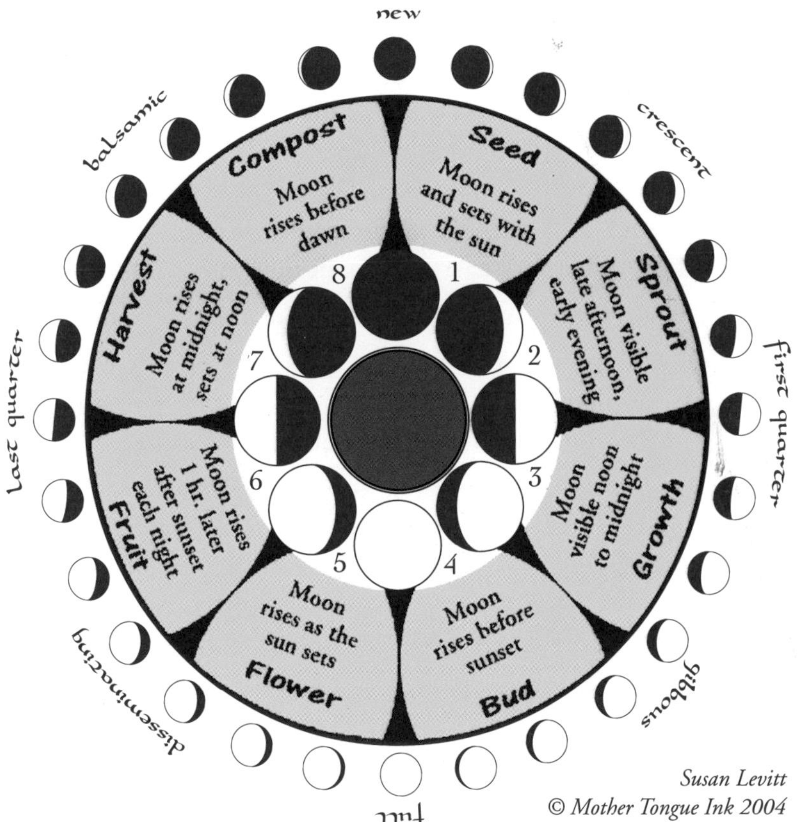

Susan Levitt

in Australia faces right (☾), while in North America, it faces left (☽). We'Moon uses a Northern Hemisphere perspective regarding times, holy days, seasons and lunar phases. Wemoon who live in the Southern Hemisphere may want to transpose descriptions of the holy days to match seasons in their area. We honor a whole Earth cultural perspective by including four rotating languages for the days of the week, from different parts of the globe.

Whole Sky Perspective: It is also important to note that all over the Earth, in varied cultures and times, the dome of the sky has been interacted with in countless ways. The zodiac we speak of is just one of many ways that hu-moons have pictured and related to the stars. In this calendar we use the Tropical zodiac, which keeps constant the Vernal Equinox point at 0° Aries. Western astrology primarily uses this system. Vedic or Eastern astrology uses the Sidereal zodiac, which bases the positions of signs relative to fixed stars, and over time the Vernal Equinox point has moved about 24° behind 0° Aries.

Musawa

ASTROLOGY BASICS

Planets: Like chakras in our solar system, planets allow for different frequencies or types of energies to be expressed. See Mooncat's article (pp.206–207) for more detailed planetary attributes.

Signs: The twelve signs of the zodiac are a mandala in the sky, marking off 30° segments of a circle around the earth. Signs show major shifts in planetary energy through the cycles.

Glyphs: Glyphs are the symbols used to represent planets and signs.

Sun Sign: The Sun enters a new sign once a month (on or around the 21st), completing the whole cycle of the zodiac in one year. The sun sign reflects qualities of your outward shining self.

Moon Sign: The Moon changes signs approximately every 2 to $2^1/_2$ days, going through all twelve signs of the zodiac every $27^1/_3$ days (the sidereal month). The Moon sign reflects qualities of your core inner self.

Moon Phase: Each calendar day is marked with a graphic representing the phase of the Moon.

Lunar Quarter Phase: At the four quarter-points of the lunar cycle (new, waxing half, full and waning half moons), we indicate the phase, sign and exact time for each. These points mark off the "lunar week."

Day of the Week: Each day is associated with a planet whose symbol appears in the line above it (e.g., ☽☽☽ for Moon: Moonday)

Eclipse: The time of greatest eclipse is given, which is near to, but not at the exact time of the conjunction (☉☌☽) or opposition (☉☍☽). See "Eclipses" (p. 18).

Aspects (□△☍☌⚹⚻) are listed in fine print under the Moon sign each day, and show the angle of relationship between different planets as they move. Daily aspects provide something like an astrological weather forecast, indicating which energies are working together easily and which combinations are more challenging.

Transits are the motion of the planets and the moon as they move among the zodiacal constellations and in relationship to one another.

Ingresses (→): When the Sun, Moon and planets move into new signs.

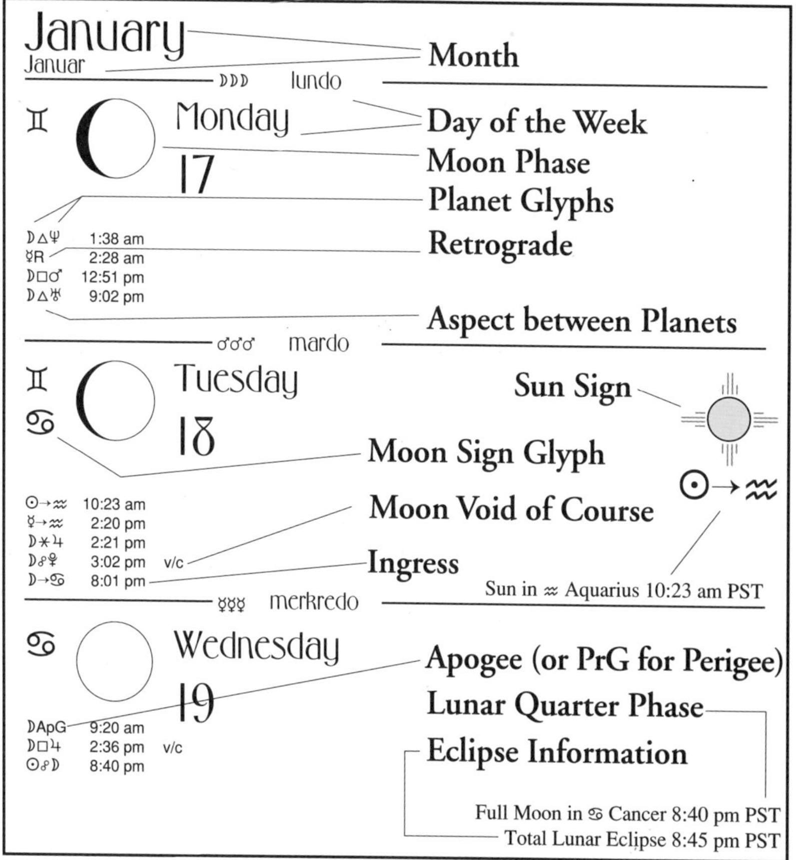

Sample calendar page for reference only

Moon "Void of Course" (☽ v/c): The Moon is said to be "void of course" from the last significant lunar aspect in each sign until the Moon enters a new sign. This is a good time to ground and center yourself.

Super Moon: A Super Moon is a New or Full Moon that occurs when the Moon is at or within 90% of perigee, its closest approach to Earth. On average, there are four to six Super Moons each year. Full Super Moons could appear visually closer and brighter, and promote stronger tides. Personally, we may use the greater proximity of Super Moons to illuminate our inner horizons and deepen our self-reflections and meditations.

Apogee (ApG): The point in the Moon's orbit that is **farthest** from Earth. At this time, the effects of transits may be less noticeable immediately, but may appear later. Also, **Black Moon Lilith**, a hypothetical center point of the Moon's elliptical orbit around the Earth, will be conjunct the Moon.

Perigee (PrG): The point in the Moon's orbit that is **nearest** to Earth. Transits with the Moon, when at perigee, will be more intense.

Lunar Nodes: The most Northern and Southern points in the Moon's monthly cycle when it crosses the Sun's ecliptic or annual path, offering to integrate the past (South) and future (North) directions in life.

Aphelion (ApH): The point in a planet's orbit that is **farthest** from the Sun. At this time, the effects of transits (when planets pass across the path of another planet) may be less noticeable immediately, but may appear later.

Perihelion (PrH): The point in a planet's orbit that is **nearest** to the Sun. Transits with planets, when they are at perihelion, will be more intense.

Direct or Retrograde (D or R): These are times when a planet moves forward (D) or backward (R) through the signs of the zodiac (an optical illusion, as when a moving train passes a slower train that appears to be going backward). When a planet is in direct motion, planetary energies are more straightforward; in retrograde, planetary energies turn back in on themselves and are more involuted. See "Mercury Retrograde" (p. 18).

Wanderlust
© Mandalamy Arts 2019

Signs and Symbols at a Glance

Planets

Personal Planets are closest to Earth.

☉ **Sun**: self radiating outward, character, ego

☽ **Moon**: inward sense of self, emotions, psyche

☿ **Mercury**: communication, travel, thought

♀ **Venus**: relationship, love, sense of beauty, empathy

♂ **Mars**: will to act, initiative, ambition

Asteroids are between Mars and Jupiter and reflect the awakening of feminine-defined energy centers in human consciousness.

Social Planets are between personal and outer planets.

♃ **Jupiter**: expansion, opportunities, leadership

♄ **Saturn**: limits, structure, discipline

Note: The days of the week are named in various languages after the above seven heavenly bodies.

⚷ **Chiron**: is a small planetary body between Saturn and Uranus representing the wounded healer.

Transpersonal Planets are the outer planets.

♅ **Uranus**: cosmic consciousness, revolutionary change

♆ **Neptune**: spiritual awakening, cosmic love, all one

♇ **Pluto**: death and rebirth, deep, total change

Zodiac Signs

♈ Aries

♉ Taurus

♊ Gemini

♋ Cancer

♌ Leo

♍ Virgo

♎ Libra

♏ Scorpio

♐ Sagittarius

♑ Capricorn

♒ Aquarius

♓ Pisces

Aspects

Aspects show the angle between planets; this informs how the planets influence each other and us. We'Moon lists only significant aspects:

☌ CONJUNCTION (planets are 0–5° apart)
linked together, energy of aspected planets is mutually enhancing

☍ OPPOSITION (planets are 180° apart)
polarizing or complementing, energies are diametrically opposite

△ TRINE (planets are 120° apart)
harmonizing, energies of this aspect are in the same element

□ SQUARE (planets are 90° apart)
challenging, energies of this aspect are different from each other

⚹ SEXTILE (planets are 60° apart)
cooperative, energies of this aspect blend well

⚻ QUINCUNX (planets are 150° apart)
variable, energies of this aspect combine contrary elements

Other Symbols

☽ **v/c**–Moon is "void of course" from last lunar aspect until it enters new sign.

ApG–Apogee: Point in the orbit of the Moon that's farthest from Earth.

PrG–Perigee: Point in the orbit of the Moon that's nearest to Earth.

ApH–Aphelion: Point in the orbit of a planet that's farthest from the Sun.

PrH–Perihelion: Point in the orbit of a planet that's nearest to the Sun.

D or R–Direct or Retrograde: Describes when a planet moves forward (D) through the zodiac or appears to move backward (R).

Constellations of the Zodiac

These stations of the zodiac were named thousands of years ago for the constellations that were behind them at the time. The signs of the zodiac act like a light filter, coloring the qualities of life force. As the Sun, Moon and other planets move through the zodiac, the following influences are energized:

♒ **Aquarius** (Air): Community, ingenuity, collaboration, idealism. It's time to honor the philosophy of love and the power of community.

♓ **Pisces** (Water): Introspection, imagination, sensitivity and intuition. We process and gestate our dreams

♈ **Aries** (Fire): Brave, direct, rebellious, energized. Our inner teenager comes alive; our adult self needs to direct the energy wisely.

♉ **Taurus** (Earth): Sensual, rooted, nurturing, material manifestation. We slow down, get earthy, awaken our senses, begin to build form, roots, and stubborn strength.

♊ **Gemini** (Air): Communication, networking, curiosity, quick witted. We connect with like minds and build a network of understanding.

♋ **Cancer** (Water): Family, home, emotional awareness, nourishment. We need time in our shell and with our familiars.

♌ **Leo** (Fire): Creativity, charisma, warmth, and enthusiasm. Gather with others to celebrate and share bounty.

♍ **Virgo** (Earth): Mercurial, curious, critical, and engaged. The mood sharpens our minds and nerves, and sends us back to work.

♎ **Libra** (Air): Beauty, equality, egalitarianism, cooperation. We grow more friendly, relationship oriented, and incensed by injustice.

♏ **Scorpio** (Water): Sharp focus, perceptive, empowered, mysterious. The mood is smoky, primal, occult, and curious; still waters run deep.

♐ **Sagittarius** (Fire): Curiosity, honesty, exploration, playfulness. We grow more curious about what's unfamiliar.

♑ **Capricorn** (Earth): family, history, dreams, traditions. We need mountains to climb and problems to solve.

adapted from Heather Roan Robbins' Sun Signs and Sun Transits

Moon Transits

The Moon changes signs every 2½ days. The sign that the Moon is in sets the emotional tone of the day.

♒ Moon in Aquarius calls us to the circle and away from private concerns; it reminds us of the sacredness of collaboration and collectivity. It's time to search for new allies, to network, and to live our philosophy.

♓ Moon in Pisces makes us aware, sometimes painfully, of our emotions. It heightens compassion, intuition. We may have to strengthen boundaries. Explore the temple of imagination.

♈ Moon in Aries accesses our fire; temper, impatience and passion. We feel an urgency to focus, but we can lose our empathy. It's time to do what truly makes us feel alive, to initiate projects and set boundaries.

♉ Moon in Taurus slows us down; roots grow deep in this stubborn, creative, sensual time. It's time to cultivate our earthly resources: garden, home, and body. Plant seeds in fertile loam, listen to the Earth's magic.

♊ Moon in Gemini speeds our thoughts and nerves. It's time to weave words: talk, listen, laugh, sing and write. Network, negotiate, rearrange; juggle possibilities; just don't get spread too thin.

♋ Moon in Cancer reconnects us with our emotions. We may get overwhelmed and defensive, or we can nourish ourselves and reconnect with our true feelings. Water is healing; bathe, hydrate, make soup.

♌ Moon in Leo gets us into the heart of the action. It's time to let our light shine, express ourselves and appreciate other's unique stories. Celebrate, ritualize, dramatize. Share with true Leonine generosity.

♍ Moon in Virgo sharpens our minds and nerves. It helps us digest information and assess the situation. Invoke Virgoan compassion and brilliant problem-solving. Clean, organize, edit, weed and heal.

♎ Moon in Libra warms our hearts and heightens our aesthetics. Beauty, fairness and balance feed us. We want everyone to get along, and we become allergic to discord in the culture and with our beloveds.

♏ Moon in Scorpio turns us inward, deepens our curiosity and focus, but gives us attitude. We need privacy, as moods may be prickly. Clear the deadwood of soul or garden. Seek deep, refreshing contemplation.

♐ Moon in Sagittarius gets us moving around the globe, or into our minds. It loans us fresh (often tactless) honesty, an adventurous spark, philosophical perspective and easy rapport with the natural world.

♑ Moon in Capricorn whets our ambition and tests our sense of humor. It's time to put sweat-equity into our dreams; organize, build, manifest. Set clear short-term goals and feel the joy of accomplishment.

adapted from Heather Roan Robbins' Moon Signs and Moon Transits

Know Yourself—Map of Planetary Influences

Most people, when considering astrology's benefits, are familiar with their Sun Sign; however, each of the planets within our solar system has a specific part to play in the complete knowledge of "The Self." Here is a quick run-down of our planets' astrological effects:

☉ **The Sun** represents our soul purpose—what we are here on Earth to do or accomplish, and it informs how we go about that task. It answers the age-old question "Why am I here?"

☽ **The Moon** represents our capacity to feel or empathize with those around us and within our own soul as well. It awakens our intuitive and emotional body.

☿ **Mercury** is "The Thinker," and involves our communication skills: what we say, our words, our voice, and our thoughts, including the Teacher/Student, Master/Apprentice mode. Mercury affects how we connect with all the media tools of the day—our computers, phones, and even the postal, publishing and recording systems!

♀ **Venus** is our recognition of love, art and beauty. Venus is harmony in its expressed form, as well as compassion, bliss and acceptance.

♂ **Mars** is our sense of "Get Up and GO!" It represents being in motion and the capacity to take action and do. Mars can also affect our temperament.

♃ **Jupiter** is our quest for truth, living the belief systems that we hold and walking the path of what those beliefs say about us. It involves an ever-expanding desire to educate the Self through knowledge toward higher law, the adventure and opportunity of being on that road—sometimes literally entailing travel and foreign or international culture, language and/or customs.

♄ **Saturn** is the task master: active when we set a goal or plan then work strongly and steadily toward achieving what we have set out to do. Saturn takes life seriously along the way and can be rather stern, putting on an extra load of responsibility and effort.

⚷ **Chiron** is the "Wounded Healer," relating to what we have brought into this lifetime in order to learn how to fix it, to perfect it, make it the best that it can possibly be! This is where we compete with ourselves to better our own previous score. In addition, it connects to our health-body—physiological and nutritional.

♅ **Uranus** is our capacity to experience "The Revolution," freedom to do things our own way, exhibiting our individual expression or even "Going Rogue" as we blast towards a future collective vision. Uranus inspires individual inclination to "Let me be ME" and connect to an ocean of humanity doing the same.

♆ **Neptune** is the spiritual veil, our connection to our inner psychology and consciousness, leading to the experience of our soul. Psychic presence and mediumship are influenced here too.

♇ **Pluto** is transformation, death/rebirth energy—to the extreme. In order for the butterfly to emerge, the caterpillar that it once was must completely give up its life! No going back; burn the bridge down; the volcano of one's own power explodes. Stand upon the mountaintop and catch the lightning bolt in your hand!

Ascendant or Rising Sign: In addition, you must consider the sign of the zodiac that was on the horizon at the moment of your birth. Your Rising sign describes how we relate to the external world and how it relates back to us—what we look like, how others see us and how we see ourselves.

It is the combination of all of these elements that makes us unique among all other persons alive! We are like snowflakes in that way! Sharing a Sun sign is not enough to put you in a singular category. Here's to our greater understanding! Know Yourself!

Melissa Kae Mason, MoonCat! © Mother Tongue Ink 2011

Goddess Planets: Ceres, Pallas, Juno and Vesta

"Asteroids" are small planets, located between the inner, personal planets (Sun to Mars) that move more swiftly through the zodiac, and the outer, social and collective planets (Jupiter to Pluto) whose slower movements mark generational shifts. Ceres, Pallas, Juno and Vesta are faces of the Great Goddess who is reawakening in our consciousness now, quickening abilities so urgently needed to solve our many personal, social, ecological and political problems.

⚳ **Ceres** (Goddess of corn and harvest) symbolizes our ability to nourish ourselves and others in a substantial and metaphoric way. As in the Greek myth of Demeter and Persephone, she helps us to let go and die, to understand mother-daughter dynamics, to re-parent ourselves and to educate by our senses.

⚵ **Juno** (Queen of the Gods and of relationships) shows us what kind of committed partnership we long for, our own individual way to find fulfillment in personal and professional partnering. She wants partners to be team-workers, with equal rights and responsibilities.

⚴ **Pallas** (Athena) is a symbol for our creative intelligence and often hints at the sacrifice of women's own creativity or the lack of respect for it. She brings to the fore father-daughter issues, and points to difficulties in linking head, heart and womb.

⚶ **Vesta** (Vestal Virgin/Fire Priestess) reminds us first and foremost that we belong to ourselves and are allowed to do so! She shows us how to regenerate, to activate our passion, and how to carefully watch over our inner fire in the storms of everyday life.

excerpt Beate Metz © Mother Tongue Ink 2009

See p. 215 for Asteroid Ephemeris

Ephemeris 101

A Planetary Ephemeris provides astronomical data showing the daily positions of celestial bodies in our solar system.

The planets have individual and predictable orbits around the sun and pathways through the constellations that correlate with the astrological signs of the Zodiac. This regularity is useful for sky viewing and creating astro charts for a particular date.

The earliest astrologers used these ephemeris tables to calculate individual birth and event charts. These circular maps plot planetary positions and the aspects—angles of relationships—in a "state of the solar system" as a permanent representation of a moment in time. The ephemeris can then be consulted to find when real-time or "transiting" planets will be in the same sign and degree as planets in the birth or event chart. For instance, use the ephemerides to follow the Sun through the houses of your own birth chart, and journal on each day the Sun conjuncts a planet. The sun reveals or sheds light on a sign or house, allowing those qualities to shine and thrive. Ephemerides can also be used to look up dates of past events in your life to learn what planets were highlighted in your chart at that time. In addition, looking up dates for future plans can illuminate beneficial timing of available planetary energies.

Read across from a particular date, ephemerides provide the sign and degree of all the Planets, the Sun and Moon and nodes of the Moon on that day. The lower box on the page offers a quick look at Astro data such as, when a planet changes sign (an ingress occurs), aspects of the outer planet, and their change in direction or retrograde period and much more. The larger boxes represent two different months as labeled.) Use the Signs and Symbols at a Glance on page 203 to note the symbols or glyphs of planets, signs and aspects.

Sandra Pastorius © Mother Tongue Ink 2018

Moon: O hr=Midnight and Noon=12PM

Planet Glyphs (p. 203)

R=Planet Retrogrades shown in shaded boxes

Ingress: January 1st the Sun moves into 10° Capricorn

Day	Sid.Time	☉	0 hr ☽	Noon ☽	True ☊	☿
1 Tu	6 41 26	10♑15 21	12♏21 35	18♏49 44	26♋52.2	23♐51.2
2 W	6 45 22	11 16 31	25 14 11	1♐35 10	26R 50.0	25 19.2
3 Th	6 49 19	12 17 42	7♐52 52	14 07 28	26 47.6	26 47.7
4 F	6 53 15	13 18 52	20 19 08	26 28 04	26 45.5	28 16.7
5 Sa	6 57 12	14 20 03	2♑34 27	8♑38 27	26 43.9	29 46.2
6 Su	7 01 08	15 21 14	14 40 17	20 40 08	26 42.9	1♑16.2
7 M	7 05 05	16 22 25	26 38 13	2♒34 48	26D 42.6	2 46.7
8 Tu	7 09 01	17 23 36	8♒30 08	14 24 32	26 42.9	4 17.6

Mars Ingress Aries January 1 @ 2:21 PM

Astro Data Dy Hr Mn	Planet Ingress Dy Hr Mn	Last Aspe[ct] Dy Hr Mn
♂0N 2 0:5[illegible]	♂ ♈ 1 2:21	1 22:27 ♀
♅ D 6 20:28	☿ ♑ 5 3:41	4 17:43 ☿
☊ D 7 0:06	♀ ♐ 7 11:19	7 6:21 ♀

2021 Planetary Ephemeris

LONGITUDE — January 2021

Day	Sid.Time	☉	0 hr ☽	Noon ☽	True ☊	☿	♀	♂	⚳	♃	♄	♅	♆	♇
1 F	6 43 27	10♑46 44	2♌43 29	9♌17 16	19♊52.7	17♑42.8	20♐24.6	27♈21.4	11♓59.6	2♒47.0	1♒37.5	6♉48.0	18♓28.4	24♑11.3
2 Sa	6 47 24	11 47 53	15 54 26	22 34 51	19R 49.3	19 20.6	21 39.8	27 47.5	12 18.2	3 00.7	1 44.3	6R 47.3	18 29.5	24 13.2
3 Su	6 51 21	12 49 01	29 18 24	6♍04 58	19 45.8	20 58.6	22 54.9	28 13.8	12 36.9	3 14.4	1 51.2	6 46.7	18 30.7	24 15.2
4 M	6 55 17	13 50 10	12♍54 25	19 46 36	19 42.6	22 36.8	24 10.1	28 40.4	12 55.8	3 28.2	1 58.1	6 46.1	18 31.9	24 17.2
5 Tu	6 59 14	14 51 19	26 41 25	3♎38 42	19 40.3	24 15.2	25 25.2	29 07.3	13 14.8	3 42.0	2 05.0	6 45.6	18 33.1	24 19.1
6 W	7 03 10	15 52 28	10♎38 20	17 40 10	19D 39.2	25 53.7	26 40.4	29 34.4	13 33.9	3 55.9	2 11.9	6 45.1	18 34.3	24 21.1
7 Th	7 07 07	16 53 37	24 44 03	1♏49 46	19 39.3	27 32.2	27 55.6	0♉01.8	13 53.1	4 09.8	2 18.9	6 44.7	18 35.6	24 23.1
8 F	7 11 03	17 54 47	8♏57 08	16 05 52	19 40.4	29 10.7	29 10.8	0 29.4	14 12.5	4 23.7	2 25.9	6 44.4	18 36.9	24 25.1
9 Sa	7 15 00	18 55 57	23 15 39	0♐26 09	19 41.9	0♒49.1	0♑26.0	0 57.2	14 32.0	4 37.6	2 32.9	6 44.1	18 38.3	24 27.1
10 Su	7 18 56	19 57 07	7♐36 55	14 47 30	19R 43.3	2 27.4	1 41.2	1 25.3	14 51.6	4 51.6	2 39.9	6 43.8	18 39.6	24 29.1
11 M	7 22 53	20 58 16	21 57 22	29 05 57	19 43.7	4 05.3	2 56.4	1 53.7	15 11.3	5 05.6	2 47.0	6 43.6	18 41.0	24 31.1
12 Tu	7 26 50	21 59 26	6♑12 41	13♑16 56	19 42.7	5 42.7	4 11.6	2 22.2	15 31.1	5 19.7	2 54.0	6 43.5	18 42.4	24 33.1
13 W	7 30 46	23 00 36	20 18 09	27 15 46	19 39.9	7 19.5	5 26.9	2 51.0	15 51.1	5 33.7	3 01.1	6 43.4	18 43.9	24 35.1
14 Th	7 34 43	24 01 45	4♒09 17	10♒58 18	19 35.4	8 55.4	6 42.1	3 20.0	16 11.1	5 47.8	3 08.2	6D 43.3	18 45.4	24 37.1
15 F	7 38 39	25 02 54	17 42 27	24 21 30	19 29.5	10 30.2	7 57.3	3 49.2	16 31.3	6 01.9	3 15.3	6 43.3	18 46.9	24 39.1
16 Sa	7 42 36	26 04 02	0♓55 21	7♓23 57	19 23.1	12 03.6	9 12.5	4 18.7	16 51.5	6 16.0	3 22.4	6 43.4	18 48.4	24 41.1
17 Su	7 46 32	27 05 09	13 47 23	20 05 52	19 16.7	13 35.2	10 27.8	4 48.3	17 11.9	6 30.2	3 29.5	6 43.5	18 49.9	24 43.1
18 M	7 50 29	28 06 16	26 19 39	2♈29 08	19 11.2	15 04.7	11 43.0	5 18.1	17 32.4	6 44.3	3 36.6	6 43.7	18 51.5	24 45.1
19 Tu	7 54 25	29 07 21	8♈34 45	14 37 01	19 07.1	16 31.6	12 58.2	5 48.1	17 52.9	6 58.5	3 43.7	6 43.9	18 53.1	24 47.1
20 W	7 58 22	0♒08 26	20 36 29	26 33 45	19D 04.8	17 55.3	14 13.4	6 18.3	18 13.6	7 12.7	3 50.9	6 44.1	18 54.8	24 49.1
21 Th	8 02 19	1 09 31	2♉29 26	8♉24 13	19 04.2	19 15.3	15 28.6	6 48.7	18 34.3	7 26.9	3 58.0	6 44.5	18 56.4	24 51.0
22 F	8 06 15	2 10 34	14 18 44	20 13 40	19 05.0	20 31.0	16 43.8	7 19.2	18 55.2	7 41.1	4 05.2	6 44.8	18 58.1	24 53.0
23 Sa	8 10 12	3 11 36	26 09 37	2♊07 16	19 06.5	21 41.7	17 59.0	7 49.9	19 16.1	7 55.3	4 12.3	6 45.3	18 59.8	24 55.0
24 Su	8 14 08	4 12 37	8♊07 12	14 09 57	19R 08.0	22 46.5	19 14.3	8 20.8	19 37.1	8 09.5	4 19.5	6 45.7	19 01.5	24 57.0
25 M	8 18 05	5 13 38	20 16 05	26 26 01	19 08.5	23 44.6	20 29.5	8 51.8	19 58.2	8 23.8	4 26.6	6 46.3	19 03.3	24 59.0
26 Tu	8 22 01	6 14 37	2♋40 10	8♋58 49	19 07.5	24 35.3	21 44.7	9 22.9	20 19.4	8 38.0	4 33.7	6 46.9	19 05.0	25 00.9
27 W	8 25 58	7 15 36	15 22 12	21 50 27	19 04.3	25 17.7	22 59.9	9 54.3	20 40.7	8 52.3	4 40.9	6 47.5	19 06.8	25 02.9
28 Th	8 29 54	8 16 33	28 23 34	5♌01 31	18 58.8	25 50.9	24 15.1	10 25.7	21 02.0	9 06.5	4 48.0	6 48.2	19 08.7	25 04.9
29 F	8 33 51	9 17 30	11♌44 05	18 31 01	18 51.3	26 14.2	25 30.2	10 57.3	21 23.4	9 20.8	4 55.2	6 48.9	19 10.5	25 06.8
30 Sa	8 37 48	10 18 25	25 21 56	2♍16 25	18 42.5	26R 27.0	26 45.4	11 29.1	21 44.9	9 35.0	5 02.3	6 49.7	19 12.3	25 06.8
31 Su	8 41 44	11 19 20	9♍13 58	16 14 04	18 33.3	26 28.8	28 00.6	12 00.9	22 06.5	9 49.3	5 09.4	6 50.6	19 14.2	25 10.7

LONGITUDE — February 2021

Day	Sid.Time	☉	0 hr ☽	Noon ☽	True ☊	☿	♀	♂	⚳	♃	♄	♅	♆	♇
1 M	8 45 41	12♒20 13	23♍16 11	0♎19 47	18♊24.7	26♒19.4	29♑15.8	12♉32.9	22♓28.2	10♒03.5	5♒16.5	6♉51.5	19♓16.1	25♑12.6
2 Tu	8 49 37	13 21 06	7♎24 23	14 29 32	18R 17.8	25R 58.7	0♒31.0	13 05.0	22 49.9	10 17.8	5 23.6	6 52.4	19 18.0	25 14.5
3 W	8 53 34	14 21 58	21 34 50	28 39 57	18 13.2	25 27.1	1 46.2	13 37.3	23 11.7	10 32.0	5 30.7	6 53.4	19 20.0	25 16.5
4 Th	8 57 30	15 22 49	5♏44 36	12♏48 37	18D 10.8	24 45.4	3 01.3	14 09.6	23 33.6	10 46.2	5 37.8	6 54.4	19 21.9	25 18.4
5 F	9 01 27	16 23 40	19 51 48	26 54 03	18 10.5	23 54.5	4 16.5	14 42.1	23 55.5	11 00.5	5 44.9	6 55.5	19 23.9	25 20.3
6 Sa	9 05 23	17 24 29	3♐55 16	10♐55 22	18 11.1	22 55.8	5 31.7	15 14.7	24 17.5	11 14.7	5 52.0	6 56.7	19 25.9	25 22.1
7 Su	9 09 20	18 25 18	17 54 16	24 51 50	18R 11.6	21 51.0	6 46.9	15 47.4	24 39.6	11 28.9	5 59.0	6 57.9	19 27.9	25 24.0
8 M	9 13 17	19 26 06	1♑47 58	8♑42 27	18 10.8	20 42.0	8 02.1	16 20.2	25 01.7	11 43.1	6 06.0	6 59.1	19 29.9	25 25.9
9 Tu	9 17 13	20 26 53	15 35 08	22 25 43	18 07.7	19 30.7	9 17.2	16 53.2	25 23.9	11 57.3	6 13.1	7 00.4	19 31.9	25 27.7
10 W	9 21 10	21 27 39	29 13 58	5♒59 33	18 01.8	18 19.2	10 32.4	17 26.2	25 46.2	12 11.5	6 20.1	7 01.8	19 34.0	25 29.6
11 Th	9 25 06	22 28 23	12♒42 12	19 21 37	17 53.1	17 09.4	11 47.5	17 59.4	26 08.5	12 25.7	6 27.0	7 03.2	19 36.1	25 31.4
12 F	9 29 03	23 29 06	25 57 30	2♓29 39	17 42.2	16 02.9	13 02.7	18 32.6	26 30.9	12 39.8	6 34.0	7 04.6	19 38.1	25 33.2
13 Sa	9 32 59	24 29 48	8♓57 51	15 22 00	17 29.9	15 01.2	14 17.8	19 06.0	26 53.4	12 54.0	6 40.9	7 06.1	19 40.2	25 35.0
14 Su	9 36 56	25 30 28	21 42 03	27 58 02	17 17.6	14 05.4	15 33.0	19 39.4	27 15.9	13 08.1	6 47.8	7 07.6	19 42.3	25 36.8
15 M	9 40 52	26 31 07	4♈10 06	10♈18 25	17 06.2	13 16.4	16 48.1	20 13.0	27 38.4	13 22.2	6 54.7	7 09.2	19 44.5	25 38.6
16 Tu	9 44 49	27 31 44	16 23 17	22 25 05	16 56.9	12 34.8	18 03.2	20 46.6	28 01.0	13 36.3	7 01.6	7 10.8	19 46.6	25 40.4
17 W	9 48 46	28 32 19	28 24 13	4♉21 12	16 50.1	12 00.8	19 18.3	21 20.3	28 23.7	13 50.3	7 08.4	7 12.5	19 48.7	25 42.1
18 Th	9 52 42	29 32 53	10♉16 35	16 10 59	16 46.0	11 34.6	20 33.4	21 54.1	28 46.4	14 04.3	7 15.2	7 14.2	19 50.9	25 43.8
19 F	9 56 39	0♓33 25	22 05 02	27 59 23	16D 44.2	11 16.1	21 48.5	22 28.0	29 09.2	14 18.3	7 22.0	7 16.0	19 53.1	25 45.5
20 Sa	10 00 35	1 33 55	3♊54 45	9♊51 48	16 43.9	11 05.1	23 03.5	23 02.0	29 32.0	14 32.3	7 28.8	7 17.8	19 55.2	25 47.2
21 Su	10 04 32	2 34 23	15 51 16	21 53 49	16R 44.1	11D 01.4	24 18.6	23 36.0	29 54.8	14 46.3	7 35.5	7 19.7	19 57.4	25 48.9
22 M	10 08 28	3 34 49	28 00 06	4♋10 45	16 43.6	11 04.5	25 33.6	24 10.1	0♈17.7	15 00.2	7 42.2	7 21.6	19 59.6	25 50.6
23 Tu	10 12 25	4 35 14	10♋26 18	16 47 16	16 41.5	11 14.1	26 48.7	24 44.3	0 40.7	15 14.1	7 48.8	7 23.5	20 01.8	25 52.2
24 W	10 16 21	5 35 37	23 14 01	29 46 51	16 36.9	11 29.8	28 03.7	25 18.6	1 03.7	15 27.9	7 55.5	7 25.5	20 04.1	25 53.9
25 Th	10 20 18	6 35 58	6♌25 54	13♌11 11	16 29.5	11 51.2	29 18.7	25 52.9	1 26.7	15 41.7	8 02.1	7 27.5	20 06.3	25 55.5
26 F	10 24 15	7 36 16	20 02 33	26 59 41	16 19.6	12 17.9	0♓33.7	26 27.3	1 49.8	15 55.5	8 08.6	7 29.6	20 08.5	25 57.1
27 Sa	10 28 11	8 36 34	4♍02 08	11♍09 18	16 07.9	12 49.6	1 48.7	27 01.8	2 12.9	16 09.2	8 15.1	7 31.7	20 10.8	25 58.6
28 Su	10 32 08	9 36 49	18 20 25	25 34 39	15 55.6	13 25.8	3 03.7	27 36.3	2 36.0	16 23.0	8 21.6	7 33.8	20 13.0	26 00.2

Astro Data	Dy Hr Mn	Planet Ingress	Dy Hr Mn
♃∠♆	4 6:59	♂ ♉	6 22:28
☽0S	6 1:11	☿ ♒	8 12:01
☊D	6 9:45	♀ ♑	8 15:42
☊R	10 20:19	☉ ♒	19 20:41
♅D	14 8:37		
♃□♅	17 22:51	♀ ♒	1 14:07
☽0N	19 5:08	☉ ♓	18 10:45
♄∠♆	20 16:59	⚳ ♈	21 5:24
☊D	20 20:50	♀ ♓	25 13:13
☊R	24 21:50		
☿R	30 15:53		
☽0S	2 6:00	♄□□	17 19:10
☊D	4 17:42	☊D	19 18:36
☊R	7 0:32	☿D	21 0:53
☽0N	15 12:51	☊R	21 1:47

Last Aspect Dy Hr Mn		☽ Ingress Dy Hr Mn
2 22:01	♂ △	♍ 3 1:14
4 21:35	♀ □	♎ 5 5:43
7 5:56	♀ ⚹	♏ 7 8:55
9 2:00	♇ ⚹	♐ 9 11:16
10 18:30	♆ □	♑ 11 13:31
13 7:23	♇ ☌	♒ 13 16:45
14 9:29	☿ ☌	♓ 15 22:18
18 3:46	☉ ⚹	♈ 18 7:08
20 8:30	♇ □	♉ 20 18:57
22 21:29	♇ △	♊ 23 7:44
25 7:18	☿ △	♋ 25 18:53
27 17:56	♇ ☍	♌ 28 2:55
30 1:54	☿ ☍	♍ 30 8:04

Last Aspect Dy Hr Mn		☽ Ingress Dy Hr Mn
1 11:11	♀ △	♎ 1 11:26
3 6:16	☿ △	♏ 3 14:16
5 9:21	♇ ⚹	♐ 5 17:18
7 6:17	☿ ⚹	♑ 7 20:53
9 17:23	♇ ☌	♒ 10 1:21
11 19:07	☉ ☌	♓ 12 7:24
14 7:30	♇ ⚹	♈ 14 15:55
17 0:18	☉ ⚹	♉ 17 3:13
19 7:29	♇ △	♊ 19 16:05
21 18:40	♀ △	♋ 22 3:54
24 4:55	♇ ☍	♌ 24 12:24
26 11:33	♂ □	♍ 26 17:08
28 15:59	♂ △	♎ 28 19:18

☽ Phases & Eclipses Dy Hr Mn	
6 9:38	☾ 16♎17
13 5:01	● 23♑13
20 21:03	☽ 1♉02
28 19:17	○ 9♌06
4 17:38	☾ 16♏08
11 19:07	● 23♒17
19 18:48	☽ 1♊21
27 8:18	○ 8♍57

Astro Data

1 January 2021
Julian Day # 44196
SVP 4♓58'15"
GC 27♐08.0 ⚵ 7♒51.1
Eris 23♈27.7R ⚴ 4♐15.0
⚷ 5♈03.6 ⚶ 20♍08.5
☽ Mean ☊ 18♊51.4

1 February 2021
Julian Day # 44227
SVP 4♓58'10"
GC 27♐08.0 ⚵ 18♒17.4
Eris 23♈29.7 ⚴ 13♐16.8
⚷ 5♈54.9 ⚶ 20♍45.9R
☽ Mean ☊ 17♊12.9

*Giving the positions of planets daily at midnight, Greenwich Mean Time (0:00 UT)
Each planet's retrograde period is shaded gray.

2021 Planetary Ephemeris

March 2021

LONGITUDE

Day	Sid.Time	☉	0 hr ☽	Noon ☽	True ☊	☿	♀	♂	⚳	♃	♄	♅	♆	♇
1 M	10 36 04	10♓37 02	2♎51 08	10♎08 55	15♊43.9	14♒06.2	4♓18.6	28♉10.8	2♈59.2	16♒36.6	8♒28.0	7♉36.0	20♓15.2	26♑01.7
2 Tu	10 40 01	11 37 14	17 27 07	24 44 54	15R 34.3	14 50.6	5 33.6	28 45.5	3 22.4	16 50.2	8 34.4	7 38.2	20 17.5	26 03.3
3 W	10 43 57	12 37 24	2♏01 29	9♏16 15	15 27.3	15 38.7	6 48.5	29 20.2	3 45.7	17 03.8	8 40.8	7 40.5	20 19.8	26 04.7
4 Th	10 47 54	13 37 33	16 28 39	23 38 18	15 23.2	16 30.1	8 03.5	29 54.9	4 08.9	17 17.4	8 47.1	7 42.8	20 22.0	26 06.2
5 F	10 51 50	14 37 41	0♐44 55	7♐48 21	15 21.5	17 24.7	9 18.4	0♊29.7	4 32.3	17 30.9	8 53.4	7 45.2	20 24.3	26 07.7
6 Sa	10 55 47	15 37 46	14 48 30	21 45 24	15 21.2	18 22.2	10 33.3	1 04.6	4 55.6	17 44.3	8 59.6	7 47.5	20 26.6	26 09.1
7 Su	10 59 44	16 37 51	28 39 04	5♑29 38	15 21.0	19 22.5	11 48.2	1 39.5	5 19.0	17 57.8	9 05.8	7 50.0	20 28.8	26 10.5
8 M	11 03 40	17 37 54	12♑17 11	19 01 48	15 19.6	20 25.4	13 03.1	2 14.5	5 42.4	18 11.1	9 11.9	7 52.4	20 31.1	26 11.9
9 Tu	11 07 37	18 37 55	25 43 36	2♒22 38	15 15.8	21 30.7	14 18.0	2 49.5	6 05.9	18 24.4	9 18.0	7 54.9	20 33.4	26 13.3
10 W	11 11 33	19 37 54	8♒58 57	15 32 31	15 09.0	22 38.2	15 32.9	3 24.6	6 29.3	18 37.7	9 24.0	7 57.4	20 35.7	26 14.6
11 Th	11 15 30	20 37 52	22 03 22	28 31 24	14 59.2	23 47.9	16 47.7	3 59.7	6 52.9	18 50.9	9 30.0	8 00.0	20 37.9	26 16.0
12 F	11 19 26	21 37 48	4♓56 36	11♓18 52	14 47.1	24 59.7	18 02.6	4 34.8	7 16.4	19 04.1	9 36.0	8 02.6	20 40.2	26 17.3
13 Sa	11 23 23	22 37 42	17 38 10	23 54 27	14 33.4	26 13.3	19 17.4	5 10.1	7 39.9	19 17.2	9 41.9	8 05.2	20 42.5	26 18.6
14 Su	11 27 19	23 37 34	0♈07 42	6♈17 57	14 19.5	27 28.9	20 32.2	5 45.3	8 03.5	19 30.2	9 47.7	8 07.9	20 44.8	26 19.8
15 M	11 31 16	24 37 24	12 25 15	18 29 46	14 06.5	28 46.1	21 47.1	6 20.7	8 27.1	19 43.2	9 53.5	8 10.6	20 47.1	26 21.0
16 Tu	11 35 13	25 37 12	24 31 38	0♉31 08	13 55.6	0♓05.1	23 01.8	6 56.0	8 50.7	19 56.2	9 59.2	8 13.3	20 49.3	26 22.2
17 W	11 39 09	26 36 58	6♉28 34	12 24 17	13 47.3	1 25.7	24 16.6	7 31.4	9 14.4	20 09.0	10 04.8	8 16.1	20 51.6	26 23.4
18 Th	11 43 06	27 36 41	18 18 44	24 12 23	13 42.0	2 47.9	25 31.4	8 06.9	9 38.1	20 21.8	10 10.5	8 18.9	20 53.9	26 24.6
19 F	11 47 02	28 36 23	0♊05 46	5♊59 30	13 39.2	4 11.7	26 46.1	8 42.3	10 01.7	20 34.6	10 16.0	8 21.7	20 56.1	26 25.7
20 Sa	11 50 59	29 36 02	11 54 10	17 50 27	13D 38.4	5 36.9	28 00.8	9 17.9	10 25.5	20 47.2	10 21.5	8 24.5	20 58.4	26 26.8
21 Su	11 54 55	0♈35 40	23 49 00	29 50 32	13R 38.6	7 03.6	29 15.5	9 53.4	10 49.2	20 59.8	10 26.9	8 27.4	21 00.6	26 27.9
22 M	11 58 52	1 35 14	5♋55 44	12♋05 17	13 38.7	8 31.7	0♈30.2	10 29.0	11 12.9	21 12.4	10 32.3	8 30.3	21 02.9	26 29.0
23 Tu	12 02 48	2 34 47	18 19 49	24 39 58	13 37.5	10 01.3	1 44.9	11 04.6	11 36.7	21 24.9	10 37.6	8 33.2	21 05.1	26 30.0
24 W	12 06 45	3 34 17	1♌06 16	7♌39 09	13 34.3	11 32.2	2 59.5	11 40.3	12 00.4	21 37.3	10 42.8	8 36.2	21 07.4	26 31.0
25 Th	12 10 42	4 33 45	14 18 57	21 05 51	13 28.7	13 04.6	4 14.2	12 16.0	12 24.2	21 49.6	10 48.0	8 39.2	21 09.6	26 32.0
26 F	12 14 38	5 33 11	27 59 53	5♍00 53	13 20.8	14 38.3	5 28.8	12 51.7	12 48.0	22 01.8	10 53.1	8 42.2	21 11.8	26 32.9
27 Sa	12 18 35	6 32 34	12♍08 32	19 22 14	13 11.2	16 13.3	6 43.4	13 27.5	13 11.8	22 14.0	10 58.2	8 45.2	21 14.1	26 33.8
28 Su	12 22 31	7 31 56	26 41 17	4♎04 45	13 00.8	17 49.8	7 57.9	14 03.2	13 35.6	22 26.1	11 03.2	8 48.3	21 16.3	26 34.7
29 M	12 26 28	8 31 15	11♎31 36	19 00 41	12 50.9	19 27.6	9 12.5	14 39.0	13 59.4	22 38.1	11 08.1	8 51.3	21 18.5	26 35.6
30 Tu	12 30 24	9 30 32	26 30 51	4♏00 53	12 42.6	21 06.8	10 27.0	15 14.9	14 23.2	22 50.1	11 12.9	8 54.4	21 20.7	26 36.4
31 W	12 34 21	10 29 47	11♏29 42	18 56 17	12 36.7	22 47.3	11 41.5	15 50.7	14 47.0	23 01.9	11 17.7	8 57.6	21 22.8	26 37.3

April 2021

LONGITUDE

Day	Sid.Time	☉	0 hr ☽	Noon ☽	True ☊	☿	♀	♂	⚳	♃	♄	♅	♆	♇
1 Th	12 38 17	11♈29 00	26♏19 46	3♐39 26	12♊33.4	24♓29.2	12♈56.0	16♊26.6	15♈10.9	23♒13.7	11♒22.4	9♉00.7	21♓25.0	26♑38.0
2 F	12 42 14	12 28 12	10♐54 44	18 05 18	12D 32.4	26 12.6	14 10.5	17 02.5	15 34.7	23 25.4	11 27.0	9 03.9	21 27.2	26 38.8
3 Sa	12 46 10	13 27 21	25 10 52	2♑11 22	12 32.8	27 57.3	15 25.0	17 38.4	15 58.6	23 37.0	11 31.6	9 07.0	21 29.3	26 39.5
4 Su	12 50 07	14 26 30	9♑06 49	15 57 18	12R 33.5	29 43.5	16 39.4	18 14.4	16 22.5	23 48.6	11 36.1	9 10.2	21 31.5	26 40.2
5 M	12 54 04	15 25 36	22 43 01	29 24 10	12 33.3	1♈31.1	17 53.9	18 50.4	16 46.3	24 00.0	11 40.5	9 13.5	21 33.6	26 40.9
6 Tu	12 58 00	16 24 41	6♒01 00	12♒33 47	12 31.5	3 20.1	19 08.3	19 26.4	17 10.2	24 11.4	11 44.8	9 16.7	21 35.7	26 41.6
7 W	13 01 57	17 23 43	19 02 46	25 28 12	12 27.3	5 10.5	20 22.7	20 02.4	17 34.1	24 22.6	11 49.1	9 20.0	21 37.8	26 42.2
8 Th	13 05 53	18 22 44	1♓50 18	8♓09 18	12 20.8	7 02.5	21 37.1	20 38.5	17 58.0	24 33.8	11 53.3	9 23.2	21 39.9	26 42.8
9 F	13 09 50	19 21 43	14 25 21	20 38 39	12 12.4	8 55.8	22 51.5	21 14.6	18 21.9	24 44.9	11 57.4	9 26.5	21 42.0	26 43.3
10 Sa	13 13 46	20 20 41	26 49 19	2♈57 31	12 02.9	10 50.6	24 05.9	21 50.7	18 45.7	24 55.8	12 01.4	9 29.8	21 44.1	26 43.9
11 Su	13 17 43	21 19 36	9♈03 23	15 07 02	11 53.0	12 46.9	25 20.2	22 26.8	19 09.6	25 06.7	12 05.4	9 33.1	21 46.1	26 44.4
12 M	13 21 39	22 18 29	21 08 37	27 08 18	11 43.9	14 44.6	26 34.5	23 03.0	19 33.5	25 17.5	12 09.3	9 36.5	21 48.1	26 44.9
13 Tu	13 25 36	23 17 20	3♉06 15	9♉02 43	11 36.2	16 43.7	27 48.8	23 39.2	19 57.4	25 28.2	12 13.0	9 39.8	21 50.2	26 45.3
14 W	13 29 33	24 16 10	14 57 54	20 52 06	11 30.6	18 44.2	29 03.1	24 15.4	20 21.3	25 38.7	12 16.8	9 43.2	21 52.2	26 45.7
15 Th	13 33 29	25 14 57	26 45 39	2♊38 54	11 27.2	20 45.9	0♉17.4	24 51.6	20 45.1	25 49.2	12 20.4	9 46.5	21 54.1	26 46.1
16 F	13 37 26	26 13 42	8♊32 17	14 26 13	11D 25.9	22 49.0	1 31.6	25 27.9	21 09.0	25 59.6	12 23.9	9 49.9	21 56.1	26 46.5
17 Sa	13 41 22	27 12 25	20 21 13	26 17 49	11 26.2	24 53.1	2 45.8	26 04.1	21 32.9	26 09.8	12 27.4	9 53.3	21 58.1	26 46.8
18 Su	13 45 19	28 11 06	2♋16 34	8♋18 04	11 27.5	26 58.4	4 00.1	26 40.4	21 56.7	26 20.0	12 30.7	9 56.7	22 00.0	26 47.1
19 M	13 49 15	29 09 45	14 22 56	20 31 46	11 29.0	29 04.5	5 14.2	27 16.7	22 20.6	26 30.0	12 34.0	10 00.1	22 01.9	26 47.4
20 Tu	13 53 12	0♉08 22	26 45 12	3♌03 50	11R 29.9	1♉11.4	6 28.4	27 53.0	22 44.4	26 39.9	12 37.2	10 03.5	22 03.8	26 47.6
21 W	13 57 08	1 06 56	9♌28 14	15 58 54	11 29.6	3 18.9	7 42.5	28 29.4	23 08.2	26 49.7	12 40.3	10 07.0	22 05.7	26 47.8
22 Th	14 01 05	2 05 28	22 36 15	29 20 39	11 27.7	5 26.8	8 56.7	29 05.7	23 32.1	26 59.4	12 43.4	10 10.4	22 07.5	26 48.0
23 F	14 05 02	3 03 58	6♍12 16	13♍11 10	11 24.2	7 34.7	10 10.8	29 42.1	23 55.9	27 09.0	12 46.3	10 13.8	22 09.4	26 48.2
24 Sa	14 08 58	4 02 26	20 17 11	27 30 02	11 19.5	9 42.5	11 24.8	0♋18.4	24 19.7	27 18.5	12 49.2	10 17.3	22 11.2	26 48.3
25 Su	14 12 55	5 00 51	4♎49 09	12♎13 51	11 14.1	11 49.9	12 38.9	0 54.8	24 43.4	27 27.8	12 51.9	10 20.7	22 13.0	26 48.4
26 M	14 16 51	5 59 15	19 43 11	27 16 07	11 08.9	13 56.5	13 52.9	1 31.2	25 07.2	27 37.0	12 54.6	10 24.2	22 14.8	26 48.4
27 Tu	14 20 48	6 57 36	4♏51 26	12♏27 54	11 04.5	16 02.1	15 06.9	2 07.6	25 31.0	27 46.1	12 57.2	10 27.6	22 16.5	26R 48.5
28 W	14 24 44	7 55 56	20 04 15	27 39 13	11 01.6	18 06.4	16 20.9	2 44.1	25 54.7	27 55.1	12 59.6	10 31.1	22 18.3	26 48.5
29 Th	14 28 41	8 54 14	5♐11 40	12♐40 33	11D 00.2	20 09.0	17 34.9	3 20.5	26 18.4	28 03.9	13 02.0	10 34.5	22 20.0	26 48.5
30 F	14 32 37	9 52 31	20 05 02	27 24 22	11 00.4	22 09.6	18 48.9	3 57.0	26 42.1	28 12.7	13 04.4	10 38.0	22 21.7	26 48.4

Astro Data	Dy Hr Mn
☽0S	1 12:41
☽0N	14 20:07
☊D	20 3:31
☉0N	20 9:38
♃⚺♆	21 1:52
☊R	21 14:33
♀0N	24 3:40
☽0S	28 22:14
☊D	2 2:42
☊R	4 10:15
⚳0N	4 15:01
☿0N	6 18:32
☽0N	11 2:43
☊D	16 5:53
☊R	20 6:55

Planet Ingress	Dy Hr Mn
♂ ♊	4 3:31
☿ ♓	15 22:28
☉ ♈	20 9:39
♀ ♈	21 14:17
☿ ♈	4 3:42
♀ ♉	14 18:23
☿ ♉	19 10:30
☉ ♉	19 20:35
♂ ♋	23 11:50
♃⚺⚺20	19:10
☽0S25	9:15
♇ R27	20:04
☊ D29	9:17

Last Aspect Dy Hr Mn		☽ Ingress Dy Hr Mn
2 14:11	♇ □	♏ 2 20:39
4 16:11	♇ ⚹	♐ 4 22:44
6 9:45	♆ □	♑ 7 2:21
9 0:54	♇ ☌	♒ 9 7:42
11 3:33	☿ ☌	♓ 11 14:45
13 16:39	♇ ⚹	♈ 13 23:45
16 3:41	♇ □	♉ 16 10:57
18 20:41	☉ ⚹	♊ 18 23:48
21 12:05	♀ □	♋ 21 12:19
23 15:27	♇ ☍	♌ 23 21:57
25 13:29	♃ ☍	♍ 26 3:27
27 23:49	♇ △	♎ 28 5:23
30 0:09	♇ □	♏ 30 5:34

Last Aspect Dy Hr Mn		☽ Ingress Dy Hr Mn
1 0:30	♇ ⚹	♐ 1 6:00
3 5:25	☿ □	♑ 3 8:14
5 7:06	♇ ☌	♒ 5 13:05
7 10:06	♃ ☌	♓ 7 20:32
9 23:49	♇ ⚹	♈ 10 6:12
12 12:08	♀ ☌	♉ 12 17:45
15 0:01	♇ △	♊ 15 6:36
17 15:04	☉ ⚹	♋ 17 19:26
20 0:05	♇ ☍	♌ 20 6:12
22 12:06	♂ ⚹	♍ 22 13:09
24 10:51	♇ △	♎ 24 16:07
26 12:41	♃ △	♏ 26 16:19
28 12:33	♃ □	♐ 28 15:44
30 13:28	♃ ⚹	♑ 30 16:17

☽ Phases & Eclipses Dy Hr Mn	
6 1:31	☾ 15♐42
13 10:22	● 23♓04
21 14:42	☽ 1♋12
28 18:49	○ 8♎18
4 10:04	☾ 14♑51
12 2:32	● 22♈25
20 7:00	☽ 0♌25
27 3:33	○ 7♏06

Astro Data

1 March 2021
Julian Day # 44255
SVP 4♓58'07"
GC 27♐08.1 ⚴ 27♒43.7
Eris 23♈40.0 ⚵ 19♐42.1
⚷ 7♈14.4 ⚶ 15♍21.6R
☽ Mean ☊ 15♊44.0

1 April 2021
Julian Day # 44286
SVP 4♓58'04"
GC 27♐08.2 ⚴ 7♓41.0
Eris 23♈57.9 ⚵ 23♐41.2
⚷ 9♈00.8 ⚶ 8♍12.5R
☽ Mean ☊ 14♊05.4

*Giving the positions of planets daily at midnight, Greenwich Mean Time (0:00 UT)
Each planet's retrograde period is shaded gray.

2021 Planetary Ephemeris

LONGITUDE — May 2021

Day	Sid.Time	☉	0 hr ☽	Noon ☽	True ☊	☿	♀	♂	⚳	♃	♄	♅	♆	♇
1 Sa	14 36 34	10♉50 46	4♑38 03	11♑45 44	11♊01.5	24♉08.0	20♉02.8	4♋33.4	27♈05.8	28♒21.2	13♒06.6	10♉41.4	22♓23.3	26♑48.3
2 Su	14 40 31	11 48 59	18 47 13	25 42 27	11 03.0	26 03.9	21 16.7	5 09.9	27 29.5	28 29.7	13 08.7	10 44.9	22 25.0	26R 48.2
3 M	14 44 27	12 47 11	2♒31 31	9♒14 37	11R 04.1	27 57.0	22 30.6	5 46.4	27 53.2	28 38.0	13 10.7	10 48.4	22 26.6	26 48.1
4 Tu	14 48 24	13 45 22	15 51 58	22 23 55	11 04.5	29 47.2	23 44.5	6 22.9	28 16.8	28 46.2	13 12.7	10 51.8	22 28.2	26 48.0
5 W	14 52 20	14 43 31	28 50 49	5♓13 04	11 03.7	1♊34.2	24 58.4	6 59.4	28 40.5	28 54.3	13 14.5	10 55.3	22 29.8	26 47.8
6 Th	14 56 17	15 41 39	11♓31 02	17 45 08	11 01.7	3 18.0	26 12.3	7 36.0	29 04.1	29 02.2	13 16.2	10 58.7	22 31.3	26 47.5
7 F	15 00 13	16 39 45	23 55 45	0♈03 15	10 58.7	4 58.3	27 26.1	8 12.5	29 27.7	29 10.0	13 17.9	11 02.2	22 32.9	26 47.3
8 Sa	15 04 10	17 37 49	6♈08 01	12 10 23	10 55.1	6 35.1	28 39.9	8 49.1	29 51.3	29 17.6	13 19.4	11 05.6	22 34.3	26 47.0
9 Su	15 08 06	18 35 52	18 10 39	24 09 09	10 51.4	8 08.2	29 53.7	9 25.6	0♉14.8	29 25.1	13 20.9	11 09.1	22 35.8	26 46.7
10 M	15 12 03	19 33 54	0♉06 10	6♉01 58	10 47.9	9 37.6	1♊07.5	10 02.2	0 38.3	29 32.5	13 22.2	11 12.5	22 37.3	26 46.4
11 Tu	15 16 00	20 31 54	11 56 49	17 50 59	10 45.1	11 03.2	2 21.3	10 38.8	1 01.8	29 39.7	13 23.5	11 15.9	22 38.7	26 46.0
12 W	15 19 56	21 29 53	23 44 45	29 38 21	10 43.2	12 25.0	3 35.0	11 15.5	1 25.3	29 46.7	13 24.7	11 19.4	22 40.1	26 45.6
13 Th	15 23 53	22 27 50	5♊32 05	11♊26 14	10D 42.3	13 42.7	4 48.8	11 52.1	1 48.8	29 53.6	13 25.7	11 22.8	22 41.5	26 45.2
14 F	15 27 49	23 25 46	17 21 07	23 17 04	10 42.3	14 56.5	6 02.5	12 28.7	2 12.2	0♓00.4	13 26.7	11 26.2	22 42.8	26 44.8
15 Sa	15 31 46	24 23 40	29 14 27	5♋13 37	10 43.1	16 06.2	7 16.2	13 05.4	2 35.6	0 07.0	13 27.6	11 29.6	22 44.1	26 44.3
16 Su	15 35 42	25 21 33	11♋14 59	17 18 59	10 44.3	17 11.8	8 29.9	13 42.1	2 58.9	0 13.4	13 28.4	11 33.0	22 45.4	26 43.8
17 M	15 39 39	26 19 23	23 26 04	29 36 40	10 45.6	18 13.2	9 43.5	14 18.8	3 22.3	0 19.7	13 29.0	11 36.4	22 46.7	26 43.3
18 Tu	15 43 35	27 17 13	5♌51 18	12♌10 24	10 46.8	19 10.4	10 57.2	14 55.5	3 45.6	0 25.9	13 29.6	11 39.7	22 47.9	26 42.8
19 W	15 47 32	28 15 00	18 34 28	25 03 53	10R 47.5	20 03.2	12 10.8	15 32.2	4 08.9	0 31.8	13 30.1	11 43.1	22 49.1	26 42.2
20 Th	15 51 29	29 12 46	1♍39 06	8♍20 25	10 47.6	20 51.6	13 24.4	16 08.9	4 32.1	0 37.6	13 30.5	11 46.4	22 50.3	26 41.6
21 F	15 55 25	0♊10 30	15 08 06	22 02 19	10 47.3	21 35.6	14 38.0	16 45.6	4 55.3	0 43.3	13 30.8	11 49.8	22 51.4	26 41.0
22 Sa	15 59 22	1 08 12	29 03 05	6♎10 19	10 46.5	22 15.1	15 51.5	17 22.3	5 18.5	0 48.8	13 30.9	11 53.1	22 52.5	26 40.3
23 Su	16 03 18	2 05 53	13♎23 43	20 42 53	10 45.6	22 50.0	17 05.0	17 59.1	5 41.6	0 54.1	13R 31.0	11 56.4	22 53.6	26 39.6
24 M	16 07 15	3 03 32	28 07 12	5♏35 54	10 44.7	23 20.3	18 18.6	18 35.8	6 04.7	0 59.2	13 31.0	11 59.7	22 54.7	26 38.9
25 Tu	16 11 11	4 01 10	13♏08 02	20 42 34	10 44.0	23 45.9	19 32.0	19 12.6	6 27.8	1 04.2	13 30.9	12 02.9	22 55.7	26 38.2
26 W	16 15 08	4 58 46	28 18 22	5♐54 13	10D 43.6	24 06.8	20 45.5	19 49.3	6 50.8	1 09.0	13 30.7	12 06.2	22 56.7	26 37.5
27 Th	16 19 04	5 56 21	13♐28 55	21 01 19	10 43.5	24 22.9	21 59.0	20 26.1	7 13.8	1 13.7	13 30.4	12 09.4	22 57.7	26 36.7
28 F	16 23 01	6 53 56	28 30 21	5♑55 02	10 43.6	24 34.3	23 12.4	21 02.9	7 36.7	1 18.2	13 30.0	12 12.7	22 58.6	26 35.9
29 Sa	16 26 58	7 51 29	13♑14 34	20 28 18	10 43.9	24R 41.0	24 25.8	21 39.7	7 59.7	1 22.5	13 29.5	12 15.9	22 59.5	26 35.1
30 Su	16 30 54	8 49 01	27 35 45	4♒36 37	10 44.1	24 43.0	25 39.2	22 16.5	8 22.5	1 26.6	13 28.9	12 19.1	23 00.4	26 34.3
31 M	16 34 51	9 46 32	11♒30 45	18 18 09	10 44.2	24 40.5	26 52.6	22 53.3	8 45.4	1 30.6	13 28.3	12 22.2	23 01.2	26 33.4

LONGITUDE — June 2021

Day	Sid.Time	☉	0 hr ☽	Noon ☽	True ☊	☿	♀	♂	⚳	♃	♄	♅	♆	♇
1 Tu	16 38 47	10♊44 03	24♒58 56	1♓33 23	10♊44.3	24♊33.5	28♊05.9	23♋30.1	9♉08.2	1♓34.4	13♒27.5	12♉25.4	23♓02.0	26♑32.5
2 W	16 42 44	11 41 32	8♓01 48	14 24 36	10D 44.3	24R 22.3	29 19.3	24 07.0	9 30.9	1 38.0	13R 26.6	12 28.5	23 02.8	26R 31.6
3 Th	16 46 40	12 39 01	20 42 15	26 55 13	10 44.3	24 07.0	0♋32.6	24 43.8	9 53.6	1 41.4	13 25.6	12 31.6	23 03.6	26 30.7
4 F	16 50 37	13 36 29	3♈04 02	9♈09 13	10 44.4	23 48.0	1 45.9	25 20.7	10 16.3	1 44.6	13 24.6	12 34.7	23 04.3	26 29.7
5 Sa	16 54 33	14 33 56	15 11 18	21 10 47	10 44.7	23 25.6	2 59.2	25 57.6	10 38.9	1 47.7	13 23.4	12 37.8	23 05.0	26 28.8
6 Su	16 58 30	15 31 23	27 08 09	3♉03 54	10 45.2	23 00.1	4 12.5	26 34.4	11 01.5	1 50.6	13 22.1	12 40.8	23 05.6	26 27.8
7 M	17 02 27	16 28 49	8♉58 28	14 52 17	10 45.8	22 31.9	5 25.7	27 11.3	11 24.0	1 53.3	13 20.8	12 43.8	23 06.3	26 26.8
8 Tu	17 06 23	17 26 14	20 45 45	26 39 14	10 46.3	22 01.7	6 39.0	27 48.3	11 46.5	1 55.8	13 19.3	12 46.8	23 06.9	26 25.7
9 W	17 10 20	18 23 39	2♊33 06	8♊27 38	10R 46.7	21 29.7	7 52.2	28 25.2	12 08.9	1 58.1	13 17.8	12 49.8	23 07.4	26 24.7
10 Th	17 14 16	19 21 03	14 23 10	20 19 58	10 46.8	20 56.7	9 05.4	29 02.1	12 31.3	2 00.2	13 16.2	12 52.8	23 08.0	26 23.6
11 F	17 18 13	20 18 26	26 18 19	2♋18 27	10 46.4	20 23.1	10 18.6	29 39.1	12 53.6	2 02.2	13 14.5	12 55.7	23 08.4	26 22.5
12 Sa	17 22 09	21 15 48	8♋20 37	14 25 04	10 45.6	19 49.6	11 31.7	0♌16.0	13 15.9	2 03.9	13 12.7	12 58.6	23 08.9	26 21.4
13 Su	17 26 06	22 13 10	20 32 03	26 41 48	10 44.2	19 16.7	12 44.9	0 53.0	13 38.1	2 05.5	13 10.8	13 01.5	23 09.3	26 20.3
14 M	17 30 02	23 10 31	2♌54 34	9♌10 35	10 42.6	18 44.9	13 58.0	1 30.0	14 00.3	2 06.8	13 08.8	13 04.3	23 09.7	26 19.2
15 Tu	17 33 59	24 07 51	15 30 07	21 53 27	10 40.8	18 14.9	15 11.1	2 07.0	14 22.4	2 08.0	13 06.7	13 07.1	23 10.1	26 18.0
16 W	17 37 56	25 05 09	28 20 48	4♍52 26	10 39.2	17 47.0	16 24.2	2 44.0	14 44.4	2 09.0	13 04.5	13 09.9	23 10.4	26 16.9
17 Th	17 41 52	26 02 28	11♍28 35	18 09 29	10 38.1	17 21.9	17 37.3	3 21.0	15 06.4	2 09.8	13 02.3	13 12.6	23 10.7	26 15.7
18 F	17 45 49	26 59 45	24 55 19	1♎46 12	10D 37.6	16 59.9	18 50.3	3 58.1	15 28.3	2 10.4	13 00.0	13 15.4	23 11.0	26 14.5
19 Sa	17 49 45	27 57 01	8♎42 13	15 43 21	10 37.8	16 41.3	20 03.3	4 35.1	15 50.1	2 10.8	12 57.6	13 18.1	23 11.2	26 13.2
20 Su	17 53 42	28 54 17	22 49 33	0♏00 34	10 38.7	16 26.6	21 16.3	5 12.2	16 11.9	2R 11.0	12 55.1	13 20.7	23 11.4	26 12.0
21 M	17 57 38	29 51 31	7♏16 07	14 35 45	10 39.9	16 15.9	22 29.2	5 49.2	16 33.6	2 11.1	12 52.5	13 23.4	23 11.6	26 10.8
22 Tu	18 01 35	0♋48 45	21 58 53	29 24 50	10 41.1	16D 09.5	23 42.2	6 26.3	16 55.3	2 10.9	12 49.9	13 26.0	23 11.8	26 09.5
23 W	18 05 32	1 45 59	6♐52 46	14♐21 46	10R 41.7	16 07.6	24 55.1	7 03.4	17 16.9	2 10.5	12 47.1	13 28.5	23 11.9	26 08.2
24 Th	18 09 28	2 43 12	21 50 52	29 19 01	10 41.5	16 10.3	26 08.0	7 40.5	17 38.4	2 10.0	12 44.3	13 31.1	23 11.9	26 06.9
25 F	18 13 25	3 40 25	6♑45 12	14♑08 25	10 40.1	16 17.7	27 20.8	8 17.6	17 59.9	2 09.2	12 41.5	13 33.6	23R 12.0	26 05.7
26 Sa	18 17 21	4 37 37	21 27 44	28 42 20	10 37.7	16 29.9	28 33.6	8 54.7	18 21.3	2 08.3	12 38.5	13 36.0	23 12.0	26 04.3
27 Su	18 21 18	5 34 49	5♒51 31	12♒54 44	10 34.5	16 46.8	29 46.5	9 31.8	18 42.6	2 07.2	12 35.5	13 38.5	23 12.0	26 03.0
28 M	18 25 14	6 32 01	19 51 36	26 41 54	10 30.9	17 08.5	0♌59.2	10 09.0	19 03.9	2 05.9	12 32.4	13 40.9	23 11.9	26 01.7
29 Tu	18 29 11	7 29 13	3♓25 34	10♓02 38	10 27.5	17 35.0	2 12.0	10 46.1	19 25.0	2 04.4	12 29.2	13 43.3	23 11.8	26 00.4
30 W	18 33 07	8 26 25	16 33 21	22 58 00	10 24.7	18 06.2	3 24.7	11 23.3	19 46.1	2 02.7	12 26.0	13 45.6	23 11.7	25 59.0

Astro Data	Dy Hr Mn
☊ R	3 20:05
☽ 0N	8 8:51
☊ D	13 10:29
☊ R	19 19:11
☽ 0S	22 19:29
♄ R	23 9:20
☊ D	26 19:23
☿ R	29 22:35
☊ R	1 1:29
☊ D	2 7:26
☽ 0N	4 15:02
☊ R	9 16:48
♄□♅	14 22:02
☊ D	18 3:49
☽ 0S	19 3:18

Planet Ingress	Dy Hr Mn
☿ ♊	4 2:50
⚳ ♉	8 8:55
♀ ♊	9 2:02
♃ ♓	13 22:37
☉ ♊	20 19:38
♀ ♋	2 13:20
♂ ♌	11 13:35
☉ ♋	21 3:33
♀ ♌	27 4:28
♃ R	20 15:06
☿ D	22 22:01
☊ R	23 6:12
♆ R	25 19:22

Last Aspect Dy Hr Mn		☽ Ingress	Dy Hr Mn
2 14:39	☿ △	♒	2 19:32
5 0:07	♃ ☌	♓	5 2:10
7 7:37	♀ ⚹	♈	7 11:54
9 22:51	♃ ⚹	♉	9 23:48
12 12:24	♃ □	♊	12 12:44
14 10:52	♆ □	♋	15 1:32
17 6:24	♇ ☍	♌	17 12:45
19 19:14	☉ □	♍	19 21:00
21 19:57	♇ △	♎	22 1:37
23 21:38	♇ □	♏	24 3:02
25 21:21	♇ ⚹	♐	26 2:40
27 17:37	☿ ☍	♑	28 2:25
29 22:16	♇ ☌	♒	30 4:05

Last Aspect Dy Hr Mn		☽ Ingress	Dy Hr Mn
1 6:15	♀ △	♓	1 9:09
3 11:12	♇ ⚹	♈	3 18:00
5 22:48	♂ □	♉	6 5:47
8 15:08	♂ ⚹	♊	8 18:49
10 17:39	♆ □	♋	11 7:24
13 11:17	♇ ☍	♌	13 18:24
15 17:28	☉ ⚹	♍	16 3:03
18 3:55	☉ □	♎	18 8:55
20 10:53	☉ △	♏	20 11:59
22 6:44	♇ ⚹	♐	22 12:57
24 2:10	♆ □	♑	24 13:06
26 12:51	♀ ☍	♒	26 14:10
27 19:09	☿ △	♓	28 17:52

☽ Phases & Eclipses Dy Hr Mn	
3 19:51	☾ 13♒35
11 19:01	● 21♉18
19 19:14	☽ 29♌01
26 11:15	○ 5♐26
26 11:20	T 1.009
2 7:26	☾ 11♓59
10 10:54	● 19♊47
10 10:43:05	A 03'51"
18 3:55	☽ 27♍09
24 18:41	○ 3♑28

Astro Data

1 May 2021
Julian Day # 44316
SVP 4♓58'00"
GC 27♐08.2 ⚴ 16♓16.8
Eris 24♈17.4 ⚵ 23♐04.9R
⚷ 10♈42.3 ⚶ 7♍08.5
☽ Mean ☊ 12♊30.1

1 June 2021
Julian Day # 44347
SVP 4♓57'55"
GC 27♐08.3 ⚴ 23♓19.3
Eris 24♈34.9 ⚵ 17♐43.7R
⚷ 12♈05.7 ⚶ 12♍48.8
☽ Mean ☊ 10♊51.6

*Giving the positions of planets daily at midnight, Greenwich Mean Time (0:00 UT)
Each planet's retrograde period is shaded gray.

2021 Planetary Ephemeris

July 2021

LONGITUDE

Day	Sid.Time	☉	0 hr ☽	Noon ☽	True ☊	☿	♀	♂	⚳	♃	♄	♅	♆	♇
1 Th	18 37 04	9♋23 37	29♓16 59	5♈30 49	10♊23.1	18♊42.1	4♌37.4	12♌00.4	20♉07.2	2♓00.8	12♒22.7	13♉47.9	23♓11.5	25♑57.6
2 F	18 41 01	10 20 49	11♈40 00	17 45 08	10D 22.6	19 22.7	5 50.1	12 37.6	20 28.1	1R 58.7	12R 19.3	13 50.1	23R 11.4	25R 56.3
3 Sa	18 44 57	11 18 02	23 46 49	29 45 39	10 23.2	20 07.9	7 02.8	13 14.8	20 49.0	1 56.4	12 15.9	13 52.3	23 11.1	25 54.9
4 Su	18 48 54	12 15 14	5♉42 16	11♉37 16	10 24.7	20 57.6	8 15.4	13 52.1	21 09.8	1 54.0	12 12.4	13 54.5	23 10.9	25 53.5
5 M	18 52 50	13 12 27	17 31 13	23 24 44	10 26.4	21 51.8	9 28.0	14 29.3	21 30.5	1 51.3	12 08.8	13 56.7	23 10.6	25 52.1
6 Tu	18 56 47	14 09 40	29 18 19	5♊12 29	10R 27.8	22 50.5	10 40.6	15 06.6	21 51.1	1 48.5	12 05.2	13 58.8	23 10.3	25 50.7
7 W	19 00 43	15 06 53	11♊07 42	17 04 24	10 28.4	23 53.5	11 53.2	15 43.8	22 11.6	1 45.5	12 01.5	14 00.8	23 09.9	25 49.3
8 Th	19 04 40	16 04 07	23 02 56	29 03 40	10 27.6	25 00.8	13 05.7	16 21.1	22 32.1	1 42.3	11 57.8	14 02.9	23 09.6	25 47.9
9 F	19 08 36	17 01 21	5♋06 53	11♋12 48	10 25.1	26 12.4	14 18.3	16 58.4	22 52.4	1 38.9	11 54.0	14 04.9	23 09.2	25 46.5
10 Sa	19 12 33	17 58 35	17 21 39	23 33 33	10 20.9	27 28.2	15 30.8	17 35.8	23 12.7	1 35.3	11 50.2	14 06.8	23 08.7	25 45.0
11 Su	19 16 30	18 55 49	29 48 39	6♌07 00	10 15.2	28 48.1	16 43.2	18 13.1	23 32.9	1 31.6	11 46.3	14 08.7	23 08.3	25 43.6
12 M	19 20 26	19 53 03	12♌28 39	18 53 39	10 08.7	0♋12.1	17 55.6	18 50.5	23 52.9	1 27.7	11 42.3	14 10.6	23 07.7	25 42.2
13 Tu	19 24 23	20 50 17	25 22 00	1♍53 41	10 01.8	1 40.1	19 08.0	19 27.8	24 12.9	1 23.6	11 38.4	14 12.4	23 07.2	25 40.7
14 W	19 28 19	21 47 32	8♍28 42	15 07 03	9 55.5	3 12.0	20 20.4	20 05.2	24 32.8	1 19.3	11 34.3	14 14.2	23 06.7	25 39.3
15 Th	19 32 16	22 44 46	21 48 43	28 33 41	9 50.5	4 47.7	21 32.7	20 42.6	24 52.6	1 14.9	11 30.3	14 15.9	23 06.1	25 37.9
16 F	19 36 12	23 42 00	5♎21 58	12♎13 33	9 47.2	6 27.1	22 45.1	21 20.0	25 12.3	1 10.3	11 26.1	14 17.6	23 05.4	25 36.4
17 Sa	19 40 09	24 39 15	19 08 27	26 06 36	9D 45.7	8 10.0	23 57.3	21 57.4	25 31.8	1 05.5	11 22.0	14 19.2	23 04.8	25 35.0
18 Su	19 44 05	25 36 29	3♏07 59	10♏12 30	9 45.8	9 56.4	25 09.5	22 34.9	25 51.3	1 00.6	11 17.8	14 20.9	23 04.1	25 33.5
19 M	19 48 02	26 33 44	17 20 00	24 30 17	9 46.7	11 45.9	26 21.7	23 12.3	26 10.6	0 55.5	11 13.6	14 22.4	23 03.4	25 32.1
20 Tu	19 51 59	27 30 59	1♐43 03	8♐57 57	9R 47.7	13 38.5	27 33.9	23 49.8	26 29.9	0 50.3	11 09.3	14 23.9	23 02.7	25 30.7
21 W	19 55 55	28 28 14	16 14 30	23 32 08	9 47.8	15 33.8	28 46.0	24 27.3	26 49.0	0 45.0	11 05.1	14 25.4	23 01.9	25 29.2
22 Th	19 59 52	29 25 30	0♑50 13	8♑08 01	9 46.1	17 31.6	29 58.1	25 04.8	27 08.0	0 39.4	11 00.8	14 26.8	23 01.1	25 27.8
23 F	20 03 48	0♌22 46	15 24 46	22 39 39	9 42.3	19 31.6	1♍10.1	25 42.3	27 27.0	0 33.8	10 56.4	14 28.2	23 00.3	25 26.3
24 Sa	20 07 45	1 20 02	29 51 53	7♒00 39	9 36.2	21 33.6	2 22.2	26 19.8	27 45.8	0 28.0	10 52.1	14 29.6	22 59.4	25 24.9
25 Su	20 11 41	2 17 19	14♒05 16	21 05 06	9 28.5	23 37.0	3 34.1	26 57.4	28 04.4	0 22.0	10 47.7	14 30.9	22 58.6	25 23.5
26 M	20 15 38	3 14 37	27 59 38	4♓48 30	9 19.9	25 41.8	4 46.0	27 35.0	28 23.0	0 15.9	10 43.3	14 32.1	22 57.7	25 22.1
27 Tu	20 19 34	4 11 55	11♓31 27	18 08 23	9 11.4	27 47.4	5 57.9	28 12.5	28 41.4	0 09.7	10 38.9	14 33.3	22 56.7	25 20.6
28 W	20 23 31	5 09 14	24 39 20	1♈04 27	9 04.0	29 53.6	7 09.8	28 50.1	28 59.7	0 03.4	10 34.5	14 34.5	22 55.8	25 19.2
29 Th	20 27 28	6 06 35	7♈24 02	13 38 27	8 58.2	2♌00.1	8 21.6	29 27.8	29 17.9	29♒57.0	10 30.1	14 35.6	22 54.8	25 17.8
30 F	20 31 24	7 03 56	19 48 10	25 53 43	8 54.6	4 06.7	9 33.3	0♍05.4	29 36.0	29 50.4	10 25.6	14 36.6	22 53.8	25 16.4
31 Sa	20 35 21	8 01 18	1♉55 42	7♉54 44	8D 52.9	6 12.9	10 45.1	0 43.1	29 53.9	29 43.7	10 21.2	14 37.6	22 52.7	25 15.0

August 2021

LONGITUDE

Day	Sid.Time	☉	0 hr ☽	Noon ☽	True ☊	☿	♀	♂	⚳	♃	♄	♅	♆	♇
1 Su	20 39 17	8♌58 41	13♉51 29	19♉46 36	8♊52.8	8♌18.7	11♍56.7	1♍20.7	0♊11.7	29♒36.9	10♒16.7	14♉38.6	22♓51.7	25♑13.6
2 M	20 43 14	9 56 06	25 40 47	1♊34 40	8 53.5	10 23.8	13 08.4	1 58.4	0 29.3	29R 30.0	10R 12.2	14 39.5	22R 50.6	25R 12.2
3 Tu	20 47 10	10 53 31	7♊28 55	13 24 10	8R 54.0	12 28.0	14 20.0	2 36.2	0 46.8	29 23.0	10 07.8	14 40.4	22 49.5	25 10.8
4 W	20 51 07	11 50 58	19 20 59	25 19 56	8 53.5	14 31.2	15 31.6	3 13.9	1 04.2	29 15.9	10 03.3	14 41.2	22 48.4	25 09.4
5 Th	20 55 03	12 48 26	1♋21 30	7♋26 07	8 51.1	16 33.2	16 43.1	3 51.7	1 21.4	29 08.7	9 58.8	14 42.0	22 47.2	25 08.1
6 F	20 59 00	13 45 55	13 34 11	19 45 59	8 46.2	18 34.1	17 54.6	4 29.5	1 38.5	29 01.4	9 54.4	14 42.7	22 46.0	25 06.7
7 Sa	21 02 57	14 43 25	26 01 44	2♌21 35	8 38.9	20 33.5	19 06.0	5 07.3	1 55.4	28 54.1	9 49.9	14 43.4	22 44.8	25 05.4
8 Su	21 06 53	15 40 57	8♌45 37	15 13 47	8 29.4	22 31.6	20 17.4	5 45.1	2 12.2	28 46.7	9 45.5	14 44.0	22 43.6	25 04.1
9 M	21 10 50	16 38 29	21 46 02	28 22 10	8 18.4	24 28.3	21 28.8	6 22.9	2 28.8	28 39.2	9 41.1	14 44.6	22 42.4	25 02.7
10 Tu	21 14 46	17 36 02	5♍01 59	11♍45 13	8 07.0	26 23.5	22 40.1	7 00.8	2 45.2	28 31.6	9 36.7	14 45.1	22 41.1	25 01.4
11 W	21 18 43	18 33 37	18 31 34	25 20 44	7 56.3	28 17.2	23 51.3	7 38.7	3 01.5	28 24.0	9 32.3	14 45.6	22 39.8	25 00.1
12 Th	21 22 39	19 31 12	2♎12 24	9♎06 16	7 47.4	0♍09.5	25 02.5	8 16.6	3 17.6	28 16.3	9 27.9	14 46.0	22 38.5	24 58.8
13 F	21 26 36	20 28 48	16 02 05	22 59 35	7 40.9	2 00.2	26 13.7	8 54.6	3 33.6	28 08.6	9 23.6	14 46.3	22 37.2	24 57.6
14 Sa	21 30 32	21 26 25	29 58 34	6♏58 53	7 37.1	3 49.4	27 24.8	9 32.5	3 49.4	28 00.9	9 19.2	14 46.7	22 35.9	24 56.3
15 Su	21 34 29	22 24 03	14♏00 22	21 02 55	7D 35.5	5 37.2	28 35.8	10 10.5	4 05.0	27 53.1	9 14.9	14 46.9	22 34.5	24 55.1
16 M	21 38 26	23 21 42	28 06 26	5♐10 48	7R 35.4	7 23.4	29 46.8	10 48.5	4 20.4	27 45.3	9 10.7	14 47.2	22 33.1	24 53.8
17 Tu	21 42 22	24 19 23	12♐15 53	19 21 31	7 35.4	9 08.2	0♎57.7	11 26.5	4 35.6	27 37.4	9 06.4	14 47.4	22 31.7	24 52.6
18 W	21 46 19	25 17 04	26 27 31	3♑33 36	7 34.4	10 51.6	2 08.6	12 04.5	4 50.7	27 29.6	9 02.2	14 47.5	22 30.3	24 51.4
19 Th	21 50 15	26 14 46	10♑39 26	17 44 39	7 31.2	12 33.5	3 19.4	12 42.6	5 05.6	27 21.7	8 58.1	14 47.6	22 28.9	24 50.2
20 F	21 54 12	27 12 29	24 48 48	1♒51 22	7 25.4	14 13.9	4 30.2	13 20.7	5 20.3	27 13.8	8 54.0	14R 47.6	22 27.4	24 49.1
21 Sa	21 58 08	28 10 14	8♒51 50	15 49 39	7 16.8	15 53.0	5 40.9	13 58.8	5 34.7	27 06.0	8 49.9	14 47.6	22 26.0	24 47.9
22 Su	22 02 05	29 07 59	22 44 17	29 35 14	7 05.9	17 30.6	6 51.5	14 36.9	5 49.0	26 58.1	8 45.8	14 47.5	22 24.5	24 46.8
23 M	22 06 01	0♍05 47	6♓22 03	13♓04 21	6 53.8	19 06.8	8 02.0	15 15.0	6 03.1	26 50.3	8 41.8	14 47.4	22 23.0	24 45.6
24 Tu	22 09 58	1 03 35	19 41 52	26 14 25	6 41.7	20 41.6	9 12.5	15 53.2	6 17.0	26 42.4	8 37.9	14 47.2	22 21.5	24 44.5
25 W	22 13 55	2 01 25	2♈41 55	9♈04 25	6 30.7	22 15.1	10 22.9	16 31.4	6 30.7	26 34.6	8 33.9	14 47.0	22 20.0	24 43.5
26 Th	22 17 51	2 59 17	15 22 03	21 35 05	6 21.7	23 47.2	11 33.3	17 09.6	6 44.2	26 26.8	8 30.1	14 46.7	22 18.5	24 42.4
27 F	22 21 48	3 57 10	27 43 51	3♉48 46	6 15.3	25 17.8	12 43.6	17 47.9	6 57.5	26 19.1	8 26.3	14 46.4	22 16.9	24 41.3
28 Sa	22 25 44	4 55 05	9♉50 20	15 49 07	6 11.5	26 47.1	13 53.8	18 26.1	7 10.6	26 11.3	8 22.5	14 46.0	22 15.4	24 40.3
29 Su	22 29 41	5 53 02	21 45 42	27 40 46	6 09.8	28 15.0	15 04.0	19 04.4	7 23.4	26 03.7	8 18.8	14 45.6	22 13.8	24 39.3
30 M	22 33 37	6 51 01	3♊34 57	9♊28 58	6 09.4	29 41.5	16 14.1	19 42.7	7 36.0	25 56.1	8 15.2	14 45.1	22 12.2	24 38.3
31 Tu	22 37 34	7 49 01	15 23 29	21 19 12	6 09.3	1♎06.6	17 24.1	20 21.1	7 48.4	25 48.5	8 11.6	14 44.6	22 10.6	24 37.4

Astro Data Dy Hr Mn	Planet Ingress Dy Hr Mn	Last Aspect Dy Hr Mn	☽ Ingress Dy Hr Mn	Last Aspect Dy Hr Mn	☽ Ingress Dy Hr Mn	☽ Phases & Eclipses Dy Hr Mn	Astro Data
☊D 1 21:21	☿ ♋ 11 20:36	30 17:41 ♇ ⚹	♈ 1 1:22	2 7:42 ♃ □	♊ 2 8:47	1 21:12 ☾ 10♈14	1 July 2021
☽0N 1 21:46	♀ ♍ 22 0:38	3 4:16 ♇ □	♉ 3 12:29	4 19:39 ♃ △	♋ 4 21:18	10 1:18 ● 18♋02	Julian Day # 44377
☊R 6 22:43	☉ ♌ 22 14:28	5 16:58 ♇ △	♊ 6 1:25	6 22:13 ♇ ☍	♌ 7 7:33	17 10:12 ☽ 25♎04	SVP 4♓57'50"
☽0S 16 8:42	☿ ♌ 28 1:13	8 4:21 ☿ ☌	♋ 8 13:52	9 12:24 ♃ ☍	♍ 9 14:57	24 2:38 ○ 1♒26	GC 27♐08.4 ♀ 27♓15.7
☊D 17 10:02	♃ ♒R 28 12:44	10 16:11 ♇ ☍	♌ 11 0:22	11 11:23 ♇ △	♎ 11 20:09	31 13:17 ☾ 8♉33	Eris 24♈45.3 ✱ 11♐20.3R
☊R 20 13:25	♂ ♍ 29 20:34	12 12:30 ♂ ☌	♍ 13 8:32	13 20:40 ♃ △	♏ 14 0:02		⚷ 12♈50.1 ⚶ 22♍39.5
☽0N 29 5:17	⚳ ♊ 31 8:14	15 6:47 ♇ △	♎ 15 14:33	16 3:06 ♀ ⚹	♐ 16 3:13	8 13:51 ● 16♌14	☽ Mean ☊ 9♊16.3
☊D 31 13:25		17 11:05 ♇ □	♏ 17 18:39	18 1:44 ♃ ⚹	♑ 18 5:59	15 15:21 ☽ 23♏01	
☊R 3 2:54	☿ ♍ 11 21:58	19 16:31 ☉ △	♐ 19 21:09	20 0:00 ♇ ☌	♒ 20 8:50	22 12:03 ○ 29♒37	1 August 2021
☽0S 12 13:25	♀ ♎ 16 4:28	21 22:27 ♀ △	♑ 21 22:37	22 12:03 ☉ ☍	♓ 22 12:44	30 7:14 ☾ 7♊09	Julian Day # 44408
☊D 15 15:09	☉ ♍ 22 21:36	23 16:35 ♇ ☌	♒ 24 0:14	24 9:14 ♇ ⚹	♈ 24 18:58		SVP 4♓57'45"
☊R 16 16:08	☿ ♎ 30 5:11	25 23:15 ♂ ☍	♓ 26 3:31	26 21:16 ♃ ⚹	♉ 27 4:28		GC 27♐08.4 ♀ 26♓50.7R
♀0S 17 11:00		28 1:14 ♇ ⚹	♈ 28 9:59	29 15:00 ☿ △	♊ 29 16:43		Eris 24♈46.8R ✱ 8♐21.1R
♅R 20 1:41		30 19:39 ♃ ⚹	♉ 30 20:09				⚷ 12♈49.0R ⚶ 5♎32.5
☽0N 25 13:17	☿0S29 13:41						☽ Mean ☊ 7♊37.9

*Giving the positions of planets daily at midnight, Greenwich Mean Time (0:00 UT)
Each planet's retrograde period is shaded gray.

2021 Planetary Ephemeris

LONGITUDE — September 2021

Day	Sid.Time	☉	0 hr ☽	Noon ☽	True ☊	☿	♀	♂	⚳	♃	♄	♅	♆	♇
1 W	22 41 30	8♍47 04	27♊16 48	3♋16 55	6♊08.4	2♎30.2	18♎34.1	20♍59.5	8♊00.5	25♒41.0	8♒08.0	14♉44.1	22♓09.1	24♑36.4
2 Th	22 45 27	9 45 08	9♋20 11	15 27 07	6R 05.8	3 52.3	19 44.0	21 37.9	8 12.4	25R 33.6	8R 04.6	14R 43.4	22R 07.5	24R 35.5
3 F	22 49 24	10 43 15	21 38 16	27 54 01	6 00.7	5 12.9	20 53.8	22 16.3	8 24.1	25 26.2	8 01.2	14 42.8	22 05.8	24 34.6
4 Sa	22 53 20	11 41 23	4♌14 43	10♌40 35	5 53.0	6 32.0	22 03.5	22 54.8	8 35.5	25 18.9	7 57.8	14 42.1	22 04.2	24 33.7
5 Su	22 57 17	12 39 33	17 11 45	23 48 13	5 42.9	7 49.5	23 13.2	23 33.2	8 46.7	25 11.7	7 54.6	14 41.3	22 02.6	24 32.8
6 M	23 01 13	13 37 45	0♍29 53	7♍16 30	5 31.2	9 05.3	24 22.8	24 11.8	8 57.6	25 04.6	7 51.4	14 40.5	22 01.0	24 32.0
7 Tu	23 05 10	14 35 58	14 07 43	21 03 05	5 18.9	10 19.4	25 32.3	24 50.3	9 08.3	24 57.6	7 48.2	14 39.7	21 59.3	24 31.2
8 W	23 09 06	15 34 14	28 02 06	5♎04 10	5 07.3	11 31.8	26 41.8	25 28.9	9 18.7	24 50.7	7 45.2	14 38.8	21 57.7	24 30.4
9 Th	23 13 03	16 32 30	12♎08 39	19 14 58	4 57.5	12 42.2	27 51.1	26 07.5	9 28.8	24 43.9	7 42.2	14 37.8	21 56.0	24 29.6
10 F	23 16 59	17 30 49	26 22 29	3♏30 39	4 50.4	13 50.8	29 00.4	26 46.1	9 38.7	24 37.2	7 39.3	14 36.8	21 54.4	24 28.9
11 Sa	23 20 56	18 29 09	10♏38 59	17 47 02	4 46.1	14 57.2	0♏09.6	27 24.7	9 48.2	24 30.6	7 36.5	14 35.8	21 52.7	24 28.2
12 Su	23 24 53	19 27 31	24 54 28	2♐00 59	4D 44.3	16 01.5	1 18.7	28 03.4	9 57.5	24 24.2	7 33.7	14 34.7	21 51.1	24 27.5
13 M	23 28 49	20 25 55	9♐06 23	16 10 29	4R 44.1	17 03.4	2 27.7	28 42.1	10 06.6	24 17.8	7 31.0	14 33.6	21 49.4	24 26.8
14 Tu	23 32 46	21 24 20	23 13 13	0♑14 26	4 44.2	18 02.9	3 36.6	29 20.8	10 15.3	24 11.6	7 28.5	14 32.4	21 47.8	24 26.2
15 W	23 36 42	22 22 46	7♑14 06	14 12 08	4 43.5	18 59.8	4 45.4	29 59.6	10 23.7	24 05.6	7 26.0	14 31.2	21 46.1	24 25.6
16 Th	23 40 39	23 21 15	21 08 25	28 02 49	4 40.7	19 53.8	5 54.1	0♎38.4	10 31.9	23 59.6	7 23.5	14 30.0	21 44.5	24 25.0
17 F	23 44 35	24 19 44	4♒55 13	11♒45 25	4 35.4	20 44.9	7 02.7	1 17.2	10 39.7	23 53.8	7 21.2	14 28.7	21 42.8	24 24.4
18 Sa	23 48 32	25 18 16	18 33 13	25 18 22	4 27.5	21 32.6	8 11.2	1 56.0	10 47.3	23 48.2	7 18.9	14 27.3	21 41.2	24 23.9
19 Su	23 52 28	26 16 49	2♓00 37	8♓39 44	4 17.4	22 16.9	9 19.6	2 34.9	10 54.5	23 42.7	7 16.8	14 25.9	21 39.5	24 23.4
20 M	23 56 25	27 15 24	15 15 29	21 47 39	4 06.1	22 57.5	10 27.9	3 13.8	11 01.4	23 37.3	7 14.7	14 24.5	21 37.9	24 22.9
21 Tu	0 00 22	28 14 00	28 16 03	4♈40 36	3 54.7	23 34.0	11 36.0	3 52.7	11 08.0	23 32.1	7 12.7	14 23.1	21 36.2	24 22.4
22 W	0 04 18	29 12 39	11♈01 13	17 17 56	3 44.3	24 06.1	12 44.0	4 31.6	11 14.3	23 27.1	7 10.8	14 21.6	21 34.6	24 22.0
23 Th	0 08 15	0♎11 19	23 30 48	29 40 01	3 35.8	24 33.5	13 52.0	5 10.6	11 20.3	23 22.2	7 09.0	14 20.0	21 33.0	24 21.6
24 F	0 12 11	1 10 02	5♉45 46	11♉48 24	3 29.7	24 55.8	14 59.7	5 49.6	11 25.9	23 17.5	7 07.3	14 18.4	21 31.3	24 21.2
25 Sa	0 16 08	2 08 47	17 48 15	23 45 47	3 26.1	25 12.6	16 07.4	6 28.7	11 31.3	23 13.0	7 05.6	14 16.8	21 29.7	24 20.8
26 Su	0 20 04	3 07 34	29 41 29	5♊35 53	3D 24.7	25 23.6	17 15.0	7 07.7	11 36.2	23 08.6	7 04.1	14 15.2	21 28.1	24 20.5
27 M	0 24 01	4 06 23	11♊29 34	17 23 11	3 24.9	25R 28.3	18 22.4	7 46.9	11 40.9	23 04.4	7 02.7	14 13.5	21 26.5	24 20.2
28 Tu	0 27 57	5 05 15	23 17 21	29 12 44	3 25.8	25 26.3	19 29.7	8 26.0	11 45.1	23 00.4	7 01.3	14 11.7	21 24.9	24 20.0
29 W	0 31 54	6 04 09	5♋10 03	11♋09 56	3R 26.3	25 17.4	20 36.8	9 05.2	11 49.1	22 56.5	7 00.1	14 10.0	21 23.3	24 19.7
30 Th	0 35 51	7 03 05	17 13 04	23 20 05	3 25.7	25 01.1	21 43.8	9 44.4	11 52.7	22 52.9	6 58.9	14 08.2	21 21.7	24 19.5

LONGITUDE — October 2021

Day	Sid.Time	☉	0 hr ☽	Noon ☽	True ☊	☿	♀	♂	⚳	♃	♄	♅	♆	♇
1 F	0 39 47	8♎02 03	29♋31 36	5♌48 08	3♊23.3	24♎37.3	22♏50.7	10♎23.6	11♊55.9	22♒49.4	6♒57.9	14♉06.3	21♓20.1	24♑19.3
2 Sa	0 43 44	9 01 04	12♌10 10	18 38 05	3R 18.7	24R 05.8	23 57.5	11 02.9	11 58.7	22R 46.1	6R 56.9	14R 04.5	21R 18.6	24R 19.2
3 Su	0 47 40	10 00 06	25 12 10	1♍52 32	3 12.1	23 26.7	25 04.0	11 42.2	12 01.2	22 43.0	6 56.0	14 02.5	21 17.0	24 19.1
4 M	0 51 37	10 59 11	8♍39 13	15 32 05	3 04.1	22 40.2	26 10.5	12 21.5	12 03.3	22 40.0	6 55.3	14 00.6	21 15.5	24 19.0
5 Tu	0 55 33	11 58 19	22 30 49	29 34 59	2 55.4	21 46.9	27 16.8	13 00.9	12 05.1	22 37.3	6 54.6	13 58.6	21 13.9	24 18.9
6 W	0 59 30	12 57 28	6♎44 00	13♎57 08	2 47.2	20 47.3	28 22.9	13 40.3	12 06.4	22 34.8	6 54.0	13 56.6	21 12.4	24D 18.9
7 Th	1 03 26	13 56 39	21 13 36	28 32 30	2 40.3	19 42.7	29 28.8	14 19.7	12 07.4	22 32.4	6 53.6	13 54.6	21 10.9	24 18.9
8 F	1 07 23	14 55 53	5♏52 57	13♏14 03	2 35.4	18 34.3	0♐34.6	14 59.2	12 08.0	22 30.3	6 53.2	13 52.6	21 09.4	24 18.9
9 Sa	1 11 19	15 55 08	20 34 57	27 54 51	2D 32.9	17 23.8	1 40.2	15 38.7	12R 08.2	22 28.3	6 52.9	13 50.5	21 08.0	24 18.9
10 Su	1 15 16	16 54 25	5♐13 04	12♐29 00	2 32.3	16 12.9	2 45.6	16 18.2	12 08.1	22 26.6	6 52.8	13 48.4	21 06.5	24 19.0
11 M	1 19 13	17 53 45	19 42 12	26 52 16	2 33.1	15 03.6	3 50.8	16 57.8	12 07.5	22 25.0	6D 52.7	13 46.2	21 05.1	24 19.1
12 Tu	1 23 09	18 53 06	3♑58 56	11♑02 02	2 34.4	13 57.9	4 55.9	17 37.4	12 06.6	22 23.7	6 52.8	13 44.1	21 03.6	24 19.3
13 W	1 27 06	19 52 28	18 01 29	24 57 13	2R 35.1	12 57.8	6 00.7	18 17.0	12 05.2	22 22.5	6 52.9	13 41.9	21 02.2	24 19.4
14 Th	1 31 02	20 51 53	1♒49 16	8♒37 39	2 34.5	12 04.9	7 05.3	18 56.7	12 03.5	22 21.6	6 53.1	13 39.7	21 00.9	24 19.6
15 F	1 34 59	21 51 19	15 22 26	22 03 41	2 32.2	11 20.6	8 09.7	19 36.4	12 01.4	22 20.8	6 53.5	13 37.4	20 59.5	24 19.9
16 Sa	1 38 55	22 50 46	28 41 29	5♓15 53	2 28.1	10 46.3	9 13.8	20 16.1	11 58.9	22 20.3	6 53.9	13 35.2	20 58.1	24 20.1
17 Su	1 42 52	23 50 16	11♓46 57	18 14 43	2 22.4	10 22.5	10 17.7	20 55.9	11 56.0	22 19.9	6 54.5	13 32.9	20 56.8	24 20.4
18 M	1 46 48	24 49 47	24 39 16	1♈00 37	2 15.9	10D 09.8	11 21.4	21 35.7	11 52.7	22D 19.8	6 55.1	13 30.6	20 55.5	24 20.7
19 Tu	1 50 45	25 49 20	7♈18 49	13 33 57	2 09.3	10 08.3	12 24.8	22 15.5	11 49.0	22 19.8	6 55.9	13 28.3	20 54.2	24 21.1
20 W	1 54 42	26 48 55	19 46 05	25 55 19	2 03.3	10 17.7	13 27.9	22 55.3	11 44.9	22 20.1	6 56.7	13 25.9	20 52.9	24 21.5
21 Th	1 58 38	27 48 32	2♉01 47	8♉05 37	1 58.5	10 37.7	14 30.8	23 35.2	11 40.4	22 20.5	6 57.7	13 23.6	20 51.7	24 21.9
22 F	2 02 35	28 48 12	14 07 01	20 06 14	1 55.2	11 07.7	15 33.4	24 15.2	11 35.6	22 21.2	6 58.7	13 21.2	20 50.4	24 22.3
23 Sa	2 06 31	29 47 53	26 03 32	1♊59 14	1D 53.7	11 46.9	16 35.7	24 55.1	11 30.3	22 22.1	6 59.8	13 18.9	20 49.2	24 22.8
24 Su	2 10 28	0♏47 36	7♊53 42	13 47 21	1 53.7	12 34.5	17 37.7	25 35.1	11 24.7	22 23.1	7 01.1	13 16.5	20 48.1	24 23.3
25 M	2 14 24	1 47 22	19 40 36	25 33 58	1 54.9	13 29.7	18 39.4	26 15.2	11 18.6	22 24.4	7 02.4	13 14.1	20 46.9	24 23.8
26 Tu	2 18 21	2 47 09	1♋27 57	7♋23 07	1 56.6	14 31.7	19 40.7	26 55.2	11 12.2	22 25.8	7 03.9	13 11.6	20 45.8	24 24.3
27 W	2 22 17	3 46 59	13 20 04	19 19 22	1 58.4	15 39.6	20 41.8	27 35.3	11 05.4	22 27.5	7 05.4	13 09.2	20 44.7	24 24.9
28 Th	2 26 14	4 46 51	25 21 40	1♌27 33	1R 59.7	16 52.7	21 42.5	28 15.5	10 58.3	22 29.3	7 07.1	13 06.8	20 43.6	24 25.5
29 F	2 30 11	5 46 46	7♌37 39	13 52 32	2 00.1	18 10.2	22 42.8	28 55.7	10 50.7	22 31.4	7 08.8	13 04.3	20 42.5	24 26.2
30 Sa	2 34 07	6 46 42	20 12 47	26 38 52	1 59.3	19 31.5	23 42.8	29 35.9	10 42.8	22 33.7	7 10.7	13 01.9	20 41.5	24 26.8
31 Su	2 38 04	7 46 40	3♍11 13	9♍50 10	1 57.4	20 56.1	24 42.4	0♏16.2	10 34.5	22 36.1	7 12.6	12 59.4	20 40.5	24 27.5

Astro Data	Dy Hr Mn
☽0S	8 19:42
♃⚺♇	11 10:07
☊D	12 16:35
☊R	13 20:35
♂0S	17 20:33
☽0N	21 21:10
☉0S	22 19:22
☊D	26 7:34
☿R	27 5:11
☊R	29 2:10
☽0S	6 4:40
♇D	6 18:30
⚳R	9 1:32
☊D	9 19:35
♄D	11 2:18

Planet Ingress	Dy Hr Mn
♀ ♏	10 20:40
♂ ♎	15 0:15
☉ ♎	22 19:22
♀ ♐	7 11:22
☉ ♏	23 4:52
♂ ♏	30 14:22
☊ R	13 3:23
♃ D	18 5:31
☿ D	18 15:18
☽ 0N	19 4:18
☊ D	23 11:49
☊ R	28 20:21

Last Aspect Dy Hr Mn		☽ Ingress	Dy Hr Mn
31 20:50	♃ △	♋	1 5:27
3 5:39	♇ ☍	♌	3 15:59
5 14:23	♃ ☍	♍	5 23:07
7 19:25	♂ ☌	♎	8 3:22
10 4:49	♀ ☌	♏	10 6:06
12 5:34	♂ ⚹	♐	12 8:36
14 10:59	♂ □	♑	14 11:35
16 5:41	♇ ☌	♒	16 15:24
18 9:16	♃ ☌	♓	18 20:24
20 23:56	☉ ☍	♈	21 3:14
23 2:06	☿ ☍	♉	23 12:39
25 13:10	♇ △	♊	26 0:38
28 4:19	☿ △	♋	28 13:35

Last Aspect Dy Hr Mn		☽ Ingress	Dy Hr Mn
30 14:50	☿ □	♌	1 0:55
2 23:44	♀ □	♍	3 8:39
5 8:47	♀ ⚹	♎	5 12:42
7 5:04	♇ □	♏	7 14:23
9 6:06	♇ ⚹	♐	9 15:25
11 4:32	♃ ⚹	♑	11 17:16
13 10:54	♇ ☌	♒	13 20:48
15 12:34	☉ △	♓	16 2:23
17 23:25	♇ ⚹	♈	18 10:05
20 14:58	☉ ☍	♉	20 20:00
22 20:36	♇ △	♊	23 7:58
25 14:12	♂ △	♋	25 21:01
28 6:03	♂ □	♌	28 9:08
30 7:06	♀ △	♍	30 18:11

☽ Phases & Eclipses Dy Hr Mn	
7 0:53	● 14♍38
13 20:41	☽ 21♐16
20 23:56	○ 28♓14
29 1:58	☾ 6♋09
6 11:07	● 13♎25
13 3:26	☽ 20♑01
20 14:58	○ 27♈26
28 20:06	☾ 5♌37

Astro Data

1 September 2021
Julian Day # 44439
SVP 4♓57'41"
GC 27♐08.5 ⚴ 21♓09.4R
Eris 24♈38.7R ⚵ 10♐31.3
⚷ 12♈01.4R ⚶ 20♎07.9
☽ Mean ☊ 5♊59.4

1 October 2021
Julian Day # 44469
SVP 4♓57'37"
GC 27♐08.6 ⚴ 13♓34.4R
Eris 24♈23.7R ⚵ 16♐31.0
⚷ 10♈46.4R ⚶ 5♏17.3
☽ Mean ☊ 4♊24.0

*Giving the positions of planets daily at midnight, Greenwich Mean Time (0:00 UT)
Each planet's retrograde period is shaded gray.

2021 Planetary Ephemeris

November 2021

LONGITUDE

Day	Sid.Time	☉	0 hr ☽	Noon ☽	True ☊	☿	♀	♂	⚳	♃	♄	♅	♆	♇
1 M	2 42 00	8♏46 41	16♍35 56	23♍28 36	1♊54.7	22♎23.3	25♐41.7	0♏56.5	10♊25.9	22♒38.7	7♒14.6	12♉56.9	20♓39.5	24♑28.3
2 Tu	2 45 57	9 46 44	0♎28 05	7♎34 09	1R 51.5	23 52.7	26 40.5	1 36.8	10R 16.9	22 41.6	7 16.8	12R 54.5	20R 38.5	24 29.0
3 W	2 49 53	10 46 49	14 46 23	22 04 12	1 48.4	25 24.0	27 38.9	2 17.2	10 07.6	22 44.6	7 19.0	12 52.0	20 37.6	24 29.8
4 Th	2 53 50	11 46 56	29 26 51	6♏53 26	1 45.8	26 56.8	28 36.9	2 57.6	9 57.9	22 47.8	7 21.3	12 49.5	20 36.7	24 30.6
5 F	2 57 46	12 47 04	14♏22 57	21 54 18	1 44.1	28 30.7	29 34.4	3 38.0	9 47.9	22 51.3	7 23.8	12 47.0	20 35.8	24 31.4
6 Sa	3 01 43	13 47 15	29 26 23	6♐58 03	1D 43.5	0♏05.6	0♑31.4	4 18.5	9 37.6	22 54.9	7 26.3	12 44.5	20 35.0	24 32.3
7 Su	3 05 40	14 47 27	14♐28 14	21 55 58	1 43.8	1 41.1	1 28.0	4 59.0	9 27.0	22 58.7	7 28.9	12 42.1	20 34.2	24 33.2
8 M	3 09 36	15 47 42	29 20 22	6♑40 42	1 44.7	3 17.2	2 24.1	5 39.6	9 16.0	23 02.7	7 31.6	12 39.6	20 33.4	24 34.1
9 Tu	3 13 33	16 47 57	13♑56 22	21 06 56	1 45.9	4 53.7	3 19.6	6 20.2	9 04.8	23 06.9	7 34.4	12 37.1	20 32.7	24 35.1
10 W	3 17 29	17 48 14	28 12 05	5♒11 41	1 46.9	6 30.5	4 14.5	7 00.8	8 53.3	23 11.2	7 37.3	12 34.7	20 31.9	24 36.0
11 Th	3 21 26	18 48 33	12♒05 40	18 54 06	1R 47.5	8 07.3	5 08.9	7 41.5	8 41.6	23 15.8	7 40.3	12 32.2	20 31.2	24 37.0
12 F	3 25 22	19 48 53	25 37 08	2♓14 57	1 47.6	9 44.3	6 02.7	8 22.2	8 29.6	23 20.5	7 43.4	12 29.7	20 30.6	24 38.1
13 Sa	3 29 19	20 49 14	8♓47 50	15 16 04	1 47.0	11 21.2	6 55.8	9 02.9	8 17.3	23 25.4	7 46.5	12 27.3	20 29.9	24 39.1
14 Su	3 33 15	21 49 36	21 39 58	27 59 50	1 46.0	12 58.1	7 48.3	9 43.7	8 04.9	23 30.5	7 49.8	12 24.8	20 29.3	24 40.2
15 M	3 37 12	22 50 00	4♈16 00	10♈28 48	1 44.8	14 34.9	8 40.1	10 24.5	7 52.2	23 35.8	7 53.1	12 22.4	20 28.8	24 41.3
16 Tu	3 41 09	23 50 26	16 38 31	22 45 28	1 43.6	16 11.5	9 31.2	11 05.3	7 39.3	23 41.3	7 56.6	12 20.0	20 28.2	24 42.4
17 W	3 45 05	24 50 52	28 49 56	4♉52 10	1 42.6	17 48.0	10 21.5	11 46.2	7 26.2	23 46.9	8 00.1	12 17.6	20 27.7	24 43.6
18 Th	3 49 02	25 51 21	10♉52 26	16 51 01	1 41.9	19 24.3	11 11.1	12 27.1	7 13.0	23 52.7	8 03.7	12 15.2	20 27.3	24 44.7
19 F	3 52 58	26 51 50	22 48 08	28 44 02	1D 41.5	21 00.4	11 59.8	13 08.1	6 59.6	23 58.6	8 07.4	12 12.8	20 26.8	24 45.9
20 Sa	3 56 55	27 52 22	4♊38 59	10♊33 15	1 41.5	22 36.3	12 47.8	13 49.0	6 46.1	24 04.8	8 11.2	12 10.5	20 26.4	24 47.2
21 Su	4 00 51	28 52 55	16 27 05	22 20 48	1 41.6	24 12.1	13 34.8	14 30.1	6 32.4	24 11.1	8 15.0	12 08.1	20 26.0	24 48.4
22 M	4 04 48	29 53 29	28 14 42	4♋09 07	1 41.8	25 47.6	14 21.0	15 11.1	6 18.6	24 17.6	8 19.0	12 05.8	20 25.7	24 49.7
23 Tu	4 08 44	0♐54 05	10♋04 24	16 00 57	1R 41.9	27 23.0	15 06.2	15 52.3	6 04.8	24 24.2	8 23.0	12 03.5	20 25.4	24 51.0
24 W	4 12 41	1 54 43	21 59 11	27 59 31	1 42.0	28 58.1	15 50.4	16 33.4	5 50.8	24 31.0	8 27.1	12 01.2	20 25.1	24 52.3
25 Th	4 16 38	2 55 22	4♌02 26	10♌08 24	1 41.9	0♐33.1	16 33.6	17 14.6	5 36.8	24 37.9	8 31.3	11 58.9	20 24.9	24 53.7
26 F	4 20 34	3 56 03	16 17 55	22 31 31	1 41.7	2 08.0	17 15.7	17 55.8	5 22.7	24 45.1	8 35.6	11 56.6	20 24.7	24 55.0
27 Sa	4 24 31	4 56 45	28 49 40	5♍12 53	1D 41.6	3 42.7	17 56.7	18 37.1	5 08.6	24 52.3	8 39.9	11 54.4	20 24.5	24 56.4
28 Su	4 28 27	5 57 29	11♍41 36	18 16 17	1 41.6	5 17.2	18 36.6	19 18.4	4 54.5	24 59.8	8 44.4	11 52.2	20 24.4	24 57.8
29 M	4 32 24	6 58 15	24 57 15	1♎44 48	1 41.8	6 51.7	19 15.3	19 59.7	4 40.4	25 07.4	8 48.9	11 50.0	20 24.3	24 59.3
30 Tu	4 36 20	7 59 02	8♎39 05	15 40 09	1 42.3	8 26.0	19 52.8	20 41.1	4 26.3	25 15.1	8 53.5	11 47.9	20 24.2	25 00.7

December 2021

LONGITUDE

Day	Sid.Time	☉	0 hr ☽	Noon ☽	True ☊	☿	♀	♂	⚳	♃	♄	♅	♆	♇
1 W	4 40 17	8♐59 50	22♎47 55	0♏02 05	1♊43.0	10♐00.3	20♑28.9	21♏22.6	4♊12.3	25♒23.0	8♒58.1	11♉45.7	20♓24.2	25♑02.2
2 Th	4 44 13	10 00 40	7♏22 13	14 47 42	1 43.6	11 34.5	21 03.7	22 04.0	3R 58.3	25 31.0	9 02.8	11R 43.6	20D 24.1	25 03.7
3 F	4 48 10	11 01 32	22 17 42	29 51 16	1R 44.1	13 08.6	21 37.1	22 45.5	3 44.3	25 39.2	9 07.6	11 41.5	20 24.2	25 05.2
4 Sa	4 52 07	12 02 24	7♐27 18	15♐04 34	1 44.2	14 42.7	22 09.1	23 27.1	3 30.5	25 47.6	9 12.5	11 39.5	20 24.3	25 06.7
5 Su	4 56 03	13 03 18	22 41 50	0♑17 50	1 43.7	16 16.8	22 39.5	24 08.7	3 16.8	25 56.1	9 17.5	11 37.5	20 24.4	25 08.3
6 M	5 00 00	14 04 13	7♑51 20	15 21 13	1 42.5	17 50.8	23 08.4	24 50.3	3 03.2	26 04.7	9 22.5	11 35.5	20 24.5	25 09.9
7 Tu	5 03 56	15 05 09	22 46 29	0♒06 18	1 40.9	19 24.9	23 35.6	25 32.0	2 49.7	26 13.5	9 27.6	11 33.5	20 24.7	25 11.4
8 W	5 07 53	16 06 06	7♒20 01	14 27 10	1 39.1	20 59.0	24 01.1	26 13.7	2 36.4	26 22.4	9 32.8	11 31.6	20 24.9	25 13.1
9 Th	5 11 49	17 07 03	21 27 30	28 20 54	1 37.4	22 33.0	24 24.8	26 55.4	2 23.3	26 31.4	9 38.0	11 29.7	20 25.1	25 14.7
10 F	5 15 46	18 08 01	5♓07 25	11♓47 15	1 36.2	24 07.2	24 46.6	27 37.2	2 10.4	26 40.6	9 43.3	11 27.9	20 25.4	25 16.3
11 Sa	5 19 43	19 09 00	18 20 42	24 48 09	1D 35.8	25 41.3	25 06.6	28 19.0	1 57.6	26 49.9	9 48.6	11 26.0	20 25.7	25 18.0
12 Su	5 23 39	20 09 59	1♈10 04	7♈26 55	1 36.1	27 15.5	25 24.5	29 00.8	1 45.1	26 59.3	9 54.0	11 24.3	20 26.1	25 19.7
13 M	5 27 36	21 10 58	13 39 15	19 47 35	1 37.2	28 49.7	25 40.4	29 42.7	1 32.8	27 08.9	9 59.5	11 22.5	20 26.4	25 21.4
14 Tu	5 31 32	22 11 58	25 52 27	1♉54 23	1 38.8	0♑24.0	25 54.2	0♐24.6	1 20.8	27 18.6	10 05.1	11 20.8	20 26.9	25 23.1
15 W	5 35 29	23 12 59	7♉53 52	13 51 24	1 40.5	1 58.4	26 05.8	1 06.6	1 09.0	27 28.4	10 10.7	11 19.1	20 27.3	25 24.8
16 Th	5 39 25	24 14 00	19 47 24	25 42 17	1 41.9	3 32.7	26 15.1	1 48.6	0 57.5	27 38.4	10 16.3	11 17.5	20 27.8	25 26.5
17 F	5 43 22	25 15 02	1♊36 27	7♊30 15	1R 42.4	5 07.1	26 22.2	2 30.6	0 46.2	27 48.4	10 22.1	11 15.9	20 28.3	25 28.3
18 Sa	5 47 18	26 16 05	13 23 59	19 17 58	1 41.8	6 41.5	26 26.9	3 12.7	0 35.3	27 58.6	10 27.8	11 14.3	20 28.9	25 30.1
19 Su	5 51 15	27 17 08	25 12 27	1♋07 42	1 39.8	8 15.9	26R 29.2	3 54.8	0 24.7	28 08.9	10 33.7	11 12.8	20 29.5	25 31.8
20 M	5 55 12	28 18 11	7♋03 56	13 01 22	1 36.5	9 50.3	26 29.0	4 37.0	0 14.3	28 19.3	10 39.6	11 11.4	20 30.1	25 33.6
21 Tu	5 59 08	29 19 16	19 00 15	25 00 46	1 32.0	11 24.6	26 26.4	5 19.1	0 04.3	28 29.9	10 45.5	11 09.9	20 30.7	25 35.5
22 W	6 03 05	0♑20 21	1♌03 11	7♌07 42	1 26.8	12 58.7	26 21.3	6 01.4	29♉54.7	28 40.5	10 51.5	11 08.6	20 31.4	25 37.3
23 Th	6 07 01	1 21 26	13 14 35	19 24 07	1 21.4	14 32.7	26 13.7	6 43.7	29 45.3	28 51.3	10 57.6	11 07.2	20 32.2	25 39.1
24 F	6 10 58	2 22 32	25 36 35	1♍52 17	1 16.5	16 06.4	26 03.6	7 26.0	29 36.4	29 02.1	11 03.7	11 05.9	20 32.9	25 41.0
25 Sa	6 14 54	3 23 39	8♍11 35	14 34 47	1 12.6	17 39.7	25 51.0	8 08.3	29 27.7	29 13.1	11 09.8	11 04.7	20 33.7	25 42.8
26 Su	6 18 51	4 24 46	21 02 17	27 34 24	1 10.1	19 12.6	25 35.9	8 50.7	29 19.5	29 24.2	11 16.0	11 03.4	20 34.5	25 44.7
27 M	6 22 47	5 25 54	4♎11 30	10♎53 53	1D 09.2	20 44.9	25 18.5	9 33.1	29 11.6	29 35.3	11 22.3	11 02.3	20 35.4	25 46.6
28 Tu	6 26 44	6 27 02	17 41 51	24 35 36	1 09.6	22 16.4	24 58.6	10 15.6	29 04.0	29 46.6	11 28.5	11 01.2	20 36.3	25 48.4
29 W	6 30 41	7 28 11	1♏35 15	8♏40 50	1 11.0	23 47.0	24 36.6	10 58.1	28 56.9	29 58.0	11 34.9	11 00.1	20 37.2	25 50.3
30 Th	6 34 37	8 29 21	15 52 13	23 09 10	1 12.5	25 16.5	24 12.3	11 40.7	28 50.2	0♓09.5	11 41.3	10 59.1	20 38.1	25 52.2
31 F	6 38 34	9 30 31	0♐31 13	7♐57 47	1R 13.2	26 44.5	23 46.0	12 23.3	28 43.8	0 21.1	11 47.7	10 58.1	20 39.1	25 54.2

Astro Data Dy Hr Mn	Planet Ingress Dy Hr Mn
☽0S 2 15:28	♀ ♑ 5 10:45
☊D 6 3:36	☿ ♏ 5 22:36
☊R 11 12:47	☉ ♐ 22 2:35
☽0N 15 10:28	☿ ♐ 24 15:38
☊D 19 17:54	
☊R 23 19:49	♂ ♐ 13 9:54
☊D 27 12:32	☿ ♑ 13 17:53
♃⚺♇ 27 16:17	⚳ ♉R 21 10:40
☽0S 30 1:49	☉ ♑ 21 16:00
♆D 1 13:23	♃ ♓ 29 4:11
☊R 3 15:05	
☊D 11 1:29	♄□□24 7:18
☽0N 12 16:16	☊D27 2:35
☊R 17 0:14	☽0S27 9:30
♀R 19 10:37	☊R31 1:10

Last Aspect Dy Hr Mn		☽ Ingress Dy Hr Mn
1 17:01	♀ □	♎ 1 23:12
3 22:33	♀ ⚹	♏ 4 0:54
5 16:11	♇ ⚹	♐ 6 0:54
7 13:45	♃ ⚹	♑ 8 1:05
9 17:53	♇ ☌	♒ 10 3:04
11 19:53	♃ ☌	♓ 12 7:55
14 5:41	♇ ⚹	♈ 14 15:49
16 15:52	♇ □	♉ 17 2:19
19 8:59	☉ ☍	♊ 19 14:34
21 15:53	♃ △	♋ 22 3:34
24 5:47	♇ ☍	♌ 24 16:00
26 16:25	♃ ☍	♍ 27 2:13
29 0:04	♇ △	♎ 29 8:56

Last Aspect Dy Hr Mn		☽ Ingress Dy Hr Mn
1 4:21	♃ △	♏ 1 11:57
3 5:23	♃ □	♐ 3 12:14
5 5:09	♃ ⚹	♑ 5 11:32
7 4:43	♂ ⚹	♒ 7 11:50
9 10:01	♂ □	♓ 9 14:54
11 19:41	♂ △	♈ 11 21:47
14 2:53	♃ ⚹	♉ 14 8:12
16 16:10	♃ □	♊ 16 20:44
19 6:03	♃ △	♋ 19 9:43
21 14:45	♀ ☍	♌ 21 21:55
24 6:41	♃ ☍	♍ 24 8:25
26 8:41	♇ △	♎ 26 16:25
28 21:12	♃ △	♏ 28 21:17
30 17:11	☿ ⚹	♐ 30 23:09

☽ Phases & Eclipses Dy Hr Mn	
4 21:16	● 12♏40
11 12:47	☽ 19♒21
19 8:59	○ 27♉14
19 9:04	◐ P 0.974
27 12:29	☾ 5♍28
4 7:44	● 12♐22
4 7:34:36	● T 01'55"
11 1:37	☽ 19♓13
19 4:37	○ 27♊29
27 2:25	☾ 5♎32

Astro Data

1 November 2021
Julian Day # 44500
SVP 4♓57'34"
GC 27♐08.7 ⚵ 9♓13.6R
Eris 24♈05.4R ⚴ 25♐24.6
⚷ 9♈26.5R ⚶ 21♏37.6
☽ Mean ☊ 2♊45.5

1 December 2021
Julian Day # 44530
SVP 4♓57'29"
GC 27♐08.7 ⚵ 10♓31.4
Eris 23♈50.1R ⚴ 5♑41.9
⚷ 8♈35.7R ⚶ 7♐47.1
☽ Mean ☊ 1♊10.2

*Giving the positions of planets daily at midnight, Greenwich Mean Time (0:00 UT)
Each planet's retrograde period is shaded gray.

2021 ASTEROID EPHEMERIS

2021	Ceres ⚳	Pallas ⚴	Juno ⚵	Vesta ⚶
JAN 1	11♓59.5	7♒51.1	4♐14.9	20♍08.6
11	15 11.3	11 11.0	7 19.3	21 07.6
21	18 34.3	14 33.4	10 15.3	21R23.1
31	22 06.5	17 57.0	13 00.8	20 51.8
FEB 10	25 46.2	21 20.6	15 34.0	19 33.5
20	29 31.9	24 43.2	17 52.4	17 33.8
MAR 2	3♈22.3	28 03.5	19 53.3	15 06.2
12	7 16.3	1♓20.7	21 33.9	12 29.6
22	11 12.8	4 33.6	22 50.9	10 05.4
APR 1	15 10.8	7 40.9	23 41.2	8 12.6
11	19 09.6	10 41.6	24 01.8	7 02.9
21	23 08.2	13 34.0	23R50.0	6D41.8
MAY 1	27 05.8	16 16.7	23 05.0	7 08.6
11	1♉01.8	18 48.1	21 47.9	8 19.4
21	4 55.2	21 06.0	20 02.6	10 09.4
31	8 45.3	23 08.0	17 57.1	12 32.8
JUN 10	12 31.2	24 51.7	15 41.8	15 24.6
20	16 11.9	26 13.9	13 29.1	18 40.6
30	19 46.1	27 11.4	11 31.1	22 16.9
JUL 10	23 12.6	27 40.7	9 56.9	26 10.3
20	26 29.8	27R38.4	8 53.3	0♎18.5
30	29 35.9	27 02.2	8 23.1	4 39.0
AUG 9	2♊28.8	25 50.9	8D26.4	9 10.4
19	5 05.6	24 06.1	9 01.8	13 51.1
29	7 23.4	21 53.5	10 06.6	18 39.8
SEP 8	9 18.7	19 22.1	11 37.7	23 35.5
18	10 47.3	16 44.8	13 32.2	28 37.3
28	11 45.2	14 15.7	15 47.0	3♏44.2
OCT 8	12 08.1	12 07.3	18 19.5	8 55.8
18	11R52.8	10 29.6	21 07.5	14 11.1
28	10 58.4	9 27.8	24 08.8	19 29.5
NOV 7	9 27.1	9 03.8	27 21.6	24 50.4
17	7 26.4	9D16.7	0♑44.3	0♐13.2
27	5 08.8	10 03.8	4 15.3	5 37.2
DEC 7	2 49.9	11 21.6	7 53.6	11 01.8
17	0 46.4	13 06.7	11 37.8	16 26.4
27	29♉11.7	15 15.3	15 26.8	21 50.1
JAN 6	28♉14.3	17♓44.5	19♑19.9	27♐12.5

2021	Ceres	Pallas	Juno	Vesta
JAN 1	15S43.3	00S31.4	11S33.3	09N42.5
21	12 29.0	00 15.6	11 45.4	10 37.3
FEB 10	09 05.9	00N31.4	11 27.1	12 47.7
MAR 2	05 39.6	01 42.2	10 39.8	15 38.4
22	02 15.3	03 08.8	09 27.2	17 54.3
APR 11	01N01.7	04 42.7	07 56.6	18 37.6
MAY 1	04 06.6	06 15.0	06 20.4	17 46.0
21	06 55.1	07 35.5	04 57.3	15 43.5
JUN 10	09 23.3	08 31.9	04 09.6	12 52.0
30	11 28.3	08 48.8	04 12.5	09 26.3
JUL 20	13 08.5	08 06.9	05 04.3	05 37.3
AUG 9	14 23.4	06 06.7	06 30.5	01 34.0
29	15 15.1	02 41.2	08 13.3	02S34.8
SEP 18	15 47.7	01S42.9	09 58.0	06 40.2
OCT 8	16 07.5	06 04.4	11 32.9	10 32.7
28	16 21.8	09 26.6	12 49.6	14 02.7
NOV 17	16 36.8	11 28.2	13 41.8	17 00.8
DEC 7	16 58.2	12 15.6	14 04.9	19 18.3
27	17N35.0	12S04.3	13S56.4	20S49.1

2021	Psyche	Eros	Lilith	Toro
JAN 1	11R30.5	8♏19.6	27♑37.2	21♎42.9
11	10♊24.2	16 13.6	1♒44.7	25 29.5
21	9 57.0	23 46.7	5 56.4	28 26.5
31	10D09.5	0♐56.9	10 11.3	0♏25.8
FEB 10	10 59.1	7 42.9	14 28.8	1 17.4
20	12 22.1	14 01.7	18 47.9	0R49.1
MAR 2	14 13.7	19 51.1	23 07.9	28♎52.3
12	16 29.6	25 07.9	27 28.2	25 25.9
22	19 05.9	29 47.2	1♓48.0	20 45.2
APR 1	21 58.8	3♑43.8	6 06.3	15 27.4
11	25 05.3	6 50.8	10 22.6	10 20.5
21	28 23.1	8 58.6	14 35.8	6 07.0
MAY 1	1♋49.8	9 57.6	18 45.0	3 10.1
11	5 23.6	9R37.6	22 49.1	1 32.8
21	9 03.2	7 52.3	26 46.8	1D08.0
31	12 47.0	4 47.1	0♈36.4	1 44.0
JUN 10	16 34.0	0 42.8	4 16.4	3 09.0
20	20 23.4	26♐17.9	7 44.2	5 13.5
30	24 14.1	22 17.3	10 57.3	7 49.5
JUL 10	28 05.5	19 14.0	13 52.5	10 50.8
20	1♌56.7	17 24.8	16 25.8	14 13.3
30	5 47.1	16D50.2	18 32.7	17 53.2
AUG 9	9 35.9	17 21.8	20 08.2	21 48.1
19	13 22.5	18 49.9	21 06.6	25 56.3
29	17 05.8	21 03.7	21R23.5	0♏16.2
SEP 8	20 45.2	23 54.6	20 55.6	4 47.0
18	24 19.6	27 16.0	19 43.7	9 28.3
28	27 47.7	1♑02.2	17 55.0	14 19.4
OCT 8	1♍08.5	5 09.2	15 42.9	19 20.5
18	4 20.1	9 34.0	13 27.4	24 31.8
28	7 20.9	14 13.8	11 29.4	29 53.3
NOV 7	10 08.9	19 07.0	10 06.0	5♐26.0
17	12 41.4	24 12.4	9 28.7	11 10.3
27	14 55.9	29 28.6	9D41.2	17 07.4
DEC 7	16 49.2	4♒55.0	10 42.1	23 18.7
17	18 17.8	10 31.1	12 27.4	29 45.7
27	19 18.3	16 16.3	14 51.4	6♑30.2
JAN 6	19♍47.4	22♒10.6	17♈48.2	13♑34.9

2021	Psyche	Eros	Lilith	Toro
JAN 1	17N52.9	21S20.6	17S50.9	17S35.2
21	18 11.4	28 07.3	15 52.4	22 35.6
FEB 10	18 52.3	33 07.6	13 25.7	26 24.6
MAR 2	19 45.4	36 28.7	10 34.2	28 19.8
22	20 37.8	38 34.3	07 23.0	26 58.7
APR 11	21 18.5	39 58.3	03 57.7	22 13.5
MAY 1	21 39.3	41 10.3	00 24.6	16 48.6
21	21 35.2	42 02.2	03N09.7	13 05.7
JUN 10	21 04.0	41 07.9	06 37.9	11 25.8
30	20 05.7	37 18.3	09 52.0	11 21.0
JUL 20	18 42.5	32 24.5	12 42.3	12 21.2
AUG 9	16 58.2	28 32.8	14 55.3	14 03.1
29	14 57.8	25 58.1	16 12.0	16 08.6
SEP 18	12 47.2	24 08.0	16 09.0	18 22.6
OCT 8	10 33.8	22 29.4	14 37.3	20 31.3
28	08 25.8	20 37.9	12 14.7	22 20.2
NOV 17	06 32.9	18 17.7	10 14.0	23 33.5
DEC 7	05 06.6	15 19.6	09 24.2	23 53.6
27	04N19.4	11S40.0	09N51.0	23S00.8

2021	Saffo	Amor	Pandora	Icarus
JAN 1	17♐01.8	1♓56.2	28♍22.7	27♐42.7
11	21 48.4	5 44.3	29 06.5	5♑26.7
21	26 35.4	9 36.0	29R15.9	12 05.0
31	1♑22.2	13 30.3	28 49.3	17 57.1
FEB 10	6 08.2	17 26.2	27 47.1	23 14.6
20	10 52.4	21 22.9	26 12.5	28 04.2
MAR 2	15 34.0	25 19.6	24 13.6	2♒29.9
12	20 12.1	29 15.7	22 01.3	6 34.5
22	24 45.3	3♈10.5	19 48.9	10 18.5
APR 1	29 12.3	7 03.4	17 49.8	13 41.9
11	3♒31.5	10 53.8	16 14.5	16 43.6
21	7 40.7	14 41.0	15 09.9	19 20.9
MAY 1	11 37.4	18 24.4	14 39.3	21 30.1
11	15 18.8	22 03.3	14D42.5	23 05.9
21	18 40.6	25 37.0	15 17.6	24 00.2
31	21 38.5	29 04.4	16 21.6	24R03.0
JUN 10	24 06.9	2♉24.6	17 51.0	23 01.0
20	25 59.1	5 36.3	19 42.7	20 38.2
30	27 08.7	8 37.9	21 53.3	16 40.0
JUL 10	27R29.3	11 27.8	24 20.1	11 00.1
20	26 57.5	14 03.4	27 00.8	3 54.1
30	25 36.1	16 22.2	29 53.1	26♑07.9
AUG 9	23 35.5	18 20.8	2♎55.4	18 45.0
19	21 16.5	19 55.0	6 06.1	12 39.6
29	19 05.5	21 00.2	9 23.8	8 16.1
SEP 8	17 26.7	21 31.3	12 47.4	5 33.5
18	16 38.1	21R22.5	16 15.7	4 19.1
28	16D47.1	20 29.6	19 47.8	4D16.6
OCT 8	17 53.3	18 50.1	23 22.8	5 12.2
18	19 52.3	16 26.1	26 59.7	6 55.3
28	22 36.7	13 26.8	0♏37.5	9 17.4
NOV 7	25 59.1	10 08.1	4 15.4	12 13.4
17	29 53.2	6 51.4	7 52.4	15 39.8
27	4♓12.7	3 58.1	11 27.4	19 34.4
DEC 7	8 52.8	1 44.5	14 59.3	23 57.0
17	13 49.5	0 20.5	18 26.7	28 47.0
27	18 59.1	29♈48.3	21 48.3	4♒00.8
JAN 6	24♓18.8	0D05.9	25♏02.6	9♒16.5

2021	Saffo	Amor	Pandora	Icarus
JAN 1	19S46.6	10S27.9	04N28.3	19S58.9
21	19 43.6	08 14.4	04 06.1	21 51.6
FEB 10	18 54.9	05 44.6	04 33.8	22 20.3
MAR 2	17 20.5	03 06.1	05 39.7	22 12.3
22	15 03.5	00 26.3	06 52.8	21 56.8
APR 11	12 10.0	02N08.4	07 37.7	21 58.3
MAY 1	08 48.7	04 31.8	07 35.3	22 44.2
21	05 11.9	06 38.1	06 45.9	24 50.3
JUN 10	01 37.4	08 21.6	05 17.2	29 02.8
30	01N27.1	09 36.6	03 18.1	35 54.3
JUL 20	03 20.2	10 17.1	00 56.0	43 54.3
AUG 9	03 17.0	10 16.8	01S42.8	48 16.1
29	01 12.7	09 28.5	04 32.8	47 24.5
SEP 18	01S46.0	07 46.4	07 29.0	44 41.4
OCT 8	04 15.6	05 12.2	10 26.3	42 07.0
28	05 31.3	02 09.8	13 20.1	39 53.5
NOV 17	05 24.4	00S25.7	16 05.9	37 39.5
DEC 7	04 03.1	01 39.1	18 39.8	34 51.9
27	01S43.0	01S17.8	20S58.7	30S31.8

2021	Diana	Hidalgo	Urania	Chiron ⚷
JAN 1	17♐25.8	8♏36.1	1♐06.5	5♈03.6
11	21 20.2	9 30.6	5 01.4	5 15.0
21	25 07.3	10 11.2	8 48.8	5 31.5
31	28 45.8	10 36.3	12 27.0	5 52.6
FEB 10	2♑14.5	10 45.0	15 54.2	6 17.7
20	5 31.5	10R36.3	19 08.1	6 46.3
MAR 2	8 34.9	10 10.2	22 06.0	7 17.6
12	11 22.7	9 27.3	24 45.1	7 51.0
22	13 52.4	8 29.1	27 01.8	8 25.6
APR 1	16 01.2	7 18.2	28 52.1	9 00.8
11	17 46.2	5 58.1	0♑11.9	9 35.8
21	19 03.9	4 33.0	0 56.5	10 09.8
MAY 1	19 51.3	3 07.4	1R02.3	10 42.3
11	20R05.5	1 45.9	0 26.7	11 12.5
21	19 44.3	0 32.5	29♐10.1	11 39.7
31	18 47.9	29♎30.5	27 17.8	12 03.5
JUN 10	17 18.9	28 42.1	24 59.7	12 23.4
20	15 23.6	28 08.7	22 31.3	12 38.8
30	13 12.0	27 51.0	20 10.1	12 49.4
JUL 10	10 56.2	27D48.6	18 12.0	12 54.9
20	8 49.6	28 01.0	16 49.1	12R55.3
30	7 03.4	28 27.1	16 08.0	12 50.6
AUG 9	5 45.5	29 05.6	16D09.8	12 40.8
19	5 00.7	29 55.2	16 53.5	12 26.3
29	4D50.0	0♏54.5	18 15.1	12 07.7
SEP 8	5 12.2	2 02.1	20 10.4	11 45.7
18	6 05.0	3 16.6	22 35.5	11 20.9
28	7 25.1	4 36.6	25 26.0	10 54.5
OCT 8	9 09.2	6 00.8	28 38.5	10 27.4
18	11 14.3	7 27.9	2♑10.3	10 00.8
28	13 37.2	8 56.4	5 58.4	9 35.9
NOV 7	16 15.3	10 25.0	10 00.8	9 13.5
17	19 06.5	11 52.5	14 15.7	8 54.7
27	22 08.5	13 17.4	18 41.4	8 40.2
DEC 7	25 19.6	14 38.3	23 16.5	8 30.6
17	28 38.2	15 53.7	27 59.9	8 26.4
27	2♒02.7	17 02.3	2♒50.3	8D27.7
JAN 6	5♒31.9	18♏02.5	7♒46.9	8♈34.4

2021	Diana	Hidalgo	Urania	Chiron
JAN 1	29S25.6	21S16.8	21S59.4	04N20.8
21	30 10.4	22 45.1	23 28.2	04 28.3
FEB 10	30 32.8	23 59.0	24 30.1	04 43.5
MAR 2	30 40.0	24 53.5	25 08.5	05 04.7
22	30 41.5	25 23.1	25 29.7	05 29.8
APR 11	30 47.8	25 24.9	25 41.6	05 56.4
MAY 1	31 08.6	25 02.4	25 50.9	06 22.2
21	31 47.0	24 26.2	25 56.9	06 45.0
JUN 10	32 32.0	23 50.5	25 48.4	07 02.8
30	32 57.9	23 27.0	25 17.9	07 14.0
JUL 20	32 42.5	23 22.4	24 38.3	07 17.4
AUG 9	31 49.7	23 38.7	24 10.6	07 12.7
29	30 40.7	24 14.6	24 01.2	07 00.3
SEP 18	29 30.4	25 07.4	24 01.7	06 41.7
OCT 8	28 21.7	26 13.9	23 58.5	06 19.7
28	27 10.1	27 30.6	23 38.0	05 57.5
NOV 17	25 49.5	28 54.5	22 49.1	05 38.5
DEC 7	24 15.1	30 22.8	21 24.6	05 25.9
27	22S24.0	31S52.7	19S21.3	05N21.3

Giving the positions of asteroids every ten days in LONGITUDE at 00:00 GMT

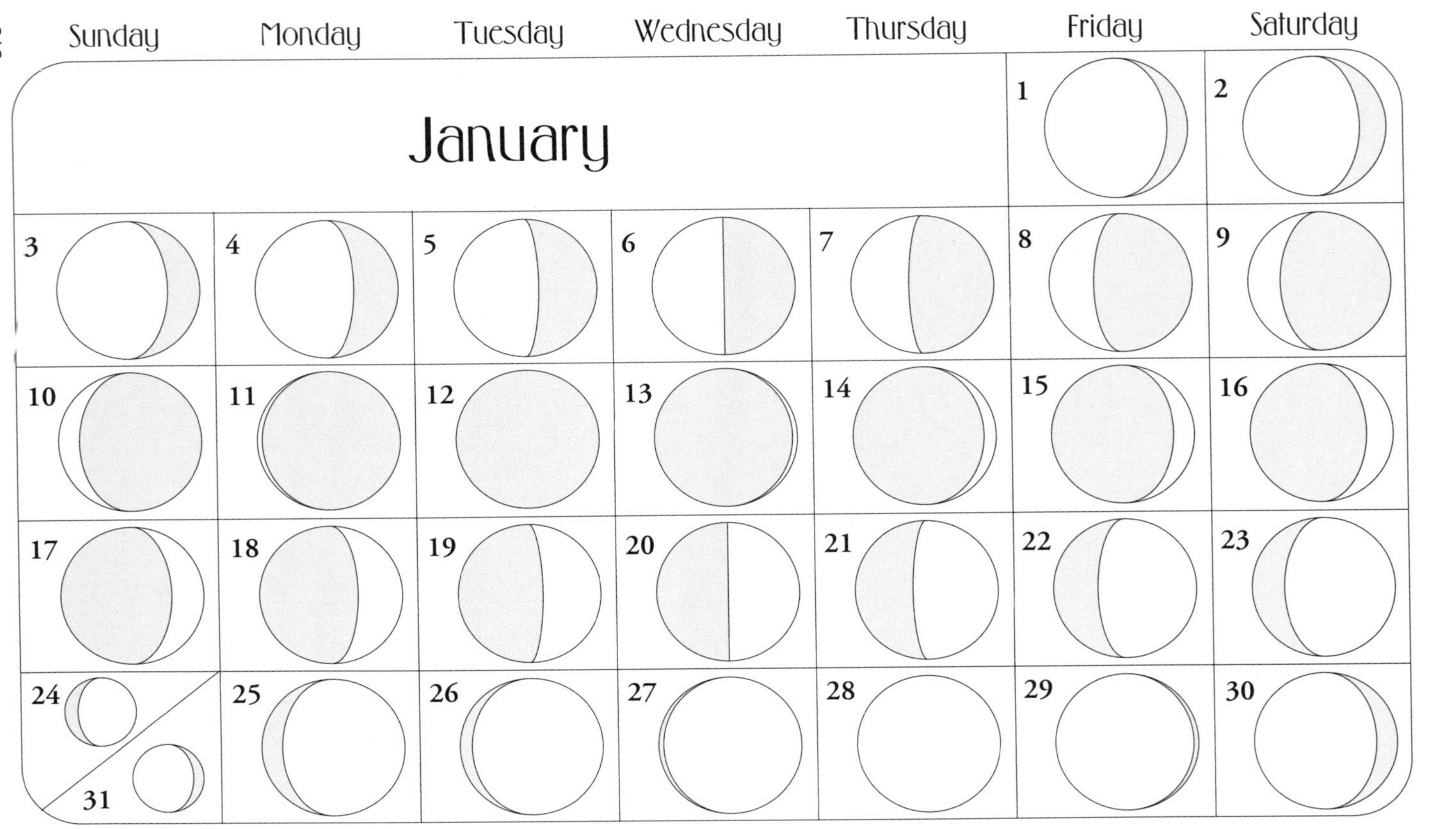
Sunday
Monday
Tuesday
Wednesday
Thursday
Friday
Saturday
January
1
2
3
4
5
6
7
8
9
10
11
12
13
14
15
16
17
18
19
20
21
22
23
24
25
26
27
28
29
30
31

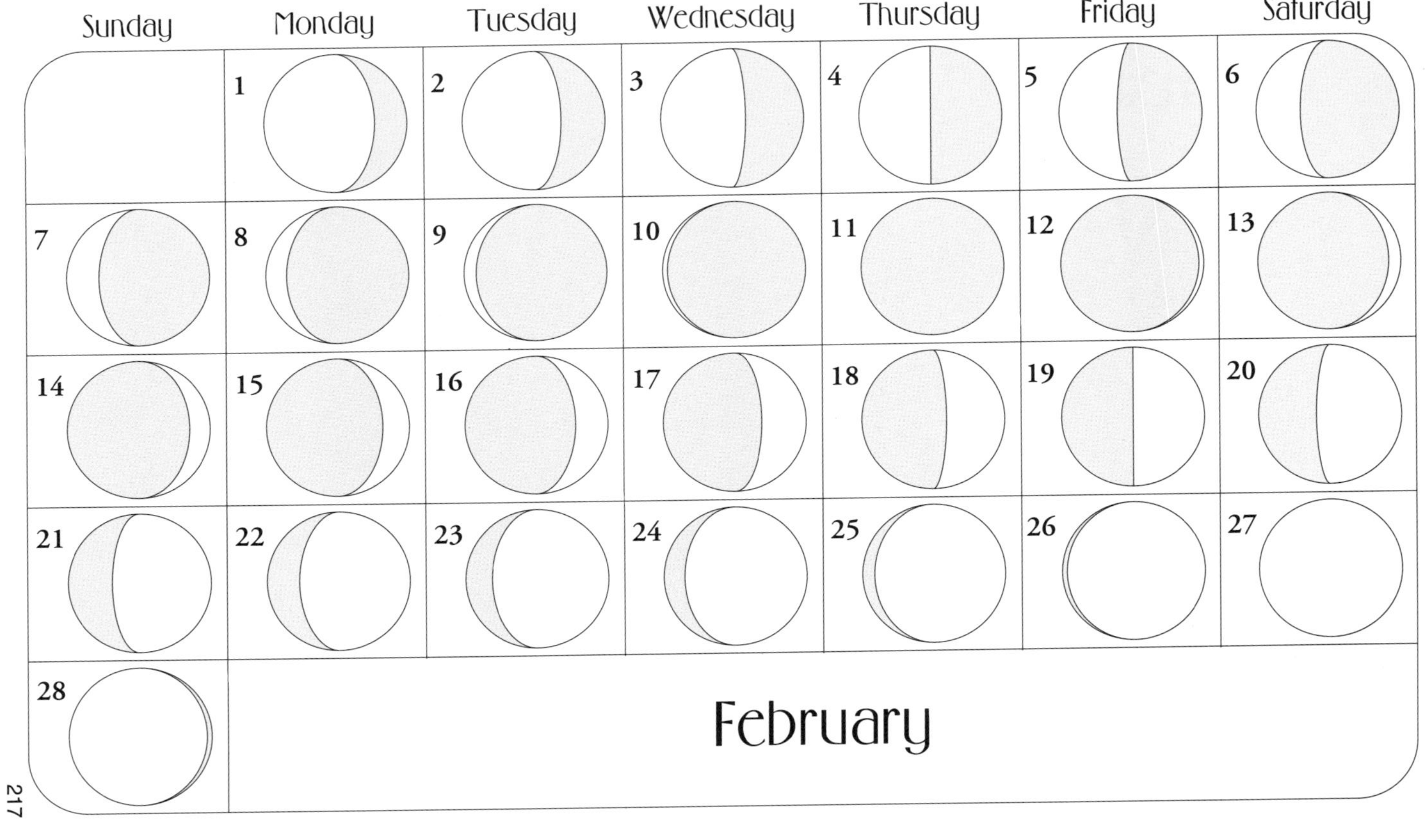

February

Sunday	Monday	Tuesday	Wednesday	Thursday	Friday	Saturday
	1	2	3	4	5	6
7	8	9	10	11	12	13
14	15	16	17	18	19	20
21	22	23	24	25	26	27
28						

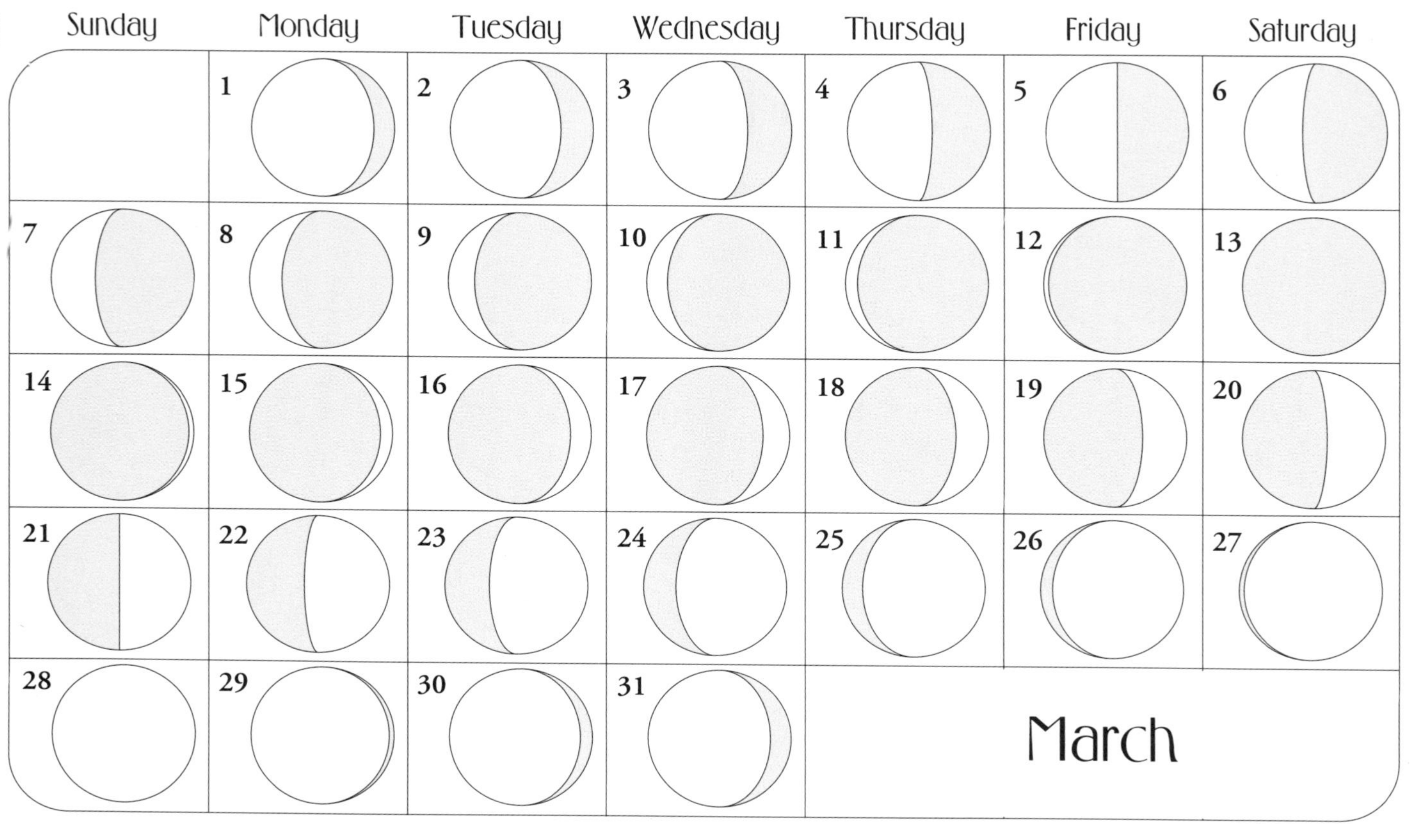
Sunday
Monday
Tuesday
Wednesday
Thursday
Friday
Saturday
1
2
3
4
5
6
7
8
9
10
11
12
13
14
15
16
17
18
19
20
21
22
23
24
25
26
27
28
29
30
31
March

April

Sunday	Monday	Tuesday	Wednesday	Thursday	Friday	Saturday
				1	2	3
4	5	6	7	8	9	10
11	12	13	14	15	16	17
18	19	20	21	22	23	24
25	26	27	28	29	30	

Sunday
Monday
Tuesday
Wednesday
Thursday
Friday
Saturday
May
1
2
3
4
5
6
7
8
9
10
11
12
13
14
15
16
17
18
19
20
21
22
23
24
25
26
27
28
29
30
31

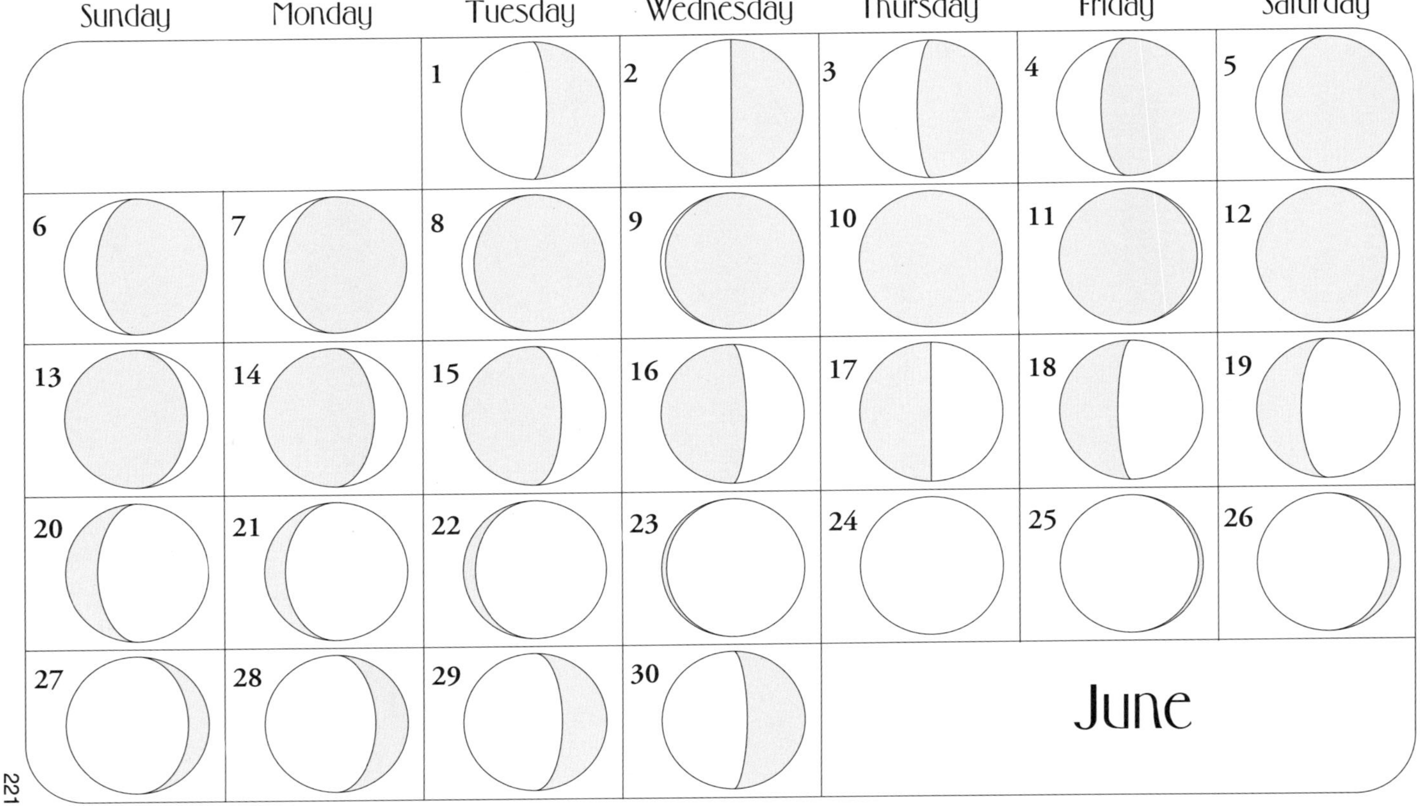
Sunday
Monday
Tuesday
Wednesday
Thursday
Friday
Saturday
1
2
3
4
5
6
7
8
9
10
11
12
13
14
15
16
17
18
19
20
21
22
23
24
25
26
27
28
29
30
June

Sunday
Monday
Tuesday
Wednesday
Thursday
Friday
Saturday
July
1
2
3
4
5
6
7
8
9
10
11
12
13
14
15
16
17
18
19
20
21
22
23
24
25
26
27
28
29
30
31

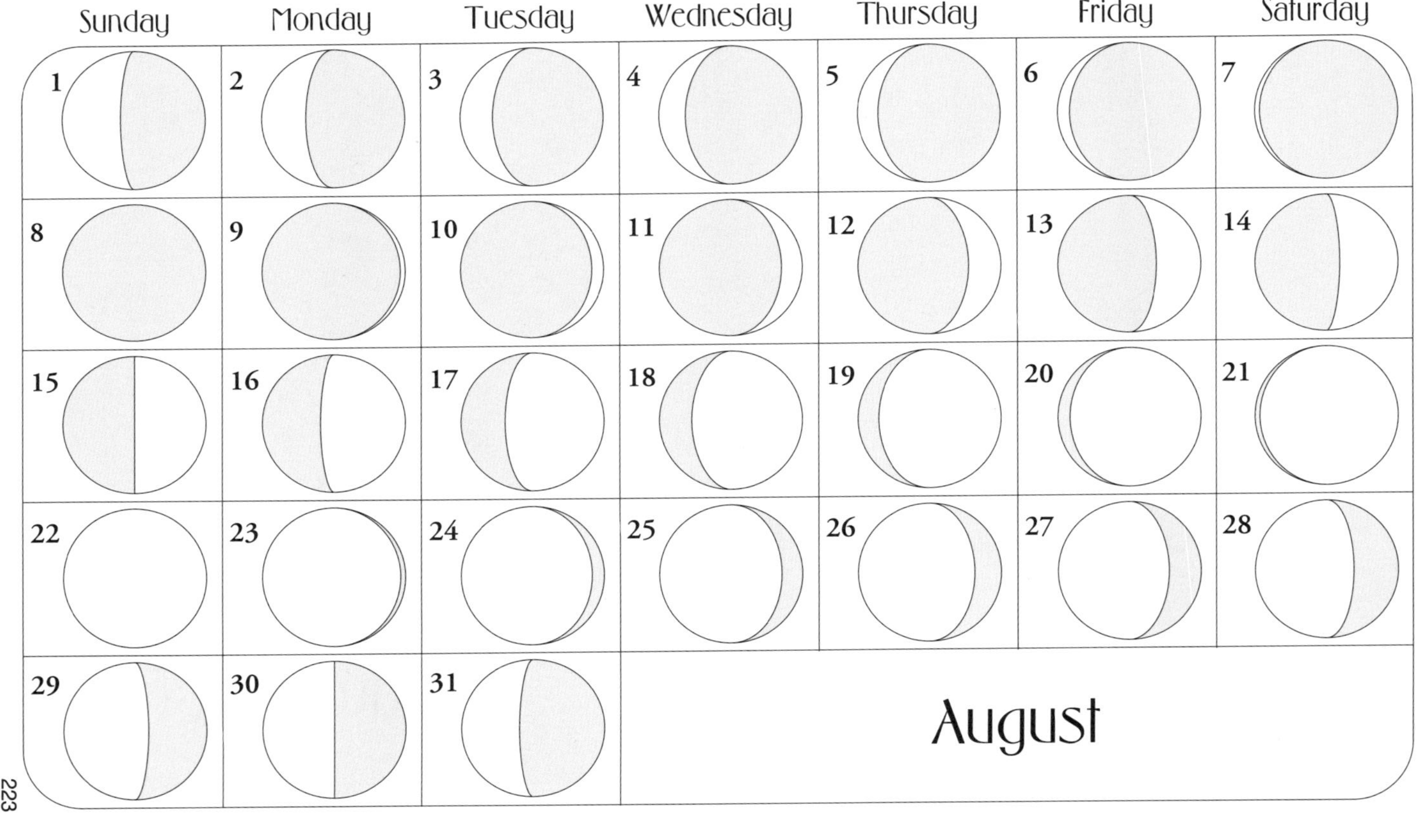
Sunday
Monday
Tuesday
Wednesday
Thursday
Friday
Saturday
1
2
3
4
5
6
7
8
9
10
11
12
13
14
15
16
17
18
19
20
21
22
23
24
25
26
27
28
29
30
31
August

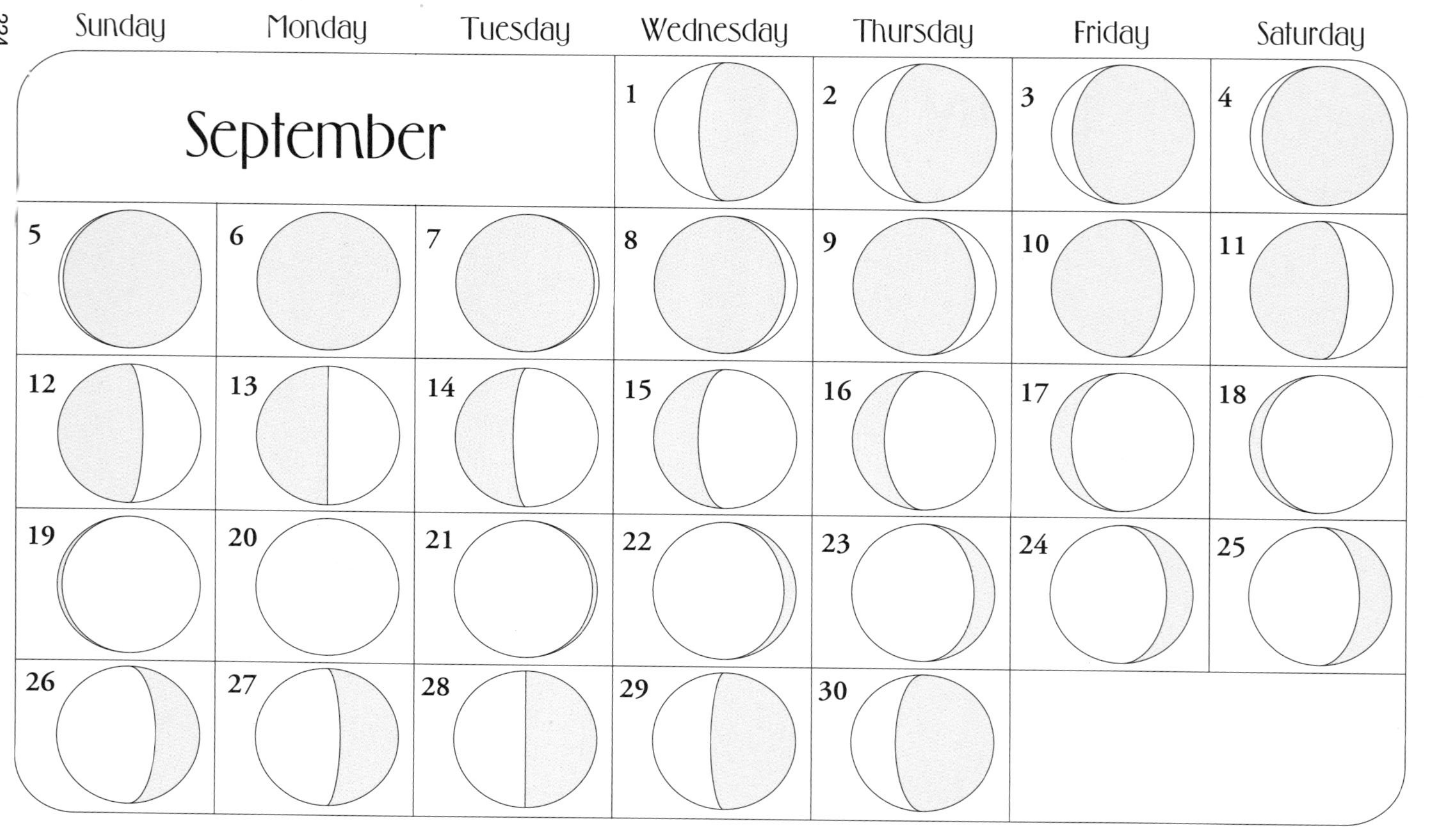

Sunday
Monday
Tuesday
Wednesday
Thursday
Friday
Saturday
September
1
2
3
4
5
6
7
8
9
10
11
12
13
14
15
16
17
18
19
20
21
22
23
24
25
26
27
28
29
30

Sunday
Monday
Tuesday
Wednesday
Thursday
Friday
Saturday
October
1
2
3
4
5
6
7
8
9
10
11
12
13
14
15
16
17
18
19
20
21
22
23
24
31
25
26
27
28
29
30

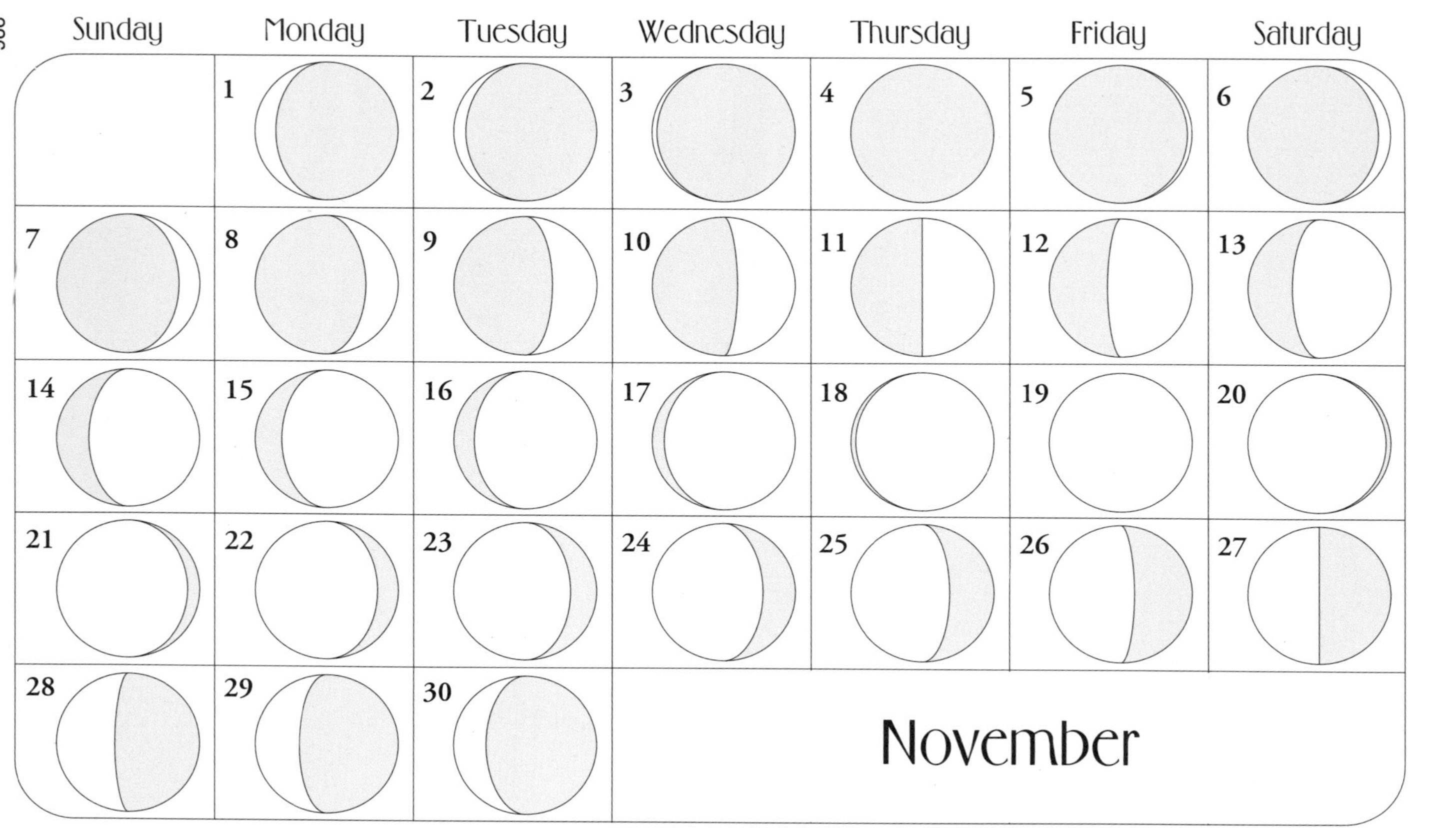

November

Sunday	Monday	Tuesday	Wednesday	Thursday	Friday	Saturday
	1	2	3	4	5	6
7	8	9	10	11	12	13
14	15	16	17	18	19	20
21	22	23	24	25	26	27
28	29	30				

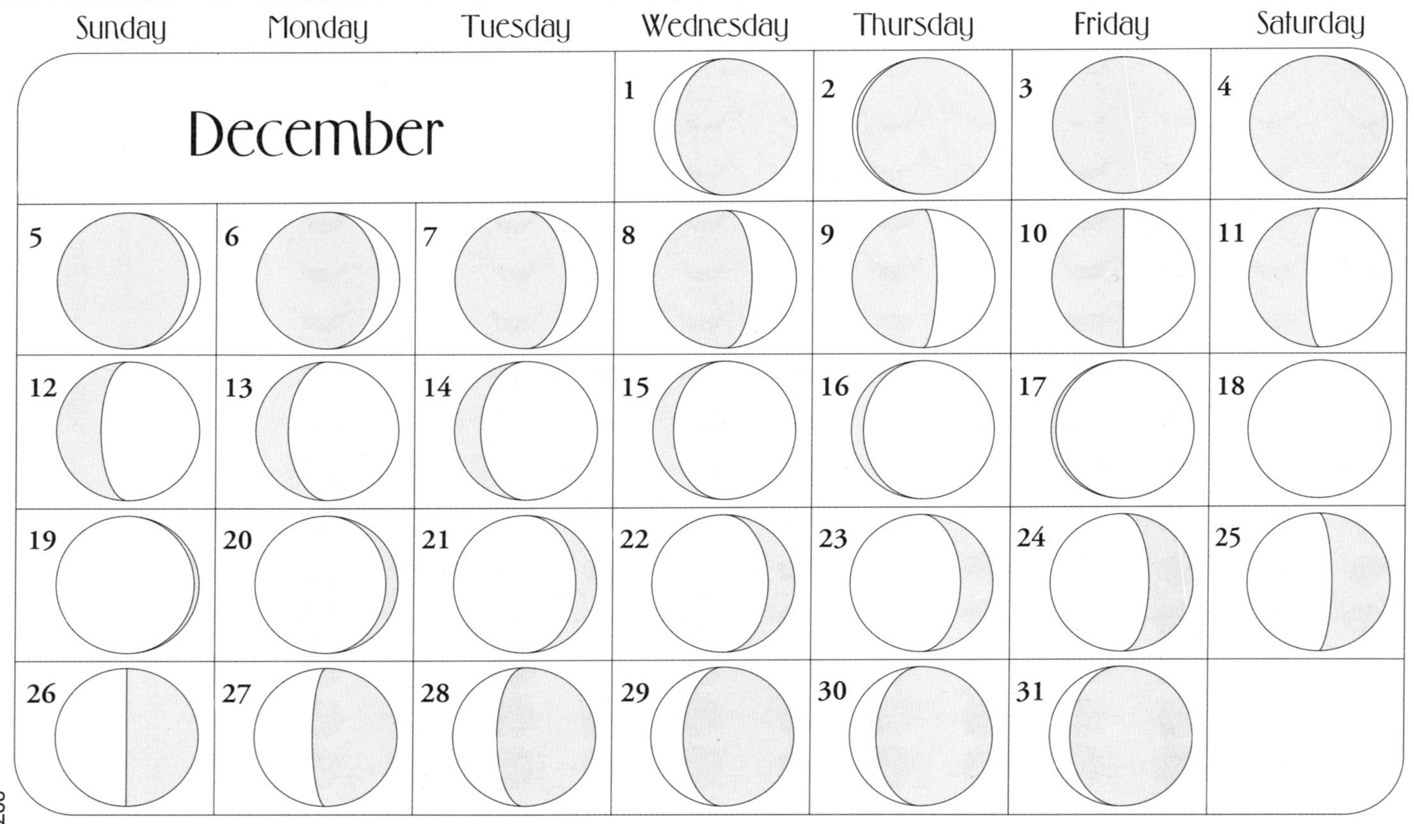
Sunday
Monday
Tuesday
Wednesday
Thursday
Friday
Saturday
December
1
2
3
4
5
6
7
8
9
10
11
12
13
14
15
16
17
18
19
20
21
22
23
24
25
26
27
28
29
30
31

Eclipse Key:

= Solar = Lunar T =Total A =Annular n =Penumbral P =Partial

Lunar Eclipses are visible wherever it is night and cloud free during full moon time.

Times on this page are in EST (Eastern Standard Time -5 from GMT) or DST, Daylight Saving Time (Mar 14 - Nov 7, 2021)

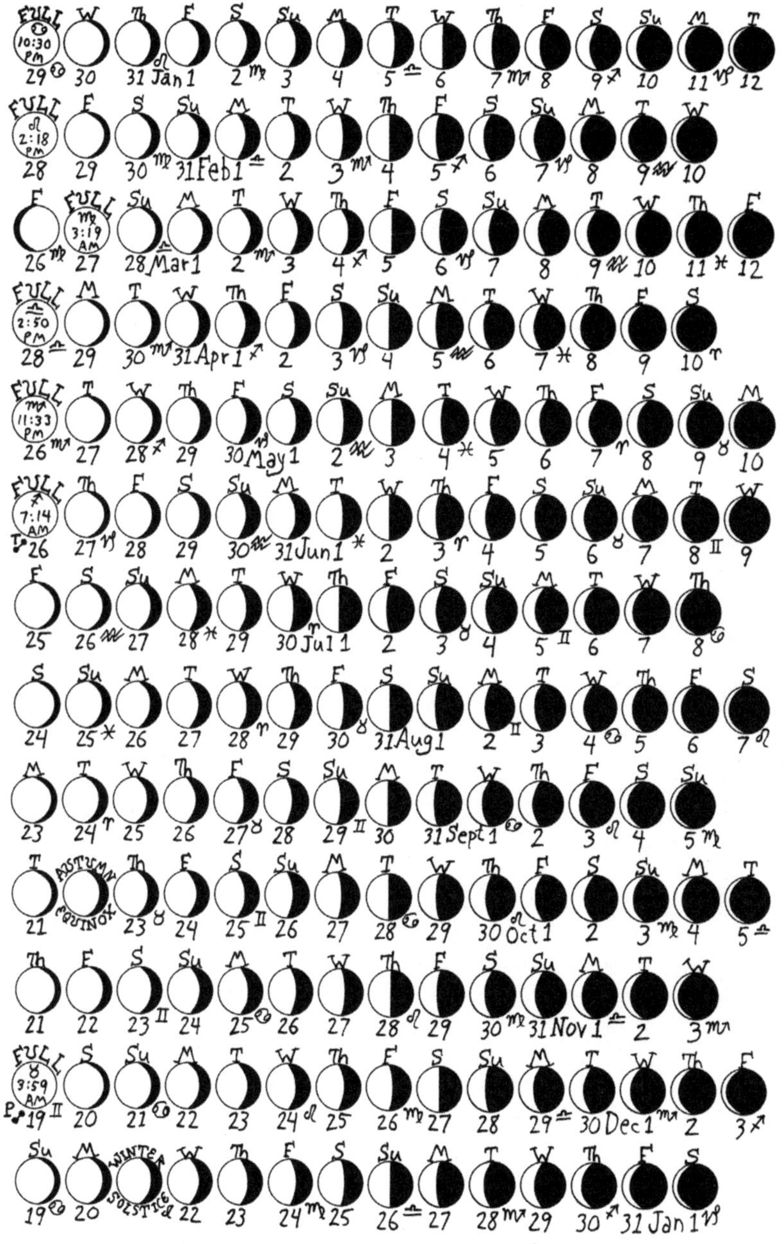

2021 Lunar Phases

This format available on cards from: **http://snakeandsnake.com**

Snake and Snake Productions 3037 Dixon Rd Durham, NC 27707

Conventional Holidays 2021

January 1	New Years Day*
January 18	Martin Luther King Jr. Day
February 11	Chinese/Lunar New Year
February 14	Valentines Day*
February 15	Presidents Day
February 17	Ash Wednesday
March 8	International Women's Day*
March 12	Mexika New Year
March 14	Daylight Saving Time Begins
March 17	St. Patrick's Day*
March 28	Palm Sunday
March 28–April 4	Passover
April 2	Good Friday
April 4	Easter
April 13–May 12	Ramadan
April 22	Earth Day*
May 5	Cinco de Mayo*
May 9	Mother's Day
May 31	Memorial Day
June 20	Father's Day
July 4	Independence Day*
September 6	Labor Day
Sept. 7–8	Rosh Hashanah
September 16	Yom Kippur
October 11	Indigenous Peoples' Day
October 31	Halloween*
November 1	All Saints' Day*
November 2	Day of the Dead*
November 7	Daylight Saving Time Ends
November 11	Veteran's Day*
November 25	Thanksgiving Day
Nov. 29–Dec. 6	Chanukah/Hanukkah
December 25	Christmas Day*
December 26	Boxing Day*
Dec. 26–Jan. 1	Kwanzaa*
December 31	New Years Eve*

*Same date every year

World Time Zones

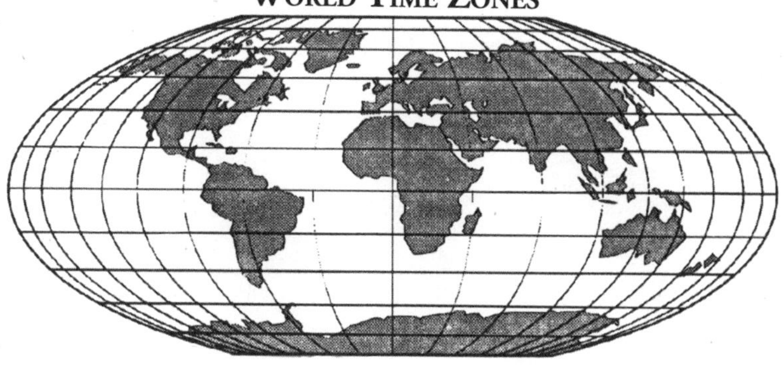

ID LW	NT BT	CA HT	YST	PST	MST	CST	EST	AST	BST	AT	WAT	GMT	CET	EET	BT	USSR Z3	USSR Z4	USSR Z5	SST	CCT	JST	GST	USSR Z10	ID LE
-12	-11	-10	-9	-8	-7	-6	-5	-4	-3	-2	-1	0	+1	+2	+3	+4	+5	+6	+7	+8	+9	+10	+11	+12
-4	-3	-2	-1	0	+1	+2	+3	+4	+5	+6	+7	+8	+9	+10	+11	+12	+13	+14	+15	+16	+17	+18	+19	+20

Standard Time Zones from West to East Calculated from PST as Zero Point:

IDLW:	International Date Line West	-4
NT/BT:	Nome Time/Bering Time	-3
CA/HT:	Central Alaska & Hawaiian Time	-2
YST:	Yukon Standard Time	-1
PST:	Pacific Standard Time	0
MST:	Mountain Standard Time	+1
CST:	Central Standard Time	+2
EST:	Eastern Standard Time	+3
AST:	Atlantic Standard Time	+4
NFT:	Newfoundland Time	+4 1/2
BST:	Brazil Standard Time	+5
AT:	Azores Time	+6
WAT:	West African Time	+7
GMT:	Greenwich Mean Time	+8
WET:	Western European Time (England)	+8
CET:	Central European Time	+9
EET:	Eastern European Time	+10
BT:	Bagdhad Time	+11
IT:	Iran Time	+11 1/2
USSR	Zone 3	+12
USSR	Zone 4	+13
IST:	Indian Standard Time	+13 1/2
USSR	Zone 5	+14
NST:	North Sumatra Time	+14 1/2
SST:	South Sumatra Time & USSR Zone 6	+15
JT:	Java Time	+15 1/2
CCT:	China Coast Time	+16
MT:	Moluccas Time	+16 1/2
JST:	Japanese Standard Time	+17
SAST:	South Australian Standard Time	+17 1/2
GST:	Guam Standard Time	+18
USSR	Zone 10	+19
IDLE:	International Date Line East	+20

How to Calculate Time Zone Corrections in Your Area:

ADD if you are **east** of PST (Pacific Standard Time); **SUBTRACT** if you are **west** of PST on this map (see right-hand column of chart above).

All times in this calendar are calculated from the West Coast of North America where We'Moon is made. Pacific Standard Time (PST Zone 8) is zero point for this calendar, except during Daylight Saving Time (March 14–November 7, 2021, during which times are given for PDT Zone 7). If your time zone does not use Daylight Saving Time, add one hour to the standard correction during this time. At the bottom of each page, EST/EDT (Eastern Standard or Daylight Time) and GMT (Greenwich Mean Time) times are also given. For all other time zones, calculate your time zone correction(s) from this map and write it on the inside cover for easy reference.

2022

JANUARY

S	M	T	W	T	F	S
						1
2	3	4	5	6	7	8
9	10	11	12	13	14	15
16	17	18	19	20	21	22
23	24	25	26	27	28	29
30	31					

FEBRUARY

S	M	T	W	T	F	S
		1	2	3	4	5
6	7	8	9	10	11	12
13	14	15	16	17	18	19
20	21	22	23	24	25	26
27	28					

MARCH

S	M	T	W	T	F	S
		1	2	3	4	5
6	7	8	9	10	11	12
13	14	15	16	17	18	19
20	21	22	23	24	25	26
27	28	29	30	31		

APRIL

S	M	T	W	T	F	S
					1	2
3	4	5	6	7	8	9
10	11	12	13	14	15	16
17	18	19	20	21	22	23
24	25	26	27	28	29	30

MAY

S	M	T	W	T	F	S
1	2	3	4	5	6	7
8	9	10	11	12	13	14
15	16	17	18	19	20	21
22	23	24	25	26	27	28
29	30	31				

JUNE

S	M	T	W	T	F	S
			1	2	3	4
5	6	7	8	9	10	11
12	13	14	15	16	17	18
19	20	21	22	23	24	25
26	27	28	29	30		

JULY

S	M	T	W	T	F	S
					1	2
3	4	5	6	7	8	9
10	11	12	13	14	15	16
17	18	19	20	21	22	23
24	25	26	27	28	29	30
31						

AUGUST

S	M	T	W	T	F	S
	1	2	3	4	5	6
7	8	9	10	11	12	13
14	15	16	17	18	19	20
21	22	23	24	25	26	27
28	29	30	31			

SEPTEMBER

S	M	T	W	T	F	S
				1	2	3
4	5	6	7	8	9	10
11	12	13	14	15	16	17
18	19	20	21	22	23	21
25	26	27	28	29	30	

OCTOBER

S	M	T	W	T	F	S
						1
2	3	4	5	6	7	8
9	10	11	12	13	14	15
16	17	18	19	20	21	22
23	24	25	26	27	28	29
30	31					

NOVEMBER

S	M	T	W	T	F	S
		1	2	3	4	5
6	7	8	9	10	11	12
13	14	15	16	17	18	19
20	21	22	23	24	25	26
27	28	29	30			

DECEMBER

S	M	T	W	T	F	S
				1	2	3
4	5	6	7	8	9	10
11	12	13	14	15	16	17
18	19	20	21	22	23	24
25	26	27	28	29	30	31

= NEW MOON, PST/PDT

= FULL MOON, PST/PDT

New Release this Fall: We'Moon Tarot!

40 years of We'Moon art distilled into a unique deck of beautiful We'Moon Tarot cards from women around the world. A boxed set of 78 cards with accompanying booklet, designed by We'Moon's founder, Musawa. Available November, 2020. Sign up for our newsletter to receive email alerts on our website: wemoon.ws

PreacherWoman for the Goddess:

Poems, Invocations, Plays and Other Holy Writ

A spirit-filled word feast puzzling on life and death mysteries—rich with metaphor, surprise, earth-passion. By Bethroot Gwynn—longtime editor for the We'Moon Datebook. Softbound, 6x9, 120 pages with 7 full color art features, $16

In the Spirit of We'Moon Celebrating 30 Years: An Anthology of We'Moon Art and Writing

This unique Anthology showcases three decades of We'Moon art, writing and herstory from 1981–2011, includes insights from founding editor Musawa and other writers who share stories about We'Moon's colorful 30-year evolution. Now in its fourth printing!

256 full color pages, paperback, 8x10, $26.95

The Last Wild Witch

by Starhawk, illustrated by Lindy Kehoe

An Eco-Fable for Kids and Other Free Spirits.

In this story, the children of a perfect town found their joy and courage, and saved the last wild Witch and the forest from destruction. A Silver Nautilus Award winner, this book is recognized internationally for helping readers imagine a world as it could be with abundant possibilities.

34 full color pages, 8x10, Softbound, $9.95

We'Moon 2021: The World

• **Datebook** The best-selling astrological moon calendar, earth-spirited handbook in natural rhythms, and visionary collection of women's creative work. Week-at-a-glance format. Choice of 3 bindings: Spiral, Sturdy Paperback Binding or Unbound. 8x5¼, 240 pages, $21.95

• ***We'Moon en Español!***
We are proud to offer a full translation of the classic datebook, in Spanish! Spiral Bound, 240 pages, 8x5¼, $21.95

• **Cover Poster** featuring art by Shauna Crandall: "*Fatima,*" raising the vibration of the Earth to the endless energy of love. 11x17, $10

• **We'Moon on the Wall**
A beautiful full color wall calendar featuring inspired art and writing from *We'Moon 2021,* with key astrological information, interpretive articles, lunar phases and signs. 12x12, $16.95

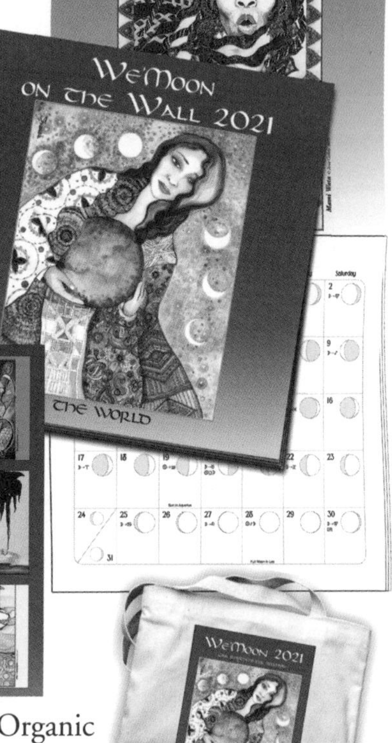

• **We'Moon 2021 Tote Bag** 100% Organic Cotton tote, proudly displaying the cover of *We'Moon 2021*. Perfect for stowing all of your goodies in style. 13x14, $13

• **Greeting Cards** An assortment of six gorgeous note cards featuring art from *We'Moon 2021*, with writings from each artist on the back. Wonderful to send for any occasion: Holy Day, Birthday, Anniversary, Sympathy, or just to say hello. Each pack is wrapped in biodegradable cellophane. Blank inside. 5x7, $11.95

More Offerings!
Check out page 233 for details on these books:

- ***The Last Wild Witch*** by Starhawk, illustrated by Lindy Kehoe.
- ***In the Spirit of We'Moon ~ Celebrating 30 Years: An Anthology of We'Moon Art and Writing***
- ***Preacher Woman for the Goddess: Poems, Invocations, Plays and Other Holy Writ*** by We'Moon Special Editor Bethroot Gwynn.

ORDER NOW—WHILE THEY LAST!

Take advantage of our

Special Discounts:

- We'll ship orders of $50 or more for **FREE** within the US!
- Use promo code: **21World** to get 10% off orders of $100 or more!

We often have great package deals and discounts.
Look for details, and sign up to receive regular email updates at

www.wemoon.ws

Email weorder@wemoon.ws Toll free in US 877-693-6666
Local & International 541-956-6052 Wholesale 503-288-3588

SHIPPING AND HANDLING

Prices vary depending on what you order and where you live.
See website or call for specifics.
To pay with check or money-order,
please call us first for address and shipping costs.

All products printed in full color on recycled paper with low VOC soy-based ink.

Become a We'Moon Contributor!

Send submissions for

We'Moon 2023

the 42nd edition!

Call for Contributions: Available in the spring of 2021

Postmark-by Date for all art and writing: August 1, 2021

Note: It is too late to contribute to

We'Moon 2022

We'Moon is made up by writers and artists like you! We welcome creative work by women from around the world, and aim to amplify diverse perspectives. We especially encourage those of us who are women of color or who are marginalized by the mainstream, to participate in helping We'Moon reflect our unique visions and experiences. We are eager to publish more words and images depicting people of color created by WOC. By nurturing space for all women to share their gifts, we unleash insight and wisdom upon the world—a blessing to us all.

We invite you to send in your art and writing for the next edition of We'Moon!

Here's how:

Step 1: Visit wemoon.ws to download a Call for Contributions or send your request for one with a SASE (legal size) to **We'Moon Submissions, PO Box 187, Wolf Creek, OR 97497.** (If you are not within the US, you do not need to include postage.) The Call contains current information about the theme, specifications about how to submit your art and writing, and terms of compensation. There are no jury fees. The Call comes out in the early Spring every year.

Step 2: Fill in the accompanying Contributor's License, giving all the requested information, and return it with your art/writing by the due date. *No work will be accepted without a signed license!* We now accept email submissions, too. See our website for details.

Step 3: Plan ahead! To assure your work is considered for ***We'Moon 2023***, get your submissions postmarked by August 1, 2021.

Notes

Mami Wata
© Zena Carlota 2013

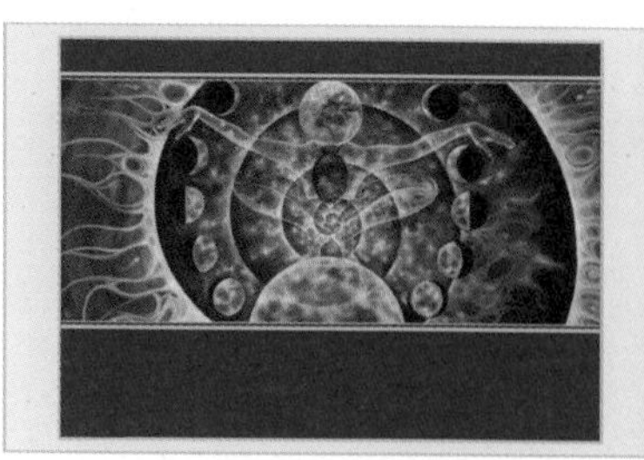

Female Strength
© Helena Arturaleza 2016

Blue Moon
© Jeanette M. French 2018

Raven's Key
© Elizabeth Diamond Gabriel 2019

Blowing Bubbles
© Robin Urton 2016

True Colors
© Darlene Cook 2017